AF316670

A LESSON BEFORE TEACHING

Phenomenology, Literary Reading
and Disenfranchised Adolescents

M. ALAYNE SULLIVAN

ISBN: 979-8-89031-288-4 (sc)
ISBN: 979-8-89031-289-1 (hc)
ISBN: 979-8-89031-290-7 (e)

One Galleria Blvd., Suite 1900, Metairie, LA 70001
1-888-421-2397

CONTENTS

Part I:
Getting Started

Chapter 1   The Beginning of Beginning 3

Chapter 2   Learning to Talk..21

Chapter 3   Learning to Trust...33

Chapter 4   Beginnings of Synthesis 40

Chapter 5   Thinking About Things...56

Chapter 6   In and Outside the Pages 67

Chapter 7   Media Stories, Personal Stories..73

Chapter 8   Running and Running 80

Chapter 9   Despair 88

Chapter 10 Looking Back and Looking Ahead.................................. 102

Part II:
Deciding on the Shape of Things

Chapter 11 Looking Back, Heading Forth 113

Chapter 12 Heroes and Demons 135

Chapter 13 Increasing Pressures 142

Chapter 14 Pastoral Reflections... 148

Chapter 15 The Power of Love... 157

Chapter 16 Taking Responsibility 167

Chapter 17 Shackled For Life... 179

Chapter 18 Realizing True Beginnings..187

Chapter 19 Continued Uncertainty...206

Chapter 20 No Matter How Educated 215

**Part III:
Transformations**

Chapter 21 Buying A Radio and Finding God 233

Chapter 22 Learning to Write and Finding God 270

Chapter 23 Mind, Memory, Heart and Life 294

Chapter 24 I Saw the Transformation..314

Chapter 25 A Lesson Before Teaching, or Final Thoughts............317

References 325

PART I

GETTING STARTED

1

THE BEGINNING OF BEGINNING

It is hard to say when this book actually began. Shortly after arriving in New York City some years ago, I was asked to teach an African American literature course for prospective English teachers, and parts of it started then I now realize. With every piece of African American literature read, I became more and more harrowed by textual renderings of indignity and survival - stories of experience over hundreds of years, bled onto the page, wrought through the bodies and souls of black Americans. At the same time, as a white, Canadian, female Assistant Professor, I was a newly arrived stranger to New York City, fumbling, trying to teach a corpus of literature with which I had no lived experience. We read, among other books, *Invisible Man* (1980) by Ralph Ellison, and I suggested that students portray critical scenes from that book through dramatic enactments accompanied by background music – jazz, blues, black gospel, and hip hop. Well before finding the trove of scholarship about how arts-based projects can intensify students' experiences and insights of literature, I'd instinctively sought to align these artistic expressions, hoping that the marriage would enrich students' explorations, that in the union we'd discover deeper resonance in the literature we were reading.

There was a moment one night during that time, in late fall, when one such reading performance had concluded. John Coltrane's jazz had been a background siren as three young men produced a dramatic reading of segments from *Invisible Man's* sorrowed allegory. We sat in silence, riveted by what had just occurred. The classroom voices were completely stilled. Beyond the open classroom windows, Harlem resounded with horns, voices, footsteps and distant urban-pistoled echoes. The mystery and bloodied power of narrative had just been rendered there viscerally in front of us. We sat in a stupor realizing that the embodiments of that fiction universe were refracted a million times over by the people just outside the windows, and by those from times past whose voices had long been stilled. We heard laments from long ago as, indeed, invisible ghosts came into the room. This book started that night.

It started and it kept growing even though I did not realize that it was being silently written over these many years since then. The nascent text moved with me to a small university town outside of Pittsburgh. There one summer, just weeks after the end of another academic year and the birth of my second daughter, money was short. I was tired but money was tight and I needed to find more work right away. My then-husband was not working and that is a whole other story. So, I was told, there are courses being offered for incoming freshmen – eighteen-year-olds who have not quite passed university entrance tests and need remedial courses before being fully admitted to the fall semester. If I passed the screening interview to teach two of these courses for "remedial readers", we'd be able to pay our stacked-up bills. 'What would be entailed in a screening interview?' I asked myself. I'd been teaching reading and literature-related courses for all of my professional life to that point. What could be forthcoming in a screening interview that might not allow me to teach a course for inexperienced adolescent readers? I found out.

"What strategies would you use to teach literal comprehension," I was first asked.

Then, "How would you teach word identification? What experience do you have teaching *these students* phonics, syllabication, spelling, vocabulary definition through dictionary usage, main idea recognition, and reading articulation and fluency?"

I was told, "Most of *these students* cannot read above a 4th or 5th-grade level."

"Do you have experience working with adolescents from the inner-city? These students are coming to us from Philadelphia and Pittsburgh, some from rural areas but mostly kids from the inner city who will be away from home living here for the first time. They need basic skills!"

My answers were satisfactory. I got the job and signed an agreement to teach *these students* the specific reading skills I had been asked about in that interview. I walked back across this new campus and … I remembered Harlem. I remembered walking up Amsterdam Avenue, and along 125th Street, past the Apollo Theater, to Malcolm X Blvd, where I turned left and proceeded to a school in East Harlem. There I had fumbled again. I was without true ballast, flailing about for a research agenda, and scared for many reasons, some of which would make for yet a whole other story. But there too, something transcendent happened.

I had carried a bundle of books with me, 20 copies of *Their Eyes Were Watching God*, which I had just finished reading for the first time merely weeks before. The pregnant and parenting teens with whom I was working then could not read that book, so I began reading it aloud for them. In time, they were willing to try reading it themselves with a partner and writing their thoughts and responses to that novel in journals I had brought for them. They became readers – they taught me, then, what I am now finally able to try writing about here. This book thus also began near Pittsburgh with that memory in mind. Books begin at odd times it seems and often much before the actual tapping of letters onto the page. Because I remembered Harlem, I left that interview near Pittsburgh fully ready to contradict everything I had just agreed to teach, and because I did that *these students* became readers given everything that happened within yet another new teaching context.

There we all were together a few weeks later on a small university campus not so far from Pittsburgh, 25 students at 8:00 a.m. and 27 more, at 10:00 a.m. *These students* were primarily African American, some Hispanic, a few Caucasian – all struggling readers, a term that will be deconstructed in many layers as this book unfolds. I had prepared a syllabus for them and listed the primary text for the course as *A*

Lesson Before Dying, by Ernest Gaines (1997). They were slouching. One student had come in late, in his pajamas. I looked at them. They looked at me. They had to pass this class and each of the three other classes that were mandatory remedial courses: math, study skills and history. I did not go over the syllabus. I began reading from the novel:

> *I was not there, yet I was there. No, I did not go to the trial, I did not hear the verdict, because I knew all the time what it would be. Still, I was there. I was there as much as anyone else was there. Either I sat behind my aunt and his godmother or I sat beside them. Both are large women, but his godmother is larger. She is of average height, five four, five five, but weighs nearly two hundred pounds. Once she and my aunt had found their places — two rows behind the table where he sat with his court-appointed attorney — his godmother became as immobile as a great stone or as one of our oak or cypress stumps. She never got up once to get water or go to the bathroom down in the basement. She just sat there staring at the boy's clean-cropped head where he sat at the front table with his lawyer* (Gaines, 1993, p. 3).

That is the whole of the first page of *A Lesson Before Dying.* I did not ask the students to get out their dictionaries (assigned by remedial-support staff much before I met with them) and define "immobile", or "verdict", or "trial". I did not ask them about the literal meaning of any of the separate sentences in what we had just heard — what we had read together as they followed along in their own books (also assigned to them before the first meeting). My times in Harlem had taught me that there is no such thing, really, as literal meaning — not in the kind of text we were reading. Whatever denotation a dictionary might set forth about immobility, verdicts, and trials would be vastly, exponentially, and experientially enlarged by a multiplicity of meanings and differing shades of those meanings as students read further into this book, and as the book lead them back into their own lives and communities. Many students in the room, for example, felt as though they were on trial in having to take this class, that a verdict about them would be passed, and that they would be immobilized academically unless they passed. Would the dictionary help them understand the many senses of these words or *prevent* them from aggregating many layers of meaning?

I looked up – not a sound. Their postures were different. There was that feeling in the room again – something was happening. They were attuned, engaged, enlivened. I kept reading. I kept reading out loud about the white man, Alcee Grope who had been killed, about Bear who had been drinking that day in the late-1940's, deep-south Louisiana, who had not enough money to buy more wine at Grope's liquor store, about Brother who was with Bear, about how Bear moved toward the counter to take the wine, about old Alcee Grope who reached for a revolver and started shooting. I read out loud about Jefferson who, in his shock, realized that Grope was calling out to him before he died, that Bear was dead, and that Brother was dead. I kept reading aloud from the book:

> *He looked from one dead body to the other. He didn't know whether he should call someone on the telephone or run. He had never dialed a telephone in his whole life, but he had seen other people use them. He didn't know what to do. He was standing by the liquor shelf, and suddenly he realized he needed a drink and needed it badly. He snatched a bottle off the shelf, wrung off the cap, and turned up the bottle, all in one continuous motion. The whiskey, burned him like fire – his chest, his belly, even his nostrils* (p. 6).

My voice read their eyes along the page – we read that the prosecutor argued Jefferson had gone there that day with the full intent of robbing and killing old Grope. Then we read that the defense argued Jefferson had been at the wrong place at the wrong time. We read and we heard that defense attorney call Jefferson a fool:

> *Would you call this – this – this a man? No. Not I. I would call it a boy and a fool. A fool is not aware of right and wrong. A fool does what others tell him to do* (p. 7).

A fool, we heard. And then I stopped reading aloud. What followed on the next two pages of the text seemed too sensitive to read publicly. What followed next in the first chapter required privacy it seemed. Each one of the students should be alone with his or her own thoughts – have a completely private moment within which they would encounter the next words of the text, which characterize Jefferson as a cornered animal who acted of the fear inherited from his ancestors in "the deepest jungle of blackest Africa" (p. 7). The defense attorney calls Jefferson a thing that acts on command, a thing to dig ditches, chop your wood, pull your corn – this is what he tells the 12-man, all-white jury. The text reads that he would just as soon put a hog in the electric chair. They should privately discover that the verdict was death by electrocution.

I told each of the two, twenty-five person classes of students that first summer that they could read the remainder of chapter one, and chapter two later that night for homework. They should write about a page in a journal that did three things: (a) identify three specific passages across chapters one and two that seemed most important to them, (b) write about why they chose those passages, why they seemed important, and (c) what their thoughts and reactions were to the chapters. They should bring their books and journals back the next day, I told both classes. We stopped reading for that first day. After that I learned their names and we reviewed the syllabus. I didn't know it at the time, but I had started writing this book then. And when the next summer came along and I was asked to teach another group of *these* remedial students, I repeated with the third group of 18-year-olds what I had done with the first two groups.

Finally, on that first day, I also presented students with what must have seemed an overwhelming range of project choices. In their syllabus they encountered several arts, and media-based projects; they would choose one that allowed them to express the thematic essence of this novel from their own perspectives, either individually or with one or two partners. They'd also write a seven-page paper that explained their thematic representation. Here are the structural details related to the project choices – all variations on an identical purpose:

Synthesis Projects	Project Descriptions
VISUAL COLLAGE PROJECT	This project will represent your interpretation of *A Lesson Before Dying* through pictures, images and small objects. Your visual collage should dramatically express your interpretation of the main idea of the text we have been reading. You can do the project by yourself or with one or two other people. Each person should contribute at least twenty-five visual details that will be organized to reflect the main idea of the text, in your opinion. You can download images from the inter-net, obtain pictures from magazines, draw pictures and collect small objects that can be embedded in your final poster-board visual collage. Your visual collage can reflect characters, major actions, key textual segments, mood, elements of setting, key objects in the story, and key dialogue among characters. You will present your project to the class in a 10-to15-minute formal presentation. You will write -- collaboratively or by yourself – a 7-to-10-page paper that presents your interpretation of the key concept of our text as reflected through your visual collage. This project will be completed gradually throughout the five-weeks we will be reading our book. Your project should be aesthetically beautiful and reflect the many activities we have completed as we read the text together.
CHARACTER MAP PROJECT	This project will present your interpretation of *A Lesson Before Dying* through a character map. This character map should reflect a deep analysis and perception of the key character(s) in your opinion. This analysis of the key character(s) should also be related to the key concept of the text in your opinion. The character's(s') (a) primary traits, (b) motivations, (c) conflicts, (d) key actions, (e) important conversations and/or inner thoughts, (f) your point of view, (g) appearance, and (h) major objects associated with the character should be presented. This character map should contain at least 5 specific page numbers associated with these details and also contain key quotes from the text about the character(s). You can embed images and objects in your character-map poster board. You will present your character map to the class in a 10-to-15-minute formal presentation. Your presentation should connect the various details of the character map with various critical details of the text. You will write a 7-to-10-page paper that persuades other readers to see your point of view as reflected through your character map. This project will be completed gradually throughout the five weeks we will be reading our text. Your character map should be aesthetically arranged and reflect the many mapping activities and discussions we completed as we read the book together. You can work on this project by yourself or with one or two other people.

FILM PROJECT	This project will represent your interpretation of *A Lesson Before Dying* by comparing four films to our book. The films' main ideas will be similar to those of our book in your opinion. You will use an assigned mapping structure to make connections between a 2-to-3-minute segment from each film with at least 4 segments from our text. The mapping structure should outline specific pages from the novel that connect to the main idea of the various film segments. The main idea of the text, in your opinion, should be connected to the main idea of each of the films. The film segments should be chosen to generally compare to details about the text's (a) characters, (b) major actions, (c) key textual segments, (d) mood, (e) elements of setting, (f) key objects in the story, and (g) key dialogue among characters. You will show one segment from each film in a final presentation. You will also connect these film segments to specific segments of the text and read from at least 4 differing segments of the text as you explain the connections between the films and the text. You will write a 7-to-10-page paper that explains the key concept of the text, in your opinion, and how each of the films connects to this main idea. You can work on this project by yourself or with one or two other people.
MUSIC PROJECT	This project will represent your interpretation of *A Lesson Before Dying* by aligning four songs with our book. The songs' main ideas will be similar to that of our book in your opinion. You will use an assigned mapping structure to make connections between a segment from each song with at least 4 segments from our text. The mapping structure should outline specific pages from the novel that connect to the main idea of the various song segments. The main idea of the text, in your opinion, should be connected to the main idea of each of the songs. The song segments should be chosen to generally compare to details about the text's (a) characters, (b) major actions, (c) key textual segments, (d) mood, (e) elements of setting, (f) key objects in the story, and (g) key dialogue among characters. You will play one segment from each song in a final presentation. You will also connect these song segments to specific segments of the text and read from at least 4 differing segments of the text as you explain the connections between the songs and the text. You will write a 7-to-10-page paper that explains the key concept of the text, in your opinion, and how each of the songs connects to this main idea. You can work on this project by yourself or with one or two other people.

PHOTOGRAPHY PROJECT	This project will represent your interpretation of *A Lesson Before Dying* through photographs you take. Your photography project should dramatically express your interpretation of the main idea of the text we have been reading. You can do the project by yourself or with one or two other people. Each person should contribute at least twenty-five photographs that will be organized to reflect the main idea of the text, in your opinion. You can collect small objects that can be embedded in your final poster-board photography project. Your photography project can reflect characters, major actions, key textual segments, mood, elements of setting, key objects in the story, and key dialogue among characters. You will present yoru project to the class in a 1o-to15-minute formal presentation. You will write -- collaboratively or by yourself – a 7-to-10-page paper that presents your interpretation of the key concept of our text as reflected through your photography project. This project will be completed gradually throughout the five-weeks we will be reading our book. Your photography project should be aesthetically beautiful and reflect the many activities we have completed as we read the text together.
SITUATION IDENTIFICATION	You will respond to *A Lesson Before Dying* through ongoing journal entries. These journal entries will focus on the similarities you see between yourself and the main character of the book. As the book unfolds for you, you will gradually see more and more of a connection between the main character's situation and your own life situation. Based on these journal entries you will write a 7-to-10-page paper that outlines major similarities between yourself and the main character of the story. It is likely that your writing will focus on the main idea of the story as reflected through the details of the main character. This is a project that can only be completed individually. Your project will be created gradually throughout the five weeks we will be reading our book. You will make a 10-to-15-minute final presentation that focuses on key similarities between yourself and the major character of our book. This presentation will conclude with your statement about the key concept of the story in your opinion.

DRAMA PROJECT	This project will represent your interpretation of *A Lesson Before Dying* through dramatic readings. One to three individuals can complete this project together. You will identify approximately 3-to-5 key scenes from the book and prepare a dramtic reading of those scenes. These scenes will be chosen because they reflect an essence of the key idea of the book in your opinion. Your dramatic reading will be accompanied by music. You will make a 10-to-15-minute formal presentation based on these dramatic readings and will also comment on how the chosen scenes represent the key idea of the book in your opinion. You will also complete a 7-to-10-paper that explains how the chosen scenes reflect a core essence of the key idea of the book in your opinion. Your project will be created gradually throughout the five weeks we will be reading our book.
SCULPTURE PROJECT	This project will represent your interpretation of *A Lesson Before Dying* through a sculpture. This sculpture should express your interpretation of the main idea of the text we have been reading. You can do the project by yourself or with one or two other people. Each person should contribute at least fifteen elements to the collage. These "elements" can be made of any substance, can be tiny or large; of various textures and medium; and of various colors. The size, shape, textures and various objects and details of the sculpture should reflect the key concept of the novel in your opinion. The sculpture should reflect (a) characters, (b) major actions, (c) key textual segments, (d) mood, (e) elements of setting, (f) key objects in the story, and (g) key dialogue among characters. The sculpture should convey a strong sense of your feeling about the text. You will present your sculpture to the class in a 10-to-15-minute formal presentation. As the creative artist your presentation should connect the various details of the sculpture with various critical details of the text. You will write a 7-to-10-page paper that explains how your sculpture conveys various critical details as well as the key idea of the book. Your project will be created gradually throughout the five weeks we will be reading our book. Your sculpture should be aesthetically beautiful and reflect the many activities we have completed as we read the book together.

MEDIA PROJECT	This project will represent your interpretation of *A Lesson Before Dying* through a combination of the various media presented. For example, you can choose to incorporate film, photography, drama, music and other elements such as visuals and sculpture. Once assembled, this project will convey your sense of the main idea of the book we have been reading. Your can do this project yourself or with one or two other people. The final version of your project should reflect (a) characters, (b) major actions, (c) key textual segments, (d) mood, (e) elements of setting, (f) key objects in the story, and (g) key dialogue among characters. You will present your media project to the class in a 10-to-15-minute formal presentation. As the creative artist your presentation should connect various details of your project with various critical details of the text. You will write a 7-to-10-page paper that explains how your media project conveys various critical details as well as the key idea of the book. Your project will be created gradually throughout the five weeks we will be reading our book. Your media project should be aesthetically beautiful and reflect the many activities we have completed as we read the book together.
THEMATIC CONCEPT MAP	This project will present your interpretation of *A Lesson Before Dying* through a concept map. This concept map should reflect a deep analysis and perception of the key idea(s) of the book in your opinion. This concept map should contain at least 5 specific page numbers associated with these details and also contain key quotes from the text about the key idea(s). You can embed images and objects in your concept-map poster board. You will present your concept map to the class in a 10-to-15-minute formal presentation. Your presentation should connect the various details of the concept map with various critical details of the text. You will write a 7-to-10-page paper that persuades other readers to see your point of view as reflected through your concept map. This project will be completed gradually throughout the five weeks we will be reading our text. Your concept map should be aesthetically arranged and reflect the many mapping activities and discussions we completed as we read the book together. You can work on this project by yourself or with one or two other people.

I was aware that I was establishing a qualitative, phenomenologically-oriented research study; in bringing video cameras into each of those three classrooms, and in obtaining students' permission to record every word of our classroom discourse, I was setting up the rudiments of the structure that has become this book. What I am now doing is sustaining a research story by depending on Ernest Gaines' fiction; his allegorical dimensions of *A Lesson Before Dying* infuse the range of characters that come forth in this true research story. It is Grant Wiggin's voice speaking to us in the first person from the pages of *A Lesson Before Dying* when he says, in the very first words of this text, "I was there and yet I was not there". In much the same way, I am the narrator of this research story about the manifold layers of engagement created through the shared reading of this novel with *those students*. I was there with them and yet I was not "there" in their deeply emotive engagements with the interior personalization they each established with this book.

Here, first, are the people from the novel – they are aligned quite deliberately, for the sake of this book, with various voices and themes of the literacy education pantheon of our current world. As each chapter of this book unfolds, it is told with three emphases: (a) close attention to the characters and plot of *A Lesson Before Dying*, (b) specific recounting of *those students'* words – their comments, questions, arguments, and feelings as expressed in video-recorded conversations, day-to-day in three, 25-hour classes over two different summers, and finally (c) commentary that places the textual elements of *A Lesson Before Dying* and *these students'* responses within a theoretical, political, historical, and literary frame. In essence, I am quite deliberately telling a qualitative, phenomenologically-oriented research story with an underlying polemic message. Readers will discover the impact of this message as it unfolds within these pages. Here is a structure outlining the three dimensions of the book, as just mentioned – each chapter contains some elements of each of these three emphases. It will all become clearer as the pages turn:

Key Characters from the novel, *A Lesson Before Dying*	Specific individuals, & societal groups, and adolescent student 'voices'	Core themes, aligned with (a) Key characters, (b) Individuals & societal groups, and (c) Adolescent voices
Grant Wiggins (African American, plantation teacher in small town of Bayonne)	Myself, a writer and teacher questioning my role within educational dynamics. Teachers struggling to define their work in light of multiple agendas.	- the roles of teachers; - backgrounds and needs of struggling students; - political agendas related to teaching.
Jefferson (African American young man condemned to die)	Disenfranchised students from various echelons of society.	- social and educational justice for struggling students; - politics of teaching "minority" students.
Miss Emma (Jefferson's godmother) & **Tante Lou** (Grant Wiggins' Aunt)	Those who fight for the dignity and literacy education rights of disenfranchised students.	- multicultural educators; - social justice advocates; - critical race theorists; - critical pedagogy, teachers and social justice advocates
Reverend Ambrose (Pastor for the plantation community) & **Vivian** (Grant Wiggins' love)	African American heroes, uplifting spiritual & emotional dignity – often, literary voices.	- Gloria Ladson-Billings; - Paulo Friere; - Jonathan Kozol; - Gholdy Muhammad; - Teachers; - Students; - Writers
Sheriff Guidry (a white leader of the community), **Henri Pichot** (sheriff's white brother-in-law) & **Dr. Joseph, Superintendent of Schools** (white man)	The authoritative status quo of literacy education and societal mores over past generations.	- hidden curriculum; - racism & education; - standardization; - high-stakes accountability
Matthew Antoine (former Mulatto schoolteacher of the community)	Past generations whose souls bear the scars of long-term disenfranchisement.	- racism and education's victims;

A word about writing method: each chapter of this book represents a range of the dialogue among students and myself that took place in the three research settings in which *A Lesson Before Dying* was experienced. Students' references to specific literary elements are set forth and methods through which they were elicited are explained. Decisions had to be made about describing one, or two or all three of the classes' classroom engagements. Writing about one class and reviewing data for only that one class would have been a far easier task. But no one class differed from another in terms of their embrace of the novel; this is a subjective statement obviously, one I cannot substantiate with a measure of the depth of each class's phenomenological aesthetic. Further, and because of my belief in this opinion, I find that there are details of each class that altogether allow me to characterize a collective depth of the literary experience of the seventy-seven students from the three classes taught by bringing an amalgam of their expressed responses to the pages. This book, then, presents one story that is a compilation of the three classrooms of students who rendered its significance in their day-to-day discussions and projects. I have chosen excerpts from the three classrooms that speak most evocatively about the zeal of embrace that was true for all of the students who read this book. That one could find a book that registered so fully with so many students is surely a rare occurrence; telling that story seems most effectively wrought by bringing across a balance of highlights from the three groups.

Readers are not likely to fully appreciate the research details without some familiarity with the novel. Synopsizing the story cannot fully convey its resonance. But, by allowing students' references to this novel to spill onto the page word-for-word, I am able to let my readers experience salient aspects of the novel while simultaneously presenting data – i.e. the students' specifically expressed references to the book. Readers can experience the novel through the student's words, through students' selections of particularly evocative phrases, passages, and segments. Italic font is used to highlight textual details that students have selected, following some guidance from me as the teacher-researcher. Each chapter of this book features what students have chosen as these critical, or most poignant elements and thus readers can both follow the evolving research story and engage the novel to a certain qualified extent.

Also, each chapter of this book corresponds to a chapter of the novel, this first one complementing the first of the novel, and so on through this book. Each chapter outlines classroom activities, methods through which they were structured, highlighted chapter details from *A Lesson before Dying*, and then theoretical and research-based comments are forthcoming. These latter comments reference such core themes as the roles of teachers who work with struggling and disenfranchised students and how political agendas must be carefully weighed as we engage such students.

The book weaves a thread of social and educational justice throughout each chapter. Sometimes that theme leaps onto the page through the words and actions of the novel's characters, sometimes through the voices of the students, and often enough as well through deliberate interpolation of theory and research thereto related. Multicultural educators have done so much to advance our awareness of the importance of our work with diverse students and their voices are brought directly into this text as well. I celebrate some in particular, thinking of them as my personal teachers through the words they have written. There are many such people but I believe I owe a special debt to Gloria Ladson-Billings (2021), Paulo Friere (2018), Jonathon Kozol (2012), and Gholdy Muhammad (2020). Ernest Gaines (1993) writes about heroes in one of his chapters and we hear Grant Wiggins strain to ask himself about the importance of such heroes in his day. I, too, ask about these heroes within literacy education and speak of many such relevant people in my own meanderings. Critical race theorists and teachers who practice critical pedagogy are numerous and attempts are made to dignify their work and honor them in this book. Then, we cannot ignore the issue of racism in education and how that plays against a backdrop related to standardization and accountability – these issues are addressed within as well.

Students of varying cultural and linguistic backgrounds participated in the project on which this book is based and yet the prevailing politic and driving energy of the work derives from an African American text and identities of African American students. The character that was formed during the reading of and response to the work was fueled by the energy of black men and women immersed in their black worlds within a white racist society. Thus, a prevailing African American collective spirit governed the affairs of our work. We were consumed by African lives in an African American world that was, in turn, portrayed as being victimized or at least profoundly influenced and affected by the white world that held power over it. This dynamic produced tensions at times but it also brought the voices of students who had analogous experiences to the forefront of our shared work. The majority of students brought life and community experience to this forum – they had all lived in a world of circumstances where one's identity had been sandwiched by prevailing power dynamics. Other students were for the first time immersed within a classroom context where societal realities were centered on a "minority" world's perspective and were themselves a minority point of view. What united everyone in an ultimately extraordinary bond was the humanity of the story and the freedom of expression that came to characterize the interactions among us. We were united in a story about the black American experience, black literature, and black power struggles even as we formed a diverse group of cultural identities.

The research objective was to discover a phenomenological literary aesthetic among disenfranchised readers that could be realized through a classroom reading methodology. The question framing this exploration was as follows:

What is the phenomenological experience of oppressed adolescents in their reading of a socioculturally relevant novel?

- would students be empowered toward clarity of energy and focus by engaging in intensive discussion and arts and media-based projects that would express their thematic synthesis of *A Lesson Before Dying;*
- what was the quality of the phenomenological experience of reading *A Lesson Before Dying* and how did this experience affect students?

- Would this experience postively affect students' stances toward and skills in academic literacy as they moved toward their fall semsters as first-year undergraduates?
- What phenomenological research methodologies facilitated the reading and classroom engagments of the students?
- What were the struggles of students as they read the book and attempted the writing and synthesis projects?
- What is the teacher's place in the classroom when facilitating a phenomenological literary reading experience?

I was determined to employ research methods that would reflect the students' reading and responsive engagements with the novel in as non-intrusvie a manner as possible. That is, I wanted to be able to record their experience with *A Lesson Before Dying* without using static methods that would dessicate their pure and spontaneously natural reading and feelings, reactions, thoughts, ideas and even stuggles with it. As much as possible I was attuned to views of phenomenological research that were respectful of researchers who had discussed some of its key tenets, however ephemeral some of those principles may have been. For example, van Manen (1990) writes that "Phenomenology, not unlike poetry, is a poetizing project; it tries an incantative, evocative speaking, a primal telling, wherein we aim to involve the voice in an original singing of the world (p. 13)." In other work (2007) he writes that "not unlike the poet, the phenomenologist directs the gaze toward the regions where meaning originates, wells up, percolates through the porous membranes of past sedimentations—and then infuses us, permeates us, infects us, touches us, stirs us, exercises a formative affect" (van Manen, 2007, p. 12). Seeking other more directive resources, while also heeding the call to present phenomenological experiential engagement with fidelity to what was being experienced, I found Groenewald (2004).

Groenewald (2004) writes that phenomenological research must respect the internal experience of being conscious of something, that the research is concerned with describing the phenomenon being experienced with as true a rendition of the facts as possible while also conveying the essence of what is being experienced. The lived experiences of ordinary people are the focus of this research exploration and, in that sense, we are in keeping with core foundational precepts of a phenomenological research study. The research objective was to 'see' and 'understand' the perspectives of the young adult disenfranchised readers' experience of a literary text, *A Lesson Before Dying*. My basic set of beliefs was that understanding their reading experiences necessitated that they read within a context that was relatively structured to varying extents so as to be able to plumb depths of reading. I worried that their reading of this novel could easily stray completely away from the novel. If I was to understand their reading of it, a relatively structured setting would prompt reading processes that might not otherwise be forthcoming in that absence. But more than that, I believed that their reading context would also prompt deepest and most complex reading processes and responses if it were collaborative in nature with the teacher acting as a co-reader. Even further, if students were able to direct themselves to some extent and if they were able to collaborate with one another, we would be involved together in a venture that was as uncircumscribed as possible, given some macrostructural guidance for each day's pursuits. These relatively non-directive pursuits will become clear as we begin to see reader's voices emerge onto the pages of this book. But, to be sure, and to be clear about the study's phenomenological paradigm the data are contained within the perspectives of the students involved and my role was that of a co-reader and participant with students most of the time. That is, in accordance with Taylor and Bogdan (1998), I was engaged in the reading with the students in the community setting of the classroom gathering videotaped data daily, to gain an understanding of the socioculturally based literary reading processes of students who had been disenfranchised from fully engaged reading in their school lives. Cresswell (2007) also offers helpful guidance and background details about phenomenological research which accords with many of these points.

2

LEARNING TO TALK

They were all there again on the second day – every one of them. I had come in earlier and set up the video recorder, placing it in the middle of the classroom. I said to them, "I'd like to hear what you think about the book so far."

"What's up with that camera?"

"Yeah, I was going to ask you – can I set this up and keep it here so that we can record a movie about your experiences with this book?"

"You makin' a movie – what for?"

"I'd like to – I've never read this book with anyone before. And none of us have read this book before – I think it'd be interesting to have a day-to-day record of how our projects work out, what we talk about, anything that comes up - anything - just – you know – be able to make a movie about our course."

"Who gonna see ah movie?"

"Prob'ly just me."

"You gonna sell this movie, make a lot a money?" They all laugh.

"You be rich – what we gonna get?"

"No. I used to do this when I worked in New York City, when I went to schools with kids. I'd record kids talking about books and I'd learn more about how to teach – just things like that. I'm really interested to hear your comments, and questions and I'd like to see how our conversations and ideas flow from one day to the next. No one's gonna see it unless you agree – maybe clips here and there – that's about it. No one's getting rich, that's for sure."

"We get to see ah movie?"

"We could do that – set up some time near the end of our five weeks together to look at some of the footage."

This was the general tenor of the introductory exchanges about the video camera; the comments included here represent a range of them from the three classes. One class member from one of the two, first-year groups seemed particularly distrustful about the idea of having the camera there, asking, "Why you wanna make a movie about us – no one ever asked us about anything we said – never."

He wasn't buying it and seemed certain I had ulterior motives. We moved along, with him being wary for the first week as the video camera was almost immediately forgotten by everyone, and this one student eventually became a part of the clamor of each day's dialogic intensities. On that second day I asked them, first, to get together with two other students and take ten minutes to read what they had written in their journals, talk about their impressions, and exchange ideas. I'd watch and listen, recording from the middle of the room as I directed the camera's focus among the eight clusters of three-person groups, and passed the microphone from one group to the other as I noticed certain patterns of conversation emerging. The presence of the microphone and recording almost certainly had some effect on their engagement, probably heightening it tacitly according import to their opinions, arguments, responses, ideas, and evolving patterns of thought. After about 10 minutes, I interrupted, directing each group to (a) choose one significant textual segment from among those they had just discussed, (b) choose someone to read it aloud, after first waiting for us to find our places on the page they identified, and then (c) explain why this particular segment seemed most critical. I explained that we would alternate speaking roles – those not speaking for their group on this day would have a turn to do so as the course continued. I called out page numbers, starting from the first page of chapter one, then chapter two, hoping that that would prompt an orderly progression of movement and revisiting of their sense of critical touchpoints of the novel. Here are some of the textual segments read aloud, primarily from chapter two of the novel:

Death by electrocution. The governor would set the date (p. 9).

When I came home from school that afternoon, I saw my aunt and Miss Emma sitting at the table in the kitchen. I was sorry now that I had come directly home, because Miss Emma was the last person I wanted to see. Just like everyone else in the quarter I knew what the sentence was going to be, and I didn't want to have to look into her face (p. 10).

I tried to think of a way to make a quick appearance in the kitchen for courtesy's sake and then leave. I didn't want to look into that face any more than I had to (pp. 10 & 11).

Miss Emma was … remembering; she was thinking; she was not seeing (p. 12).

"Called him a hog" (p. 12).

She said that and it was quiet again. My aunt looked at me, then back down at the table. I waited (p. 12).

She turned her head slowly and looked directly at me. Her large, dark face showed all the pain she had gone through this day, this past weekend. No. The pain I saw in that face came from many years past (p. 12).

"I don't want them to kill no hog," she said. I want a man to go to that chair. On his own two feet" (p. 13).

"What do you want me to do," I asked her. "What can I do? It's only a matter of weeks, a couple of months maybe. What can I do that you haven't already done over the past twenty-one years?"

"You the teacher," she said.

"Yes, I'm the teacher," I said. "And I teach what the white folks around here tell me to teach — reading, writing, and 'rithmetic. They never told me how to keep a black boy out of a liquor store" (p. 13).

I sat back in the chair and looked at both of them. They sat there like boulders, their bodies, their minds immovable (p. 14).

"Tante Lou, Miss Emma, Jefferson is dead. … There's nothing I can do anymore. Nothing any of us can do any more" (p. 14).

I stood back from the table and looked at the both of them. I clamped my jaws so tight the veins in my neck felt as if they would burst. I wanted to scream at my aunt; I was screaming inside. I had told her many, many times how much I hated this place and all I wanted to do was get away. I had told her I was no teacher, I hated teaching, and I was just running in place here. But she had not heard me before, and I knew that no matter how loud I screamed, she would not hear me now (p. 15).

The last passage on p. 15 was read aloud many, many times — many students had identified this passage as a significant one.

I waited.

"What do you think?" I asked.

They looked at me. I continued to wait.

"Can we talk about why you chose those segments?"

"He gotta make things right."

"Who," I asked.

"Grant," someone answered, "That teacha."

"Why him — why Grant?" I asked.

"He's their - he's the one - he the teachah – he be the only one that white folks back then – they won't have nuthin' ta do with those women. They know that."

"What do they want him to do?"

"Just like they say – he go there and - "

"They think he get Jefferson outa that jail- he - ". They all laugh.

"Naw. They want him – they pressurin' him …"

The video camera swings from one student to the next, and they quickly learn to pass the microphone as I point to it, and each one of them in turn, as they begin to speak.

"He don't want to be there – he be runnin' from there first chance he get."

"Why," I ask. "Why would be run."

"That's what they say - "

"Where?" I interject. "Where does it say that?" Some of them page through chapter two. I want them to become accustomed to pinpointing specific elements from the text.

"There," someone exclaims, "There, they say, *'all I wanted to do was get away … I hated teaching, and I was just running in place'* …"

"What do they mean by that?" I ask, repeating a phrase, 'Running in place'. "Who's running in place."

"He don't know what they want – he's bein' pressured."

"Is that it? Is that what they mean by running in place? I wonder," I say.

"It ain't gonna do no good. He gonna die, like he say."

Then someone says, "I got a question …". The microphone is passed to him from the other side of the room.

"How does a man die any different – it don't matter – you still die."

"I gotta – I got a response to that - "

"No - "

"They want they dignity - "

"Grant – he be like – he the only one they got –

"Jefferson is the whole black race - " Many voices speak at once

Someone else claims the microphone: "Some people are saying that he represents the whole black race because – like him – like his situation – and everything that went on – how he's in jail – that represents a stereotype – on the whole – um – black race and when she's – and - ".

The camera pans among the faces in one room – most are either listening intently or waiting to speak. Some are not waiting to speak and voices overlap.

Another hand shoots up: "They want him – he be their last hope for they respect."

"Yeah but they pressurin' him – he don't wanna do it. He, like, be wanna go from there."

The conversation among the differing classes of students all veered among similar points of conversation in different ways at this point of the course(s). I asked them all, "What do you think will happen?"

"What do you mean, like, happen?"

"So it seems as if the author is setting up some things for Grant and for Jefferson, and for Miss Emma and Grant's aunt, right? I'm just wondering what you think will happen." I was prompting predictions that might provide an impetus directing a path of synthesis, bearing their final projects in mind. But I did not want to suggest how their projections ought to be shaped, or to imply that there was a "correct" answer. I wanted to affirm the energy of their engagement with the text thus far, to encourage their ownership of its elements, to empower their voices, their thoughts, their authoritative interpretations – as well as nudge their attention toward questions that arose for me as a co-reader with them. I was aware at all times of the fragile balance between ensuring the centrality of *their* lived experience of the text, and also molding the classroom environment so that their "Synthesis Projects" would assimilate as broad a range as possible of salient details from the text.

* * * *

We know from the outset of *A Lesson Before Dying* that Jefferson is condemned to die for a crime he did not commit, and we see that Miss Emma, with the support of Tante Lou, enlists Grant Wiggins to redeem Jefferson's soul so that he will walk like a man toward his fate.

These women are bent on salvaging Jefferson's dignity by coercing the most obvious resource they can muster, the one and only educated -- and resistant -- black man in their community. Analogously we also know that Jefferson's plight is one that has been borne time-upon-time by ever so many young black men, and by many citizens whose lives hurtle them toward unfair circumstances, most certainly including unfair educational opportunities.

Just as Grant Wiggins balks at the task set for him by Miss Emma and Tante Lou, so am I as a teacher troubled by the nature of the work inflicted upon us by authority figures, especially over past years. We must ask about students who do not have what some might call cultural capitol, or those who come to school already at a disadvantage due to cultural, linguistic, economic, and experiential variables. It is *always* the most disenfranchised who are least nourished by educational programs - they are most pushed up against the barriers of dictated curriculum and skills programs (Nieto, 2000; Sleeter, 2005).

Surely, we see readily enough that Ernest Gaines' work in *A Lesson Before Dying* might be read as an allegorical text: Jefferson is not a single man, nor are Grant Wiggins, Miss Emma and the other characters single entities. They represent hundreds upon thousands of lives and circumstances. Jefferson's plight symbolizes that of so many others who have been similarly shrifted by an unfair world. Grant is not one literal man but a metaphor: his conflicted dimensions represent the work and struggles of so many others - teachers, writers, artists, and humble folks who have bent over under the burden of carrying and upholding the well-being of their people. Miss Emma and Tante Lou are singular women within the novel whose words, actions, and characters embody the manifold experiences of mothers, and sisters - women who have watched and waited for the opportunity to do whatever they could to redeem dignity and humanity for their people in ways that have been big and small. So, it must also be said that Sheriff Guidry, Henri Pichot and Dr. Joseph, as we will see, are characters surely representing the racist world-view so long in place on this continent (if not others), and still in varying degrees of latent-to-overt influence.

In this book I hyper-extend what I am guessing was Ernest Gaines' intention in writing his story. *A Lesson Before Dying* represents not one finite set of circumstances, it is conjectured, but thousands upon thousands of lives as it establishes a collective regard for the experiences of African Americans within this country. I am guessing that Gaines was not intending to enlarge his point beyond this already broad scope. In expanding the allegorical potential of this text to also embrace myself and other teachers, along with disenfranchised students, those who fight for them, African American and other heroes, and the status quo of literacy education and societal mores I am creating a new story. It is one that prompts realizations about teaching – its power to shape the character of a nation. As this research tale is encountered, it is hoped that we solidify differing realizations, as well, about our responsibilities toward those who have not yet been afforded fully expansive opportunities for deeply meaningful educational experiences. Even further, we may feel inclined to pause for reflection about how we can begin to truly find the varied resources needed to undertake this work.

Few of the seventy-seven readers who participated in this research experience had had positive or successful literacy experiences; most read at reading levels that ranged between grade two to grade eleven in what we might describe as a perfect bell curve distribution. All of these students had been involved in what Bartolome (2009) refers to as the methods fetish; she says, "the solution to the current underachievement of students from subordinated cultures is often reduced to finding the "right" teaching methods, strategies, or prepackaged curricula that will work with students who do not respond to so-called "regular" or "normal" instruction" (p. 338). These words capture the professional sentiments of scores of other theorists and researchers. Ladson-Billings (2006) claims that we are indebted to *these students*; she refers to the work of Clark (1965) who first challenged teachers and teacher educators to make education engaging and relevant for "underachieving" students. Ladson-Billings claims that "we do not have an achievement gap; we have an education debt" (p. 5), and she further states, "I am arguing that the historical, economic, sociopolitical, and moral decisions and policies that characterize our society have created an education debt"

(2006, p. 6). In her view the history of education for Native American, Latina/o, and African American students, among others, has been replete with injustice, as education has been legally denied, poorly (if at all) funded, and culturally insensitive. A legion of other theorists, researchers and practitioners also speak of such oversight, among them teacher-educators (Oakes and Lipton, 2007; Cochran-Smith, 2004, 2013; and Sleeter, 2005), sociolinguists (Au, 1980; and Delpit, 1995), multicultural education researchers (Banks, 1994; and Gay, 2002), and curriculum theorists (Apple, 2004). But in using a metaphor of debt owed to *these students* I find Ladson-Billings argument most highly evocative. Akin with such sentiments, Bartolomé writes that until we create schools that are "true culturally democratic sites ... situated in the students' cultural experiences, [subordinated] students will continue to show difficulty in mastering content area that is not only alien to their reality, but is often antagonistic toward their culture and lived experiences" (p. 352). The prevailing image here is one of an education debt incurred by educators who fail to recognize and act on these realities.

In undertaking this literary-reading, research endeavor, I am keeping the ideas of the previously mentioned writers closely in mind. While the literature might discuss *these readers* as struggling (Allington, 2001), Alverman (2011) writes "the term *struggling reader* is one that ... means different things to different people. It is sometimes used to refer to youth with clinically diagnosed reading disabilities as well as to those who are English language learners (ELL's), "at-risk", underachieving unmotivated, disenchanted, or generally unsuccessful in school literacy task" (p. 196). She further states that these labels "tell us very little about the reader though they do suggest ways of thinking about culture and adolescents" (p. 196). With historical background in mind, I am thinking of *these readers* as disenfranchised or subordinated as previously expressed by Bartolomé.

As will be made clear as we proceed through these chapters, the students with whom I worked had had virtually no reading experiences that they could remember much less ones that engaged them in culturally relevant literacy instruction. As we entertain thoughts about the students in a research context, I want to emphasize that schools have not reached them and have largely exposed them to a methods fetish approach to education. Thus, in framing thoughts about the specific research undertaking, I bear that realization closely in mind and take this moment to isolate this conceptualization: *these readers* have been disenfranchised from a full intellectual, cultural, and aesthetically nourishing school literacy experience. In querying their phenomenological experience with literary reading, we have to take into account that the work described herein was largely a first-time experience for them and that we are further indebted to them, yet again, for teaching us about how a socioculturally based literary reading event resonated for them.

About phenomenology: Creswell tells us that a "phenomenological study describes the meaning for several individuals of their lived experiences of a concept or phenomenon. Phenomenologists focus on describing what all participants have in common as they experience a phenomenon" (2007, pp. 57 & 58). Moustakas' work (1994) establishes a core methodological approach for such research investigations. The phenomenological experience in question is the students' reading of the literary text, *A Lesson Before Dying* – I wanted to know what the essential dimensions of their experience of this book were. Knowing that the consciousness of the students would be most fluidly accessed if I could hear their spontaneous thoughts through free-flowing conversations, I introduced the video camera and was thus able to "hear" and "see" their embodied responses as well as observe and make inferences about how this experience grew over the five weeks of the reading.

Van Manen tells us that phenomenology is a "poetizing project"; it tries to convey a telling of the story of engaged experience so that the original sense of that is conveyed for readers/listeners. He suggests that, "not unlike the poet, the phenomenologist directs the gaze toward the regions where meaning originates, wells up, percolates through the porous membranes of past sedimentations—and then infuses us, permeates us, infects us, touches us, stirs us, exercises a formative affect" (van Manen, 2007, p. 12). This is what I have attempted to do in my telling of the story; I do so by bringing the words of students directly to the page so we can hear them. I do so as well with reference to Rosenblatt's notion of aesthetic reading and attempt to convey the "live circuit" between readers and *A Lesson Before Dying* in a way that allows the readers' "fully lived-through fusion with the text to come through" (1978, p. 47). I want to be able to show that the aesthetic life of the students in this book is one that is highly active and is an actual experience being lived through, a "moment-to-moment participation" (1978, p. 28) that "draws upon past experiences and calls forth meaning from the coded symbols" (1978, p. 22) that are the words on the page. Also, I want not to topple the primacy of the readers' experiences of the book with philosophical weight but rather allow their words to convey the "associations, feelings, attitudes, and ideas that these words and their referents arouse" (Rosenblatt, 1978, p. 25). I believe we see this aesthetic conjured as we hear the students speaking – this happens throughout this book as their words show what is stirred up for them and how "the fusion of thought and feeling, of cognitive and affective ... constitutes the integrated sensibility" (Rosenblatt, 1978, p. 46). But I also must respect the noble traditions of philosophical roots of phenomenology and briefly refer to the work of Husserl (1931) and Moustakas (1994). John Dewey's (1910) influence must be mentioned, especially as it affected Rosenblatt's views, as should Roman Ingarden's influence in his *The Literary Work of Art* (1973).

Influenced by Descartes, Hume and Kant, Husserl's work (1931) most deeply influenced this project in terms of his insistence on the fundamental role of intersubjectivity in our conceptual system. In order to understand linguistic systems, he said, we would study the units of consciousness that respective persons give voice to. These he termed intentional acts or experiences. The words and eventual projects of the students were the intentional content that expressed their experiences of *A Lesson Before Dying*. These "nominal" acts produced "nominal meanings". The students' subjective and intuitive perceptions of this book were fueled by their life experiences which are conjoined with the descriptions I am offering to produce an accumulating description of their reading. The quality of their experience swims onto the page through their words that are reproduced exactly as they were heard thus allowing readers to feel the essence of this collective experience. The shared meaning of the work was produced in the collaborative dynamic of the verbal exchanges and private readings of the students. In Husserl's terms the mental files – the students' words, interior thoughts, emotional responses, and project expressions – become the common intentional object of the experiences which become more and more complicated as we read further and further into the book. Their structures of experience are expressed through words primarily and ultimately in varying projects. My phenomenological descriptions come onto the page in a first-person point of view as he insisted and we hear exactly the words of the students exactly as intended and expressed by them. The reality of the literary object becomes fused with the students' experience of it achieving a union of subject-object oneness.

These comments point to my awareness of the history and essence of phenomenology but they are offered as backdrop commentary. The essence of the phenomenological experience accumulates over the course of this book and cannot be fully conveyed through an analytic account of its intellectual roots but rather will become more and more apparent as the pages turn.

3

LEARNING TO TRUST

T here we were again on our third day together, becoming deeply involved in an experience that was taking shape moment by moment. Ostensibly, I had promised to teach basic skills, reading comprehension, and academic literacy as a means of fostering greater preparedness for the upcoming fall semester. Subverting that surface-level agenda, I was seeking profundity of a deeper kind – that feeling again, that sense of innocent trust that occurs when collectively, everyone is enthusiastically building literary communion. The construction process was collaborative in nature, involving diverse students some of whom connected profoundly with the text in deeply personal ways, and others who, though curious, interested, and involved, were not necessarily invested with the same degree of socio-cultural kinship. As each day became another, I tended the ongoing reading engagement with structures that would nudge a focused energy toward project syntheses, yet not direct predetermined interpretive conclusions. Journal writing was ongoing through this process. The video camera was turned on, the microphone ready.

"I know you have read the 3rd chapter and have your journals – can we – can we take them out and your books – and let's – for today can we do this – can we focus on Grant today maybe – I know we have Miss Emma and Tante Lou and others in this chapter – but I have to say I'm curious about him – what's he going through 'cause it's him talking here right? Did you write anything about him – can you talk together about that for about 5 minutes in your groups before we do something altogether, and I'll read your journals tonight. What are you seeing about him in this chapter – can you find places that help see things from his perspective?"

As wc move from small-group processes to whole-class conversation, I ask them, "Can we kind of find the places from the beginning of this chapter that you notice about Grant? Can we read those segments as we pass the mike around?"

Here is what was read aloud, again, choosing representative snippets from the three classes:

> *Not only was I going up to Henri Pichot's house against my will, but I had to perform all the courtesies of a chauffer as well (p. 16).*

> *I could feel my aunt's eyes on the back of my head for shutting the door as I did (p. 16).*

> *When my aunt started to get out of the car to open the gate for me, I told her to keep her seat because I had nothing to do all that day but serve. I felt her eyes on the back of my neck again, then on the side of my face as I opened the gate (p. 17).*

> *I was not aiming for the ruts but I was not avoiding them either (p. 17)*

> *I looked around the kitchen. I had come into this kitchen many times as a small child, to bring in wood for the stove, to bring in a chicken I had caught and killed, eggs I had found in the grass, and figs, pears, and pecans I had gathered from the trees in the yard ... Miss Emma was the cook up here then ... she cooked; she ran the house; my aunt washed and ironed; and I ran through the yard to get the*

things they needed to cook or cook with. As a child growing up on this plantation, I could not imagine this place, this house, existing without the two of them here (p. 18).

"They called my boy a hog Mr. Henri. ... I want the teacher make him know he's not a hog, he's a man. I want him know that 'fore he go to that chair, Mr. Henri (p. 21).

"And what do you plan to do?" he asked me (p. 21).

I shook my head. "I have no idea". He stared at me and I realized that I had not answered him in the proper manner. "Sir", I added (p. 22).

"I'm not beggin' for his life no more; that's over. I just want to see him die like a man. This family owe me that much Mr. Henri. And I want it. I want somebody do something for me one time fore I close my eyes, Mr. Henri," (p. 22).

As the varied voices in the room called out segments of text, I video-recorded their words, waiting quietly for another voice to take over the reading of each subsequent segment; they are presented in a sequential order from one page-to-another of this chapter. Then I stood and drew a simple concept-map circle into the center of a sheet of chart paper, taped it to a bare wall, and asked what words they'd use to describe Grant (with his name in the middle of the circle), given what had been read from this chapter, and what had happened so far in the book:

"We be makin' a Grant-flower," one called out.

"Yes, a Grant flower," I laughed along with them, realizing that what I'd drawn looked like a daisy, with its petals extending from a circular hub.

"It's not just him – it's all a them – those women – what they be wantin'."

"It's like my cousin," one young man called out, "He's in prison upstate and he got, like - life!"

Several other comments pass, many referring to life stories, effects on families, and some talk about getting away: "Um gonna get my education; my father tell me to leave they mess; I be here – you know what I'm sayin' I'm be – this is – I am the one goin' - go back there with my degree!"

"So, OK, let's talk about Grant now, let's see if we can start in a little bit on one of the projects you got in your syllabus on that first day – what do you think? Give me some words – some adjectives for Grant." I ask if anyone can video-record as I write and comments are forthcoming – someone quickly steps in after some arguments about why "he" was chosen instead of them.

"OK tell me and give me a page number and I'll be a scribe for you," I quickly interject, "Give me some adjectives, and a page number, and then see if you can read one of the lines from a page over the first 3 chapters that go with your adjectives."

"What do you mean!?"

"OK, for example, I think he's, like, no – you look and tell me what word describes how Grant is feeling in this chapter, OK?"

"He be angry!"

"OK – look through and give me a sentence about that from what we just heard"

"He hit them bumps – he mad at his Aunt for makin' him go there!"

"Find the place it says that," I direct them.

The students bustle, having been diverted from discussing their own life stories in this instance. Adjectives are forthcoming:

"Angry, disrespectful, resentful, unwilling, preoccupied, confused, nostalgic …"

I create a concept map, aligning page numbers beside adjectives – sometimes the page numbers are searched for by those who call out the adjectives, sometimes not. It is loud, disorganized, and messy. I call out directives to those who seem to be overwhelmed, suggesting partnerships, asking certain shyer, non-verbal members of the classes to be a page finder for certain other people. It works. I create a map and then as things calm down after 35 or so minutes, I ask them to write about Grant in their journals for 3 minutes, using adjectives from the board, and referring to pages that are noted there. Then, I refer them to their syllabi – particularly to the description for the **CHARACTER MAP PROJECT.** As each day unfolds, I want to introduce activities that gently frame assimilation processes associated with each of the major projects for this course. By starting a character analysis of Grant, I am hoping that our beginning constructions of the "Grant flower" will allow students to easily see how such work might be extended should they decide to produce a character map such as the one we have started here. Students might decide to build a character map of Jefferson, Miss Emma or other characters, for example, and I wanted to frame a process for them that would sharpen their attention to textual details about key characters, as well as offer them a structure that would organize such impressions.

* * * *

Our work on a character analysis of Grant Wiggins is three fold in nature and purpose: (a) it models a strategic process through which his character (and other characters) might be systematically explored, (b) it may heighten readers' attention to evolving aspects of this central character as their reading continues and their appreciation for his being evolves, and (c) it may augment readers' attention to textual details of language and description, character development, *and* other literary elements. By taking a few moments to set up rudimentary foundational work related to the thinking and attention that could be the beginning of one of the synthesis projects, we have used the collaborative energy of the class to establish dynamic character focus. They are having focused fun to put it very simply and the energy generated with one another fuels the continued work to complete this activity.

We are aware that culturally relevant instruction is a necessary ingredient for students who have been stampeded with standards-based instruction. Many also speak of the need for culturally relevant literature; Tatum writes that "[u]sing culturally relevant literature is the key to a culturally relevant approach" and that "[t]here is a fundamental tension between a basic skills approach to meet standards and a culturally relevant approach" (2000, p. 53). In other work,

Wilhelm (2008) writes that adolescents are meaningfully engaged in visual techniques, drama, and symbolic story representations. Franzaks' (2006) work on "marginalized" readers points to adolescent reading as a socially constructed process, commenting, in Moje's words, (2000) that marginalized readers are those "who are not connected to literacy in classrooms and schools. Specifically, we identify as marginalized adolescents those who are not engaged in the reading and writing done in school" (Moje et al, 2000, p. 211). Franzak suggests that, while cognitive psychologists, socioculturalists, reader-response and critical literacy theorists, and developmentalists all describe reading in their own image, she pays fair attention to those who "hold that reading is not a stand-alone practice, but rather one embedded in socially situated activity" (p. 221). Also, Franzak discusses policy issues related to marginalized readers; she documents a sense of crisis among policy associations, commenting that policy texts do not sufficiently "explore how the institution of schooling contributes to the creation of marginalized readers or how schools are but part of a systematic unequal distribution of achievement and power" (pp. 234 & 235). She concludes by affirming the important role of qualitative research in exploring the literacy lives and lived experiences of adolescents.

As we draw some of these strands of thought together and connect them to the literary readers featured in this book it becomes obvious that I am situating them in realms of thought pertaining to sociocultural, critical literacy, and reader-reponse perspectives. At the same time that I write this thought, I am also realizing that we have to look at the critical role of the teacher in providing contexts which allow the students to bring their worlds into the classroom. To quote Franzak one more time, "it is easy to overlook the fact that struggling or marginalized readers are, in fact, individuals" and we need to see "the students at the center of our work" (p. 239). Given the qualitative phenomenological lens through which this literary reading experience is being framed and explored, the students' varied experiences of *A Lesson Before Dying* lie at the center of this shared literary reading venture. We are reading a highly culturally relevant text, exploring it through various arts-based media and paying careful attention to students who have most certainly been marginalized or "disenfranchised" from the education system that they are all trying very hard to stay connected to through their summer "remedial" classes. Learning more about their phenomenological aesthetic with this novel helps us appreciate yet more about how other similar readers engage the world of multicultural literature.

4

BEGINNINGS OF SYNTHESIS

t is Thursday. A fourth chapter read and reflected upon. Students are tired; each day of this week, they've been through three, 2-hour classes, and another hour of study skills. Some come in late, others sleep in class that day – it shows up clearly on film! The phenomenological reading experience still needs tending - shepparded guidance that helps students amass focus yet resists telling them what that focus should be: structure without dictatorship, suggestion without commandments, and questioning without a necessarily right or wrong answer. This is the nature of such a classroom-based, literary reading experience. Despite some grumpy resistance, we have to move forward into this experiential territory, for another four weeks after this first week! Is one text sufficiently absorbing to be the basis for this course, I wonder? Are the reading and writing structures and final-project activities sufficiently focused, encouraging, and sustaining for each 2-hour class meeting? Are we invested enough in this literary universe to keep things working?

The day begins: "If I asked you to find one word or phrase from this chapter [chapter 4] that seemed to kind of – you know – kind of be the one concept – the one idea for this chapter that brings everything together so far in your opinion, what would it be?"

"We looking for another Grant-flower?!" someone teased.

"Good idea," I retorted, smiling, "Let's do that – let's get together with our groups today or work by yourselves for awhile and see if you can – when you're ready – come up here and write onto the board what you think is the word, or phrase or a whole sentence that seems to be the most important one in this chapter." Secretly I worried that group work might be too stale already.

"What you mean – you want a word, a phrase a sentence – what you mean!?"

"See if there's one word – I can think of one – or maybe a phrase – maybe it's what one of the characters says – or a whole passage – maybe a sentence or more – try it out – ten minutes, then I'll interrupt you – try it out. When you come up to write make sure you put page numbers beside your words or phrases, OK?"

"What's your word?!"

"Not telling – go ahead and try it out – be careful not to wake up James!" They laugh.

Then when it seemed they were ready – or not ready as the cases varied - they moved toward the boards all around the room with their 3-person group members. Here are the varied segments they wrote onto the board from the text, again, from beginning to end of this chapter:

I needed to be with Vivian (p. 25).

... movie theatre for whites on the riverbank ... back of town to the colored section (p. 25).

We're teachers and we have a commitment ... a whole fucking barrel of commitment ... I don't feel alive here ... I'm tired of feeling committed (p. 29).

"They gave him death" (p. 30).

"Now his godmother wants me to visit him and make him know – prove to these white men – that he's not a hog, that he's a man. I'm supposed to make him a man. Who am I? God?" (p. 31).

> *"If they say yes, I want you to go for me – for us Grant – I*
> *don't know if I can take it – I know you can – I'll need*
> *you every minute – I'll be here"* (p. 32).

"So," I begin after the varying elements are scribbled onto the board (reflecting an amalgam of core segments that were selected from among the three, twenty-five-or more classroom groups), "Let's look at what you have – can we read these words, and phrases out loud – I want to do something – I want to try out an idea with you."

Various students read aloud what has been written onto the board.

"Let's read the first one again," I direct them. "Let's read it more slowly – can you do that?" I ask the person who has read the first phrase to reread it. She complies. As she does this I walk to a bare patch of wall and tape an extra-large, twenty-by-thirty-inch sheet of chart paper onto the wall. The students are curious.

"Can you read that again?" I ask, and the phrase, 'I needed to be with Vivian,' is read again and then once again. I have by now looped a circle into the middle of the sheet of chart paper.

I repeat the phrase out loud now, "I needed to be with Vivian". And I ask them, "What's really going on here? What is the underlying idea here? Why is Ernest Gaines – why is the author writing that here?"

"What do you mean – writing what – why – what?!" They look bewildered.

I know what I am getting at but all too often (habitually?) I am vague, and struggle to convey clearly what I mean to my students. I try again, pointing now to the inner part of the circle I have placed onto the chart paper:

"I mean Ernest Gaines seems to be saying something about 'need' here, right?" Is there something about that idea, 'need', that is perhaps a big idea, a main concept, a key theme of the book so far?"

Silence.

"Need," I repeat, "Is this idea about 'need'? -" I ask, writing that word into the center of the concept map I am trying to start, " – is this a big idea in the text so far – is it something we could associate with many or all of the characters so far?"

"Yeah – prob'ly," says one person tentatively.

"Really? Who?" I ask, now standing in front of the chart paper and the blank circle there, in which I write "N-E-E-D" in upper case text.

"Grant – he need Vivian. That's why we write that!"

Quickly I draw an arrow outward from the circle and write "Grant & Vivian", asking, "What do they need?"

"Love, strength, confidence, power – "Various other ideas come forth.

"Who else has need?" I ask.

"Miss Emma, Jefferson, the whole black community …"

I scribble on our concept sheet about "N-E-E-D," as various other sheets of chart paper are taped up at my request – various things happening simultaneously again.

"OK, now let's look at the other phrases you have written onto the board – look at them and give me an idea about another key concept that might be going on in the book so far – can one of you read one of the other statements written there?"

A hand goes up. "Great, which one can you read?" I stand back ready to hand over my marker to a student in the class.

A young man reads in a strong, yet mechanical voice: "… *movie theatre for whites on the riverbank … back of town to the colored section*" (p. 25).

"What's a word, a key concept that we'd associate with those phrases?" I ask.

"Racism!" Two or three have exclaimed at once, without hesitation. I pass the marker to one of them and point to one of the new sheets of chart paper now taped onto the wall, "Let's start a thematic concept map for 'R-A-C-I-S-M,'" I suggest, now deliberately using terminology that is linked to another of the synthesis projects that were all too briefly reviewed during our first class, and also purposely attempting to channel the students' ongoing conscious focus to governing ideas.

"Look at what you've written onto the board and give me another key concept from the sentences we have here."

"Commitment," someone yells out. I toss another marker, as someone else adumbrates, "A whole fucking barrel of commitment," which is what the text literally says. The class bursts into raucous laughter and I caution, "Let's write out only one of those words here – other classes will be coming into this room for this afternoon after we leave." They get the censoring intent of my last comment, writing the word 'C-O-M-M-I-T-M-E-N-T' into the middle of another sheet. Now we have the rudiments of three concept maps taped around the room.

"Anything else?" I ask. "Can any one read another of the sen- "

"Love!" a girl decisively calls out, cutting me off. I toss another marker. She rolls her eyes and walks to another blank sheet of paper: 'L-O-V-E,' she writes.

"So," I ask them, walking to the first map, we have begun to make associations or connections between 'N-E-E-D,'" I say, "and Grant and Vivian".

"What details could we add to our maps on commitment, love, racism, and need – what are some details from the book that might be associated with – which one of these maps would you want work on together first?"

"Racism!"

"OK, let's have teams of people write in details for each map," I suggest organizing the room into 4, 6-person teams, one team for each of the four core concepts generated so far: 'N-E-E-D, C-O-M-M-I-T-M-E-N-T, R-A-C-I-S-M, AND L-O-V-E'.

"Take your books with you," I direct them. "Work first with 3 people from each group doing the writing onto the chart paper for 3 minutes, as the other 3 people find details and page numbers from the book about the key idea you are working on. Then we'll switch, taking turns as scribes and readers and detail finders." This explanation, and the previous activities make good sense to everyone, though they argue about which concept they want to start working on – I quickly assign students to one of the 4 key concepts that have emerged from chapter four of the novel, telling them that as the reading continues, they will all have a chance to develop details on other days about an idea they might not be working on today.

The ensuing several minutes are busy. I circulate from one group to the next affirming, suggesting, prodding, organizing, cajoling, and especially calling attention to those who are readily noting page numbers and specific phrases from the text as the four sheets of chart paper's concept maps expand with details. There is a lot of argument. Sometimes one person's written detail is crossed out — that generates differing responses! Not everyone is completely involved but those who aren't (aside from James who is still sleeping through it all) are attentive to what is going on, enjoying the spectacle of activity. Much rereading takes place. New impressions are formed about what has really been happening so far; some admit to others that they really didn't "get" what Miss Emma was asking Grant to do. Others realize that the story takes place at a time of the recent past (the late 1940's). Some pose questions to one another. Some sit reading quietly to catch up, hoping I won't notice. Of course, salacious details are offered about the course of Grant and Vivian's relationship.

Then, after about 35 or more minutes, I call for their attention and ask each person in the class to explain one or two of the details that have been scribbled onto their map. I want to establish some informal channels of presentation for them. Thus, I direct them to one of the maps that seems to have been most developed — the one where group cohesion and productivity was smoothest. I ask the group that worked on the "L-O-V-E" concept map to offer brief comments about their map, asking for one member at a time to pinpoint a detail, *and* related page number from the novel and tell us how that detail relates to their key concept. I choose this group, knowing that the most confident and articulate members will speak first, and that they will model language and actions that others will emulate when it is their turn to speak.

* * * *

At this point in our conversation we can turn to several veins of thought to gain further perspective about the readers and activities being presented. First of all, it is critical to look at work on adolescent literacy, in general, realizing that we are talking about disenfranchised readers. Secondly, we need to think carefully about the range of processes being asked of the students at this time: reading, collaboration, discussion and presentation elements, to summarize areas of their asked-for focus. Then thirdly, we have to consider the work on literary reading processes for such readers. A lot is going on for my students at this time and, as most will be heard to say, they had never been involved in such a range of activity with a literary text before, or any other genre of text for that matter. The varieties of viewpoints that can be brought to bear are thus multifacted. I'd like to borrow some further perspective, first, from the field of adolescent literacy, then glance, secondly, at work regarding reading theory and research specifically, while also then, thirdly, peeking at literary reading processes, all the while bearing in mind that we are discussing students whose school lives have not engaged them in the acts of mind that we have seen them being prompted toward as they read *A Lesson Before Dying*.

Research-based policy regarding adolescent literacy advises us to provide meaningful choice to adolescents, engage them with real-world practices, affirm multiple literacies, have supportive learner-centered environments and foster social responsibility through multicultural literacy. This we hear from the National Council of Teachers of English (NCTE, 2012) who, in commenting on teachers' preparedness, outlines the need to integrate literacy processes, base teaching on some degree of information-rich and media-based resources, assessment alignments, and respect for context and students' diverse identities. The Alliance for Excellent Education (AEE) discuss literacy, broadly speaking, as the corner stone of adolescents' secondary lives (Wise, 2009). Alverman and Hinchman (2011) pay particular attention to the lives that adolescents lead, emphasizing that our educational plans for them must respect their digital and media savvy and the diverse contexts of their lived realities in the world outside of school.

A perusal of reading research scholarship reveals a much more delineated focus on specific attention to finite reading processes. For example, Scammacca et al (2007) focus on interventions for struggling readers; they summarize such emphasis at the word and text level, speaking of reading difficulties that may be benefitted by comprehension strategies, and "gains" in reading comprehension. The first volume of the *Handbook of Reading Research* (1984) puts primary emphasis on technical models of the reading processes, including focus on word recognition, structures of text, metacognition and cognitive processes, as well as various instructional practices thereto related. The second such volume (1991) has a complementary focus on reading research variables, constructs of reader process, and literacy and schooling. While the third volume (2000) broadens its focus to include literacy research, processes, practices, and policies, we don't find work that helps us construe a broader understanding of literary reading, especially that of disenfranchised adolescents. While the 5th edition of *Theoretical Models and Processes of Reading* (2004) pays heed to sociocultural contexts of reading with fair attention, we do not necessarily gain insights about literary reading, nor was it the focal intention of any of these texts to explore such phenomena.

Looking further afield, Rayner and Pollatsek's (1989) work describes various approaches and a history of reading research as "an emphasis on the different components of a complex skill" (p. 8), referring to "information processing" as they outline retinal processing, pattern recognition, sensory storage, short-term memory, long-term memory, and stages of information processing. This text offers a thorough overview of what have come to be known as top-down, bottom-up and interactive models of reading. Bottom-up models, they say, portray information as flowing "in a passive manner through the information-processing system" (p. 25), whereas information in top-down models passes slowly due to "bottlenecks" which force readers to slow down as they stop to align incoming information within their own memory and experiences. From an interactive perspective, a reader relies both on the information represented in the visual dimensions and patterns of the letters on the page and his/her own memory and experience to process and comprehend the meaning of what is being read. Gibson's and Levin's book (1975) by the same name presents an analogous cognitive representation of reading.

Frank Smith's *Understanding Reading* (2004) offers another view of reading, also much consulted in the field. He allows that reading is a phenomenon that entails appreciation for "language, memory, learning, the development of spoken language ability, and the physiology of the eye and brain" (*vii*) but also writes about psycholinguistic variables. He refers to schemata (organized structures of various experiences, including story schemes), which we rely on as we read - as we predict and apply our experiences of the world to the page. Smith helps us see that as we read psycholinguistically, merging thought and language to make sense of text, we are performing a host of naturally occurring processes: predicting, organizing, inferencing, literally comprehending, imagining, thinking, reasoning, problem solving, forming and enlarging and building new concepts. We are classifying, categorizing, metacognating, and reflecting as we simultaneously process surface and deep structures of language. Goodman (1976) referred to such processing as a psycholinguistic guessing game.

While my students are certainly reading, per se, thus inviting me to look back at all of my work in this specific field of study, they are reading literature. I am distinguishing between a focus on more finite reading processes and literary reading processes to lead us into the broader terrain related to the reading of literature. Smith's and Goodman's (2004; 1976) work makes for a gentle transition into this peek at literary reading processes; they help us to see reading as a highly complex activity that entails the experience and worldviews of readers. But they do not speak specifically about the reading of literature and right now a glimpse of some fundamentals of that field may widen our regard for the specific activity going on with readers featured in this book. Let's see.

If we look to a highly influential work that introduces the fundamentals of literary reading and a background on literary theory, we'd find Eagleton (1983). As he summarizes a formalist regard for literature we begin to see their point of view through his words: "[t] he Formalists started out by seeing the literary work as a more or less arbitrary assemblage of 'devices'" (p. 3). They saw literature as a "special kind of language" (p. 4); they began to "think of all literature as poetry" (p. 5), as "non-pragmatic discourse" (p. 7). He then goes on to comment on the difficulty of objectively characterizing literature when he brings readers into the equation: "one can think of literature less as some inherent quality ... than as a number of ways in which people relate themselves to writing" (p. 8). Continuing with this evolving point of view we hear him musing about the relativity of literary definition; after all, he says, literature is ultimately unstable given that its value and interpretation relies on the highly variable "re-writing" of works in accordance with differing societies and contexts in which "literature" is read. Readers bring variable assumptions, beliefs, or "ideologies" to a text: "subjective differences of evaluation work within a particular, socially structured way of perceiving the world" (p. 14). In eighteenth century England, for example, literature gained importance as a way of socializing the middle classes to "correct taste and common cultural standards" (p. 15).

Eighteenth and nineteenth century Romanticism is described by Eagleton as a solitary and creatively imaginative "alternative ideology" (p.17) to the harsh realities of industrial capitalism with its "wage-slavery" (p. 17), and "alienating labor-process" (p. 17) mechanisms. The notion of a unity of aesthetic experience came to be seen as an apposite complement to 19th century empiricist rationalism. The weakening relevance of the church's ideological powers to pacify and inspire a "contemplative inner life" (p. 20) meant that the church was losing its ideological power and control – its "*pacifying* influence [that fostered] meekness, self sacrifice and the contemplative inner life" (p. 20, original italicis). Literature, then, took on the function of delighting and instructing but also to save souls and heal the state. Matthew Arnold (in Eagleton, 1983) speaks of the power of schools to tame the working class and the power of literature within schools to provide this salve. Eagleton writes that "literature becomes more than just handmaiden of moral ideology: it *is* moral ideology for the modern age" (p. 24). And when the first great war ended with an English victory over Germany, he submits that "[l]iterture would be at once solace and reaffirmation, a familiar ground on which Englishman could regroup both to explore, and to find some alternative to the nightmare of history" (p. 26).

We are surely waiting for the arrival of the baleful adolescent in our midst at this point. Where does this sojourn through European literary evolution join the tide of work on adolescent literary reading process and theory? One more quick glance at Eagleton's synthesis helps us along the road there. We move through T. S. Eliot's emphasis on the poem as an object that can suggest "enigmatic images which would penetrate to those primitive levels at which all men and women experience alike" (p. 35) to the close reading and practical criticism of detailed analytic interpretation that implies that "any piece of language, 'literary' or not can be adequately studied or even understood in isolation" (p. 38). American New Criticism brings us to a renewed emphais on the poem, which was seen to exist "as a self-enclosed object, mysteriously intact in its own unique being" (p. 40). The authors' intentions were regarded as having "no relevance to the interpretation of his or her text" (p. 41), while "[r]escuing the text from author and reader went hand in hand with disentangling it from any social or historical context" (p. 42). In the figure of Empson, then, we find shadows of regard for the reader's process and experience of literature: his work is described by Eagleton as a kind of "pre-run" (p. 46) toward phenomenology, hermeneutics and reception theory. As we peruse this territory we can allow ourselves brief annoyance with Eagleton now, as he seems to completely overlook one very important woman in the vast field of white male literary theorists.

We are offered an incisive snapshot of phenomenology through the lens of its key proponent, Edmund Husserl and in this picture are able to appreciate another view of literary reading as we wade toward our waiting adolescents and a lone female theorist. Husserl's view is that "consciousness is not just a passive registration of the world, but actively constitutes or 'intends' it" (Eagleton, 1983, p. 48) while "put[ting] in brackets anything which is beyond our immediate experience" (p. 48). It is helpful to even further recognize that "[w]hat is presented to phenomenological knowledge is not just, say, the experience of jealousy or of the colour red, but the universal types or essences of these things" (p. 48). In my work, thus, I attempt to get at, if you will, the very essence of the aesthetics of the phenomenonon of literary reading experience for marginalized or struggling adolescents, to bring this intention forth now momentarily. The literary object and subjective reader(s) are really two sides of the same coin – not separate entities but united. We read that "[p]henomenology ... restored the transcendental subject to its rightful throne" (p. 50) and that within phenomenological criticism "the unifying essence is the author's mind" – "the way an author experiences time or space" (p. 51). We are thus penetrating to the "very interior of a writer's consciousness" (p. 51). The reader becomes subsumed in the essence of the *author's* experience.

Critiquing Husserl, Eagleton submits that the sphere of language and experience is "ineradically social" (p. 52) and thus where phenomenology with Husserl "wishes to keep 'pure' internal experiences free from the social contaminations of language" (p. 53), the theory runs into trouble in its reluctance to fully come to terms with language other than in "imagining a language which would be purely expressive of consciousness" (p. 53). In contrast, Heiddegger's phenomenological view begins with a regard for subjects "inside a reality which we can never fully objectify" (p. 54, In Eagleton), and so human existence is a "dialogue with the world, and the more reverent activity is to listen rather than to speak" (p. 54). Language is the "very dimension in which human life moves" (p. 55) and has an existence all its own" in which humans come to participate, and only in that participation do they come to be human at all" (p. 55). Language preexists and is where reality "unconceals itself" (p. 55). The human subject is merely the medium where the 'truth' of literary art object speaks itself and in this view is something we let happen. By yet another phenomenologist, Hans Georg Gadamer, the question is raised: what is the meaning of a literary text? For him, such a text is not solely attributed to an author but is 'unstable' and slippery, "shaped and constrained by the historically relevant criteria of a particular culture" (p. 60) and thus ultimately unknowable as such - dependent on the questions asked of it and always *'productive'* in the realization that there is a constant new meaning there. But, points out Eagleton, this approach focuses on works of the past and refuses to recognize that literary "discourse is always caught up with a power which may be by no means benign" (p. 64).

As we move forward here inch by inch, we encounter reception aesthetics or reception theory that does not focus almost exclusively on works of the past but blatantly asks what happens when we read literature. In this view the reader makes inferences, speculates, builds hypotheses, makes "implicit connections, fills in gaps ... and to do this means drawing on a tacit knowledge of the world in general and of literary conventions in particular" (p. 66). For reception theorists, the reader 'concretizes' the literary work of art "which in itself is no more than a chain of organized black marks on a page" (p. 66). As we read literature we:

> Shed assumption, revise beliefs, make more and more complex inferences and anticipations; each sentence opens up a horizon which is confirmed, challenged or undermined by the next. We read backwards and forwards simultaneously, predicting and recollecting, perhaps aware of other possible realizations of the text which our reading has negated (p. 67).

To bring this voyage around to a point of summary, we might say that modern literary theory has moved from "a preoccupation with the author (Romanticism and the nineteeth century)" (p. 64) to "an exclusive concern with the text (New Criticism)" (p. 64) to "a marked shift of attention to the reader over recent years" (p. 64). The reader, Eagleton tells us, "has always been the most underprivileged of this trio – strangely since without him or her there would be no literary texts at all" (p. 64).

Why Eagleton would not have referred to Rosenblatt's 1938 and 1978 work is both curious and vexing. For it was Rosenblatt's 1938 original work in *Literature as Exploration* which brought the every day reader fully into view as the flesh and blood reality that realizes the elements of the literary text – not the author, not reader as concretizer of an author's meaning, not reader as predetermined by the textual schemas, and not reader as filling in the indeterminacy of the text, but reader as explorer and personally vested individual each with a unique mindset and social context. While Eagleton tells us that "[f]or literature to happen, the reader is quite as vital as the author" (1983, p. 65), Rosenblatt writes that there are millions of readers and millions of texts, that a work "remains merely inkspots on paper until a reader transforms them into a set of meaningful symbols" (1978, p.

25). Further she explains that a "live circuit" between reader and text creates an imaginative experience that is a result of many factors: the author's life, literary traditions, and the form, structure and method of the work, but these variables are "expendable unless they demonstrably help to clarify or enrich individual experiences" (p. 27). The infinitely vast range of responses is born of social origins and effects arising from "particular social systems and … groups such as age, sex, occupation and nation" (p. 28). Even more, literary responses are shaped by "forces of social conditioning [that are] pervasive in the formation of specific emotional drives" (p. 28) and which are, "socially patterned, so the literary work, like language itself, is a social product" (p. 28). The teaching of literature, in turn, she argues must facilitate a rich and dynamic exploration that respects this vast range of dynamics. More will be said later in this book about the even more mature 1978 work. Having now encountered a range of work on ideologies of reading, and literary reading per se we are next door to the vestibule of adolescent literary reading and the teaching of such.

We are outright exclaiming at this point: "Where is the adolescent reader in this rather vast spectrum of literary thought, and reading theory?" One might begin by situating focus on adolescent reading solidly in the latter half of 20th and these first years of the 21st centuries. The *Handbook of Adolescent Literacy Research* (2009) puts the spotlight on adolescents' literacies with an overview on sociocultural constructions of adolescence, commenting that, "adolescent literacy emerges in the culture in which young peoples' development takes place; literacy practices are afforded and constructed by what is available in their settings; and research is a cultural practice that reflects local goals and practices" (pp. 3 & 4). With such a comment, the editors situate the ideological thumbprint of this volume as minds in society much like Vygotsky (1978), i.e. steeped in the amniotic social, linguistic, economic, political and cultural environments in which they begin and live their lives. Highly varying school contexts complement and enlarge adolescent literacies – or not. Adolescents' workplace, academic, virtual and media literacy lives are critical variables in a comprehensive appreciation for their literate identities. Also, a fully comprehensive view of diverse adolescent identities looks at gender roles, sexualities, cultural selves, and the distinct voices of girls, Latina/os, American Indians, and multiplicity of cultural contexts in which these varying identies have been shaped.

Alvermann (2009) refers to the deluge of attention paid to adolescent literacy over past years, referring to two dominant models: the autonomous and the ideological. The prevailing autonomous model, she says "views reading and writing as neutral processes that are largely explained by individual variations in cognitive and physiological functioning" (p. 15, and as we have seen earlier), whereas, in referencing Street, (1995), she comments that "the ideological model subsumes the autonomous model and simultaneously incorporates an array of social and cultural ways of knowing that can account for seemingly absent but always present power structures (p. 16). Johannessen and McCann (2009) complement this view when they discuss struggling adolescent readers: "the learners for whom English is a second language and learners from low-income homes are the adolescents who appear to be struggling with literacy" (p. 65). Latina/os and African Americans are embraced by the humble socioeconomic echelons that include a preponderance of "struggling readers" snagged within the power structures of schooling and society.

These readers whom we see as inexperienced and assisted by guiding structures toward concept identification and enlargement are those who have emerged out of history onto the stage of our reflections here. They are enmeshed within contrasting constructions of an autonomous view of reading, as described here and in a quick review of reading theory earlier, and an ideological model of reading working with me. Over all of the years of their schooling, they had been involved in autonomous reading programs that emphasized word lists, syllabication, morphemic analysis, dictionary definition, isolated skills emphasis, and reading short passages on which they were tested for literal memory of arcane facts. In our reading environment, ideologically, they were reading a culturally resonant text that they were guided to respond to, deciding on critical concepts and aligning their own life experiences thereto. For the first time, they were awakened to literary reading and able to explore the characters' engagements, core thematic threads, historical significance, myriad layers of setting, and phenomenological resonance of *A Lesson Before Dying*. Had they been habitually involved in a literary-reading discourse community (as per Gee, 2008) over the course of their lives, embedding critical literacy skills in such contexts, one might surmise I would not have had the privilege and pleasure of working with them. I risk suggesting that they had been enforced within autonmous discourse settings in which they did not find community, and almost never been touched by ideological reading contexts that invited them to read *within* a discourse community that embraced their lives and identities. The evolving story of their life within the novel will continue to rebound against this backdrop.

5

THINKING ABOUT THINGS

Today is Friday. Everyone straggles in, most on time. They have all read the first 5 chapters of the book – or most of them have. Even as I write now, with reams of videotape to remind me of the many moments and many colors of this collaborative reading experience, I resist being too married to the belief that 'all' students were fully involved and completely invested. Yet I would be hard-pressed, reviewing the data, to find more than three students who shirked it, who did not complete the novel, journal writings, classroom activities, or the final synthesis project. It is Friday, and today we are ready to frame acts of mind that look back on the five chapters read thus far, and move ahead into deeper waters – new chapters - that build on themes generated. We will delve further into Grant's character, the setting and furor related to his struggles and commitments, and the students' encounters with the text. We watch their phenomenological engagement unfold and are continuously aware of the shaping influence of the classroom context, its influence on the constructions that students are asked to make of their reading through their synthesis projects.

"Another day," I say to them.

"Another day," one of them repeats.

"We've read a lot of this text so far; we've only been here together for a few days."

"Uh huh," they all seem to say at the same time.

I wait. They wait as well.

"So far so good?" I ask.

"So far so good," one person affirms. They are quieter today, tired, waiting for something to happen. I worry that their listlessness may be due to lagging engagement – either with the novel or with activities that have taken place so far. Perhaps they are fearful about these synthesis projects that have been presented to them on the first day, and to which I have referred over the past few days. Here is what the data reveals for this day, primarily for two of the three classes:

"How are you feeling about the work you have been doing so far?"

"You mean this work in this class, or all the work for all the classes?"

"Well, I was thinking about this class I guess. How is it going overall for all of your classes?"

"It's a *lot!*"

Many voices.

I have set up the camera and have the microphone in my hand when one student asks, "I just wanna hear the opinions of different people. I want to know do they think this is a true story – I mean - "

Someone answers right away: "Personally I think this story is … all … non-fiction."

"Non-fiction?" I ask.

"I think - but it's all true," responds A.K., "You know what I'm sayin' – I don' think these are the characters, you know – but I mean I think this happened – I - and that that's why – the guy – is - the guy's name is Ernest Gaines – you know I – I think he wrote this book – you know what I mean."

Someone else jumps in: "Well I don't because what black woman you know back then is goin' ta have *that* much power to do or say **any**thing to a white man – be for real!"

A.K. responds: "You know what I'm sayin' – I just want to have a discussion – you know what I'm sayin' so you could see it in your eyes - that you could see it in your mind that this could be true, you know what I mean?"

Such banter continues for several minutes with varied anecdotes about related community experience forthcoming.

A young woman says, "And that – that happens – that happens in my community and it's happenin' everywhere around the world and that's how - how – some people grow and change different in the community or -"

"That's life!" says another.

"It's like he said – she said – they said – this is real!"

"No - it ain't -" says the young woman who reasoned that a black woman back then would not have the power to say *anything* to a white man, referring to Miss Emma. Someone cuts her off.

"But we have to listen to each other," I caution them.

"I hear what she sayin'," says another, "About that – about that."

"Yeah, but this is what goes on all the time. All the time!"

I don't say anything for a while. One person holds the microphone back and forth, content with his role in facilitating the recording process as I swipe the camera lens back and forth, catching some voices as they speak. The data is a blur of movement, voices captured with felicity while one person's face and then another's appears at various angles, sometimes centered in the lens, sometimes not.

Finally, I interject, "What about chapter 5?!" I ask. What's going on there? Is there anything happening there that tells us more about any of these ideas," I refer to the maps that are taped around the room, completed yesterday. "Or about Grant?" I pause.

"Or," I ask them, "Anyone or anything else that we need to focus on?" No one answers.

I ask, "Is he committed?" Do you think Grant is committed?"

"He got no choice, he want to eat." They laugh. "He lives there with his Aunt – she feedin' him."

"Yeah, but he got Vivian sometimes …".

"When he need her – ain't that the truth," someone chortles, referring to Grant and Vivian's arrangements for privacy, referred to at the end of chapter 4.

"Well, let's look at what we've written here: love, commitment, racism, and need," I read from the posters on the wall.

"What's in the book – what did you find here – last night? About Grant, or about Jefferson or anything else that's happened so far? Can we just read – talk altogether today a bit about that?"

The videotaped data reveals two differing scenarios: two classes read from the text and form a rambling, series of exchanges based on specifically identified passages from chapter 5 of the text. The third class wants to go to the board and write there: "Let's do what we did – like with those posters yesterday."

What follows in italic print are snippets of students' pinpointing of particular literary elements from the novel, selected from the most frequently identified details, either verbally read aloud from the text or written onto the board and "mapped" as was done for core concepts identified from chapter 4 on the previous day:

We have pledged allegiance to the flag (p. 33).

The sky was ashy gray and the air chilly … (p. 33).

I knew which of them would do something for themselves and which of them never would … I listened for a moment then turned it off … (p. 34)

I still felt bad about the problem I was having at home with my aunt (p. 35).

Every little thing was irritating me (p.35).

At the door, I turned to look back at the other classes [within the one-room schoolhouse]. *They all knew I was in a pretty rotten mood today, and they kept their heads down* (p. 37).

"Do you all know what is goin on in Bayonne," I asked them, back at my desk. "Do you know what is going to happen to someone just like you who sat right where you're sitting only a few years ago? All right, I'll tell you. They're

going to kill him in Bayonne. They're going to sit him in a chair, they're going to tie him down with straps, they're going to connect wires to his head, to his wrists, to his legs, and they're going to shoot electricity through the wires into his body until he's dead" (p. 39).

The chapter concludes as a handyman for Henri Pichot at the 'big house' has come to the school and tells Grant Wiggins, "it be all right if you come up there 'bout five" (p. 41).

One class has scribbled the word "cynicism" onto the board and various lined tentacles from the center of this map point to the words "Jefferson", "tyrant", and just about everyone in all three classes has noted the phrase, "Every little thing was irritating me," as they align details to that phrase about Mr. Wiggin's whacking of students with his Westcott ruler, his cruel words about Jefferson, and how that he has made one of the girls (Jefferson's cousin) cry. Now he is about to see Henri Pichot who will – or won't – extend permission for Grant to visit Jefferson in the jail cell.

At this point, a weekend looms and I want to move the reading ahead. I ask the students to read chapters 6, 7, and 8 over the weekend and to continue writing in their journals, one page for each chapter following the simple guidelines I offered to them at the beginning of the course. Now, I know that they will write with more confidence and involvement. Then, I assign students a mini-project and refer them to their syllabi, to the series of synthesis projects outlined there.

"Over the weekend, can you choose a picture, film, or piece of music, or media – a radio, TV, newspaper, internet site – that you can connect with one of the key ideas that are going on for you so far in this book?" Most appear interested, some uncertain.

"OK, so you will do three things over the weekend as you prepare – each person will complete about a 3 to 5-minute presentation - " many groans. I speak more slowly, a little more deliberately, "You might want to take some notes about what you're being asked to do." They comply – most of them.

"So, you will each find a film, song, or TV program, or visual image …," I repeat what I said before, then add, "find a particular point in the film, or play a segment of a song, or media, or detail of the visual image," I continue, outlining some details onto the board for them, "And be prepared to (a) play/show your piece for about a minute, maybe longer, then (b) read a segment from chapter 6, or 7 or 8 that connects with what you play/show us, and then (c) tell us how the book and your film, or song, or media or picture are connected – what is the connection between what you show us and a key idea from the book?" I suggest that images can be found in magazines or the internet.

Someone asks, "Does that mean we can't read out anything from chapters 1 through 5?"

"Good question." I think about it.

"For this presentation, focus on those 3 chapters – any one of those three chapters for your presentation. Remember, in your journal writing you will most likely refer to details from previous chapters, and then after each person has a chance to present, we'll – we'll – you'll want to respond to what you see and hear and then you'll – you'll absolutely be talking about everything that's happened in the book so far but - ".

"OK," someone says. "This gonna take some time – we all make a presentation?"

"It'll probably take us three days of next week – Monday, Tuesday, and Wednesday. But what we are doing with these projects does – is – it helps us explore the book and focus on Grant, or Jefferson maybe, or one of the other characters, and even more, it gets us going – gets a start on what will become expanded as your synthesis projects."

I then explain that what we have done to this point of the class (and will do next week) explores aspects of the process that will be entailed in producing the final version of each student's synthesis project. By next week, I say, we will have attended to work on the (a) Visual Collage project, (b) Character Map project, (c) Thematic Concept map, (d) Film Project, (e) Music project, and (f) Media project.

A young man asks, "Can we do – like Chris Rock and one of his things?"

"As long as you can present that media, and read a segment from chapter 6, or 7 or 8 that connects with what you play for us, then tell us how your comedy sketch – is it one of his comedy sketches?"

"Yeah."

"As long as you can, in your own words, really make a solid connection between the comedy sketch and the segment from the book you read – what you all present for us with a visual image, or TV segment, or music, or film – that has to be intricately connected to - "

"You be usin' them big words again." Laughter from everyone.

"Yeah," I giggled, "I know I am – ah – you know, what you show us or play for us, it has to – it has to you know, have some kind of real connection to one of the key ideas in the chapters you are reading over this weekend." I pause.

"Does that make sense?" I ask.

Some are intrigued, some resistant, some a little uncertain, some not sure about this assignment. It is one they have never been asked to do before.

"And we can do it with anything we read before – in the book I mean?

"Here's the thing," I respond. "This book you know, it's gonna be about one overall idea – you may each have differing opinions about what that overall idea is - and we already know a lot about what some of the big ideas are, right?" I ask them, pointing to the maps around the room, and holding up one of the journals from someone's desk.

"So," I continue, "It's pretty likely that the key ideas in the next three chapters will be connected to some of the big ideas – one of the concepts so far in the book, right?"

"So, you mean we can talk about stuff in the first five chapters?"

"Focus on a specific idea in chapter 6, or 7, or 8, find music, or film, or images that connect to one of those specific ideas, then tell us the connection you see between what you show us and a specific segment of the book. When we respond to your presentation, we are likely to make our own connections to what has gone on in the book so far."

They waited.

"Try it out, OK?" They nod, and head out of the classroom, ready now for the weekend to start.

One last question from a young girl who has waited for everyone else to leave: "Miss when you keep sayin', like, segments, I'm not sure what you mean - Miss what's a segment?" She pronounced the word 'segment' as though it was a foreign food.

"Well, you know, for what we're doing for this weekend, find a few sentences, or a paragraph."

"Sentences, like some sentences altogether, or sentences like one here and one there, from different parts of the chapter?" she asked.

"Well it's up to you but it might be easier to just choose one passage - " she frowned.

"I mean, maybe it's – it will work best I think to just choose," I picked up the book from my table, "Here you see," I pointed to some sentences from chapter one that I had first read to them, and then another passage from chapter two, and three, and said, "These are all segments – sometimes it's people talking, sometimes just the author's words narrating - " I stopped there, realizing that might matters worse.

"Oh," she said, "I get it – like one part of the book, right?"

"Yeah," I said, "One part that seems like it's saying something important – like it has - "

"Yeah, like there's somethin' goin' on there, right."

"Yeah, somethin' goin' on," I said, leaving things like that. If this one student had asked, then others were also confused about the terminology I was using.

* * * *

Vygotsky (1978) teaches us that human beings are embryonically shaped by their environments, both as social and physical beings. The role of speech in the development of human thought is fundamental; though he speaks of children when he explains himself, it is recognized that he offers us foundational principles about the evolution of all human thought and language. He says, "speech and action are part of *one and the same psychological function,* directed toward the solution of the problem at hand (p. 25, original italics). Speech is of such vital importance that "if not permitted to use it, young children cannot accomplish the given task" (p. 26). Even further, he elucidates: "[t]he unity of perception, speech, and action, which ultimately produces internalizations of the visual field, constitutes the central subject matter for any analysis of the origin of uniquely human forms of behavior" (p. 26). Talking, then, we learn can be thought of as an auxililliary tool as difficult tasks are solved and solutions to problems are planned "especially in social contact with other people" (p. 28).

As questions are asked, outlooks discussed, insights shared, and arguments engaged we learn to sort through and plan complex activities. Over all of the conversations heard so far – from seemingly simplistic questions, to discussion of text segments to be selected and presented, to disagreements shared, to interpretations articulated, to instructions offered and repeated – we have seen these principles play out in the students' verbal exchanges. Language in a highly social context was and is the constant emollient related to all of the activity ongoing in more and more complex ways thus far, and as the weeks unfold. Vygotskian, or social constructivist perspectives related to thought and language are articulated by many educators (Sullivan Palinscar, 1998; Wertsch, 1991; Wells, 1995). Another of Vygotsky's key tenets is also considered by John-Steiner and Mahn (1996) who emphasize "the semiotic (signs and symbols including language) mediation in human development" (p. 191). These words align quite nicely with those of Vygotsky: "children direct the objects of their attention with words and sticks, demonstrating the fundamental and inseparable tie between speech and action" (1978, p. 30). Let's continue this discussion with some focus on the role of the symbolic and visual and its connection with thought and language.

Vygotsky refers to "pivots" (p. 98) writing that they are instrumental in transfer of meanings from words to objects; the pivot acts as a symbol or "designation" (p. 99) and thus "through play the child achieves a functional definition of concepts or objects, and words become parts of things" (p. 99). For example, in play a stick can act as a pivot, or represent a horse. He speaks of self-control, spontaneity and freedom, self-restraint, self-determination, and "action/meaning ratios" (p.

100). This is to say that conscious and intentional making of meaning becomes predominant: "imagination, interpretation and will are the internal processes carried by external action" (p. 100). Actions become the pivot through which "the meaning of *things* leads to abstract thought" and "the ability to make conscious choices occurs when the child operates with the meaning of *actions*" (p. 101, original italics). Meaning, then, "subordinates all real objects and actions to itself" (p. 101) and purposefully predominates in play; thus, meaning intention in play developmentally creates a zone of proximal development: "play contains all developmental tendencies in a condensed form and is itself a major source of development" (p. 102). Again, as explained by Vygotsky, action and voluntary intentions, real-life plans and volitional motives all manifest in play that continues toward "conscious realization of its purpose" (p. 103) and leads toward abstract thought.

I want to align these thoughts of Vygotsky's with the activities of the readers who are the focus of this book. At this point of their experience of the novel, I am asking them to purposefully use media, images, and graphic representations as pivots that will express their perceptions of key moments in the novel. Another way of putting it would be to say that they are being asked to deliberately express their perceptions of core themes (core meanings) through such visuals and media and make deliberate connections between such elements and the novel. I am also asking them to present these conscious choices verbally – to articulate their thoughts in a semi-formal verbal expression to the class. It also bears mentioning that their progress toward such a point has been scaffolded relatively well; with recognition for the fact that they have never engaged in any such work before, they have been taken through a series of events leading toward their relative comfort with what they are being asked to do. This comfort derives partially from the fact that they now feel confident enough about identifying crucial segments (from their perspectives) and partially because their lives have been saturated in traffic with the pivots – the visual and media and graphic symbols. Even further, these meaning-based actions are set forth with some degree of rules-based, or structure-based logic: (a) first the art/media/visual segment, (b) then the explanation of the novel's connecting idea and segment, and (c) then an explanation of how the pivot expresses the meaning or critical idea the student sees as central to both the symbol/pivot and the text.

Many have taken up the essential ideas presented by Vygotsky's conceptual model. Suhor (1984) writes that one has "a range of media theoretically at one's disposal in encoding various experiences" (p. 250). Zoss (2009) emphasizes that adolescents have various sign systems available such as "linguistics, gestural, pictorial, musical and constructive" (p. 185). Eisner (2002) claims that from a semiotics perspective individuals ought to be exposed to a curriculum that allows them to access their integrated linguistic/pictorial pathways and thus be able to make meaning through such diverse media. Others speak about mask making as a means through which to express identity (Smagorinsky, Zoss, and O'Donnell, 2005). Several others write about the power of the visual and multi-media modalities in meaning-making potential for students and humans in general (Arnhein, 1969; Callow, 1999; Callow, 2003; Kress, 2000; Flood, Heath, and Lapp, 1997; New London Group, 1996). In writing about cognition and its relation to all ranges of visual stimuli Arnheim is describing "all mental operations involved in the receiving, storing and processing of information: sensory perception, memory, thinking and learning. ... This eminently active performance is what is truly meant by visual perception" (pp. 13 & 14). Considering these thoughts and linking them to Vygotsky's ideas, we can even more fully appreciate how meaning making for my readers becomes facilitated through their "pivots" – the range of arts and media based, and graphic symbols that they will use to express the abstract concepts they see in *A Lesson Before Dying*.

6

IN AND OUTSIDE THE PAGES

It's another Monday as Grant goes to Mr. Pichot's home and waits in the kitchen. The students' presentations begin. Knowing that of the twenty-five students in each class, some will have focused on chapter 6, some chapter 7, and some chapter 8, I ask, "Who has a presentation related to a key idea in chapter 6?" I want to have the order of presentations follow the order of the chapters: first those related to chapter 6, then, 7, then 8 so that the novel's structural flow can be considered sequentially.

A hand is raised. Another.

"OK, let's get set up - what do we need – who has film? Music? Visual Images? Anything else? No? Nothing else." A hand is raised, "Something else?" One young man nods, smiling; he has written a poem and has music to play while he reads it for us.

Scufflings: some students ready their CD's, others DVD's, others page through their books finding passages. I go over the directions – again, reminding them of what is expected for these presentations.

Someone gets the mood jump-started as he walks in, a few minutes late, and playfully draws a concept map on the board to tease me - "We know you like these bubbles Miss – chapter 6 we're comin' to the word 'Dignity'"," writing it onto the board, annotating p. 49 beside it, as students giggle at him. Another student stands up, claps and hums loudly, triumphantly.

"OK, I'll go first," says one student, having readied his CD disc and wanting to move things along.

"Great." I call people to one point of focus.

Jerome says, "I really - this song that happens is not really a song – it's like a comic piece you know what I'm sayin' – it's like a comic piece - it's called Born Suspect. It's basically talking about how different black people and white people are and I think it goes good with the book because ah … you'll see." He hits the play button and everyone is completely attentive right away.

Chris Rock's voice: "All black people born a suspect, came out of my mother's stomach - anything that happened within a 3-block radius I was a suspect."

The comic riff continues for about 5 or 6 minutes and I let it play, not wanting to interrupt and hoping the presentation will model the expectations outlined for them on Friday.

He lowers the volume and hits the stop button. Right away, he picks up the book (microphone in hand the whole time, being held against the speakers of the CD player) and says, "This goes good with the book right here on p. 47 – you know Grant's been waiting for 2 and a half hours for Sheriff Guidry to see him as he – you know he's got people there – at the house, and the book says – it's Grant - he's sayin' – he's thinkin' you know," Jerome reads " *I tried to decide how I should respond to them. Whether I should act like the teacher I was, or the nigger I was supposed to be. I decided to wait and see how the conversation went. To show too much intelligence would have been an insult to them. To show a lack of intelligence would have been a greater insult to me'* and then on p. 49, it's Sheriff Guidry talking and he says, *'I don't like it and I want you to know I don't like it. Because I think the only thing you can do is just aggravate him, trying to put something in his head against his will. And I'd rather see a contented hog go to that chair than an aggravated hog'* it's like you know the whole book is sayin' – this chapter and the other chapters are sayin' that we read - that we got to fight back against the 'pinions, the whole thing for black people is to - "

A student calls out – the one that came in and wrote on the board: "To find they dignity no matter what and - "

"OK," I ask them, now intent on orchestrating the collective classroom energy inspired by students' attentive responses, "We have heard Jerome comment on a connection between his comic sketch and his segment from the book – now – how – what other connections do you see between what he played – his media piece – and this novel we're reading? Does anyone – do you – is there anything else you want to say?"

"He got to deal with everything – everyone pressin' on him."

"The whole world be waitin' on him."

"Chris Rock's makin' it funny but – it's true what he say."

"He all mad and confused and -"

"Can you find someplace in particular in this chapter that shows this?"

"The whole chapter show it!"

"Go someplace in particular," I tell them.

"I gotta place – it's what I'm - I – my segment got that."

"Read it."

"He say, *'Believe – believe me Mr. Guidry if it was – if it was left* [up] *to me, I wouldn't have anything to do with it at all'*" [p. 49]

I ask, "Do you think Ernest Gaines is telling a story about one man, one situation or is he being allegorical - "

"She doin' it agin," says someone.

"What you mean, 'gorkygull'?" another calls out.

"So is this story about one particular person, particular people, or is it about a broad general situation – is the author talking about Grant and Jefferson literally or about a deeper underlying situation in society, history maybe in this country – and that word," I turn to the board, 'Is a-l-l-e-g-o-r-i-c-a-l,' I spell it out for them.

"Why you gotta be axing us questions like that?!" says one young lady, annoyed.

"I know," I say, "All these questions. We don't have to answer them right now, but maybe we can think about it – it will - can be something we come back to but maybe we can think about it – if this is one literal story, or if Ernest Gaines and Chris Rock, for that matter, are talking about bigger situations – I'm gonna keep asking questions like that and we won't necessarily always have the answers right away but we can keep questions like this in mind."

Class periods proceed as film clips, music, and visual images from magazines and the internet are played and presented, segments of the text aligned, and commentary offered. Various students offer a presentation based on the guidelines offered; some are broadly related to impressions the students have made of the book so far or offered in response to analogous situations in their own lives that are related to the general conceptual territory of the book, and tied less tightly to specific concepts in chapter six. Their presentations thus sometimes take us directly to particular details of the text and sometimes not. My job is to ask those pesky questions that prod and prompt students to find particular connections between what they show us and play for us, and the literary elements of the novel. Always, I feel I am walking a tightrope, balancing the constantly shifting dynamics that sway between the risk of being too directive, too text-bound, too literal, or allowing wildly chaotic, and undisciplined literary reference to life circumstances, when sometimes one might say that the media and arts-based projects become strictly entertainment vehicles. We veer back and forth between these two poles, it seems, in an organically evolving pattern of activity.

Constantly on my mind is the moment-to-moment dilemma of facilitating a genuine phenomenological aesthetic literary experience grounded in the students' self-ordered engagement with the novel's elements, yet also nudging them to organize, shape, and expand these personal touchpoints through the projects, discussions and writing activities suggested. With respect to phenomenological ontology, I constantly struggle with the paradoxical challenge of conducting an action-oriented, teacher-as-researcher exploration that respects the precepts of this qualitative research domain. For, while it is true that the students' experiences of this novel are governed primarily by their own feelings, thoughts, and ideas, it is also true that their responses are being influenced by the strictures of journal writing, projects, discussions, pesky questions, idea mapping, and so forth. Thus, I am continuously intent on allowing students' owned literary phenomenology *and* shaping the direction and expression of that experience at one and the same time, a delicate conundrum throughout the work. Moreover, there are limitations on how deeply one can probe the depths of experience given the confines of the classroom space that may not, in fact, allow insights into such depths.

* * * *

Let's take another step along the path of Vygotskian sociocultural theory. John-Steiner and Mahn (1996) are helpful in clarifying key signposts in his thinking. The first, of course, is the primacy of social interaction on the individual; in progressing through the various contours of schooling and life: "learners depend on others with more experience" (p. 192) and "synthesize several influences into [their] novel modes of understanding and participation" (p. 192). They internalize the words and actions of others as new scenarios ensue. Secondly, and of particular relevance to the story being woven here, the notion of semiotic mediation presents and is described as the "key to all aspects of knowledge co-construction" (p. 192). Vygotsky (1981), himself, refers to a range of semiotic channels: "language; various systems of counting; mnemonic techniques; algebraic symbol systems; words of art; writing; schemes; diagrams, maps and mechanical drawings; all sorts of conventional signs and so on" (p. 137). Given that his writings took place in the 20's and 30's (before his early death) and only brought to us through translation and editing in the 70's and 80's it seems fair to suggest that he'd include current media and online symbolic systems in addtion to those referred to here. So, inviting my adolescent readers to express the meaning of what they'd read through visuals and various media as well as their own written words, they are given access to what Wertsch (referring to Vygotsky's work, 1991) refers to as a socially provided toolkit of semiotic means.

Moving along, now is the time to come clean about the idea that I am deliberately offering my young adults their own sociocultural semiotic of art, media, visual, and graphic representation as one of the critical means of expressing their phenomenological experience of this novel. They are reading the written language of the text and interpreting it through socially based verbal language with one another and also using a range of other semiotic systems to express their sense of the abstract concepts of the novel. Their inexperience with reading (which I had guessed at even before I met them, given my Harlem days) prompted me to facilitate their expression of the meaning of the text through such conduits. Recalling for a moment Vygotsky's "pivots", I believe that the students' experience of the novel was focally heightened due to the employment of such psychological tools which the students most certainly had access to in their home and school communities. John-Steiner and Mahn write that "[t]he diversity of these means and the psychological tools that they represent are of special interest to educators who work in multicultural settings" (p. 193). I believe that the semiotics of arts, media, visuals, and graphics resulted in the deeply realized internalization of the concepts of the novel and the transformation of the students' awareness of the novel's elements as both relevant to their own lives *and* explicit abstract ideas that they would eventually moor to ongoing reading, if not eventual constuction of their final synthesis projects.

Phenomenologically, their experience of the text is transmediated by written and verbal language, their own sounds, poetry, visual collages, film clips, and other media. The videotaped data for this day, and the next, and the next is pumped with sound and image: rock, punk, comedy routines, rap, film segments, and visual color of images projected from internet pictures and various magazine pictures.

7

MEDIA STORIES, PERSONAL STORIES

The presentations continue as we move to a new day in the week. A rhythm had been established on the previous one. Conversation had been ongoing in response to the presentations and my questions. Students were becoming more accustomed to grounding their comments and responses to specific textual elements and it was also becoming increasingly clear that the boundaries between this text and most students' lives was thin. They were reading the book, yes, but most of the students were responding to it as a chord within their own beings. It resonated for them as a life text, a tale of their own history, a page within their own community script. So as this day and the next moved along, conversation about the book became a tableau of exchanges about themselves and the people in their worlds. Rather than impinge too much on this gravity, I listened and allowed the conversational energy to emerge with relatively less insistence on strict media-text alignment. The goal was to establish students' familiarity with the structures of the synthesis projects, strengthen the classroom collaborative dynamic, and move toward a point where each would invest in the assimilation processes called for with the final project that would express a synthesis of the novel's elements. Many of these intentions were being realized as they shared their film, music, visuals, and other media *and* conversational exchanges as the presentations ensued.

The camera reveals sound, color, movement, talk, panning faces around three differing classrooms as lyrics from a punk song are heard: "The little jump nigger doin' bad shit, so much shit 'cause I never had shit. I remember being' …"

Then James, who is awake today, comments and reads from the text: "It - he's sayin' this song's talkin' about what he done, a lot a stuff and …" he laughs. Other students laugh too – they know the tune. Then he reads from the book: "It reads here on page 52 – it's the day the Superintendent – what's his name?" He looks into the book.

"Mr. Joseph," someone else responds.

"Yeah, him," says James, then "He there to – I don't know he comes once a year to see them and he fat – it reads here, '*he would have the poor children spreading out their lips as far as they could while he peered into their mouths. At the university, I had read about slave masters who had done the same thing when buying new slaves, and I had read of cattlemen doing it when purchasing horses and cattle. At least Dr. Joseph had graduated to the level where he let the children spread out their own lips rather than letting using some kind of crude metal instrument. I appreciated his …*" James stops and someone else, who has been reading along, supplies the word, '*humanitarianism*' [p. 56].

> James continues, "They – he – Grant Wiggins he gotta watch while this man doing this and my song – the kids are poor – they're all poor and this white man comes and – he – he like - he ah makes them feel dirty - they ain't got nuthin' and that's what my song's talkin' about too."

"I have another one of those questions – like yesterday sort of. Is. Mr. Joseph one man or does he represent a whole lot of people? We can think about that. I'm just wondering."

"That's the same question you axe us yesterday!"

"No," I say, "Not quite – yesterday I asked you about Grant – now I'm asking you if Mr. Joseph is just one person or if he might also, represent a whole lot of people. And we don't have to answer that right now either – I'm just planting thoughts."

"I got somethin' that connects to that," says Andrew.

He plays a clip from Amistad, then says in simple and clear words, "It's just like the man here in this film who is slowly and gradually thinking about making a connection with the slaves the same way Grant will slowly and gradually make a connection with Jefferson."

"Someone has been reading ahead in the book," I tease – "How do you know he makes a connection with Jefferson?"

"Cliffnotes," someone accuses.

"No. No," says Andrew, "It says here on the back that the two men forge a bond, so I'm guessing that's all."

"So what segments from chapter 7 are you connecting with your film segment?" I ask.

"Here," he says, seeming nervous that I might think he's not completely attuned to pertinent details of the focus for today's work, "It say's right here on page - where ..." he looks up at me. "It's like Mr. Wiggins – the superintendent calls him Higgins – he's tryin' to explain to him that they're poor and they need books and that's why – he's tellin' him that their pages are missing – he's trying to explain it to him here where it says, like on page 57, *I do the best I can with what I have to work with Dr. Joseph' I said. 'I don't have all of the books I need. In some classes, I have two children studying out of one book. And even with that, some of the pages in the books are missing. I need more paper to write on, I need more chalk for the blackboards, I need more pencils. I even need a better heater'.*"

"It's like Grant is tryin' and the superintendent won't listen, it's like how the man is trying in the film, and in the end he does make communication – so I'm just making a comparison – like how they're communicating – not – trying to communicate."

So a complex concept (communication) is the focus of this student's analogous thinking process as he articulates the connection between his media segment and the text. I must resist yet again. I want to ask this class, 'Do you think that the book and the film segment we've just seen each in differing ways focus on cultural and political challenges that fundamentally impede human rights and dignity?' But that question would have forwarded *my* sense of those texts' themes, at least partially. Asking that question or another along those lines (and phrasing it in such elevated terms) would have shortchanged the students' current stage in their interpretive process, or worse, intruded on the fabric of trust among us that was becoming solidified at this point. It would have pulled the exploratory rug out from under their feet. But how, then, do we both guide the ongoing journey of literary interpretations in circumstances like these without becoming a micromanager, a controlling beadle who wrestles the minds-eye of our students' thoughts toward our own authoritative opinions? How can we establish relational zones that validate students' engagement processes and emotional investments while also prompting them to expand, even further enrich these frameworks?

I said, "Let's do this – let's – start recording some details – some of these questions I'm asking on more chart paper around - "

"This room look like a shack – a ..."

"Naw, I got this." Two young men have quickly come to take over the camera from me.

"Just very quickly," I say, taping another sheet of chart paper to the wall, "Let's just write out 'communication'," I start to walk toward the wall.

"I'll write it out," says a young lady, rising, "You want that whole question – what was that – who's one person?"

"No," I say, "Just – I asked if Mr. Joseph the superintendent was one person or represented a whole lot of people - no – but just write 'communication' – that's right, right?" I ask turning to Andrew.

"Yeah," he says.

"Just put that word at the top of the sheet."

We continue. Another presentation booms out a black man's rap lyric: "race against time ..."

And another. Each time we talk, refer to the book, and I respond with questions, trying to highlight core conceptual elements and themes that arise from the literal surface of the work that has been done. Often enough as well, I realize it is wise to wait ...

* * *

Now we must wrestle with a boodle of interconnected ideas. I have so far talked about the importance of such theoretical concepts as the development of thought and language within social contexts and the premise of semiotic mediation. Often, these ideas are put forth by Vygotsky and others in connection with learning and knowledge. And of course I am interested in my students' knowledge and learning but my primary research focus is on their experience of literature of a particular novel in a particular setting, issues I struggle with to some extent. I wonder, for example, if a presentation of Vygotsky's ideas may compromise the intent of my phenomenological study. I offer his thoughts, though, with respect for the ontological core of his thinking; I read his work not so much as a formal treatise on learning as acquisition of knowledge but as core reflections about how thought and language function within social spheres of experience. I put them forth as applicable to the ongoing reading experience in which we are co-engaged and do so with a dual appreciation for these notions and those related to semiotic mediation. Even more so, I am thinking about how he emphasized his approach as process oriented - that we need to focus "not on the *product* of development but on the very *process* by which higher forms are recognized. ... To study something historically means to study it in the processes of change; that is in the dialectical method's basic demand" (1978, pp. 64-65, original italics). And then I am more and more realizing that this work, though resting on these core realizations, also takes place within a theoretical quilt of other colors. We are, after all, talking about teaching literature with a recognition of the diverse literacies in adolescents' lives, and that these readers are most certainly inexperienced – inexperienced or disenfranchised. It is far more the latter I realize with more and more certainly each day.

Visiting spheres of thought about 'struggling' or 'inexperienced' or 'disenfranchised' readers must be taken into account here too. In the varying concentric circles that represent the scholarship related to this work, let's turn a moment toward such issues while also bearing in mind some core assumptions about social context and semiotics and the process of literary reading in connection with respect for varying classroom moments.

Citing work by Heath (1983), Gee (1991), Cazden (1988), Moll and Whitmore (1993), and Friere (1970), John-Steiner and Mahn (1996) speak quite directly about how an absence of socioculturally sensitive teaching may cause students to be disenfranchised:

> (a) discontinuities between the culture (values, attitudes and beliefs) of the home and school; (b) mismatches in communicative practices between nonmainstream children and mainstream teachers, which lead to miscommunication and misjudgements; and (c) the internalization of negative stereotypes by minority groups who have been marginalized and often see school as a site for opposition and resistance (p. 202).

More recently Intrator and Kunzman (2009) comment that adolescents are largely excluded from the discourse around schooling while having a consumerist outlook about it. They offer research related to the insight that literacy evolves an ecology of relationships and that adolescents yearn to express their distinctive youth voices in school. Moreoever, they write, "experience of adolescence varies according to sociocultural environment" (p. 29). They continue: "the growing research on "youth voice" suggests to us that the relationships between teachers and their adolescent students must be *dialogical* in nature, a cultivation of listening and learning by both adults and teens" (p. 31, original italics). Goodlad (1984) comments that "boredom is a disease of epidemic proportion" (p. 9) in schools. About African Americans who struggle with school literacy Tatum (2000) writes that many teachers are forced to adopt a skills approach due to the influnce of standardized testing. Citing a litany of statistics about school dropout rates, deaths, and the paucity of rigor in high schools, Lee (1995) writes that "[s]tudents who enter high school with long histories of underachievement often have internalized expectations for what schooling is that are not a useful foundation for complex learning" (p. 32). She helps us appreciate the complexities of the teaching of literature and lead us to infer that such teaching does not occur for students who are perceived through typical assessment measures as "low achievers". We will soon enough come to a full realization that *these readers*, sadly, had not ever engaged such rich teaching in their recollections. Even more stark a truth is that they had been systematically led to expect that schooling did not include *any* reading of literature at all.

8

RUNNING AND RUNNING

The few students who have not yet offered us a presentation do so today. Many of them have brought the same movie clips, and in some cases the same segments of those films are played and discussed: *Stand and Deliver, Lean on Me, Dangerous Minds, and Dead Poet's Society* seem to have been selected because of their focus on teachers and teaching which is reflectively considered by Grant Wiggins in chapter eight. Others feature stories broadly related to societal and historical contexts of African Americans: *The Color Purple, Boys in the Hood, What's Love Got to Do With It?, A Soldier's Story, Do the Right Thing, Rosewood,* and others. The classes proceed.

One young woman who had been paging through this chapter called out, "You're all missin' something – there".

"Where?" someone asked.

"There on page sixty-three, it's talkin' about 'she' – this chapter – it's about her."

"Her – his aunt – it's just one word."

"Where," I asked?"

"It all seems all about him – Grant- what he's thinkin' but that one part – it's not about that other teacher – it's about her."

"Where – what do you mean?" I ask, thinking that this chapter was solely about Grant's reflections about a former African American teacher of his, the embittered Matthew Antoine, who had unwittingly become a key person in his life.

"There – there," the young woman said, "There it says, '*She told me I would not be one of the others, that I would learn as much as he could teach me, then I would go away to learn from someone else*' – that's sayin' that he's thinkin' about why he has to go and visit with Jefferson like his aunt and Miss Emma want him to – it's cause a her – that's what this chapter is talking about – what he's remembering."

They argue: "He thinkin' about teachin' – he's watching the old men come with the wood for the school outside and he's rememberin' that other teacher - one a his teachers – that none of it matter."

Then someone says, "Dr. Sullivan you should a done a presentation – this chapter's Grant and thinkin' about teachin' – you should a done one for us."

"I wonder if he is thinking about teaching," I respond. "I'm not so sure."

Maybe I should have worked on a presentation. Grant's words in this chapter are about memories and confusion it seems to me. He stands in his one-room schoolhouse watching two old men unload poles of wood near the segregated plantation school. He asks himself: '*What am I doing? Am I reaching them at all? Is it just a vicious circle? Am I doing anything?*' (p. 62). He thinks about his visits to see Matthew Antoine, what that man had told him when he'd returned to the plantation, after his university days away from there and remembers that old mentor's words: '*I stayed here. You have to get away to know about life. There's nothing but ignorance here. You want to know about life? Well, it's too late. Forget it. Just go on and be the nigger you were born to be but forget about life*' (p. 65). Matthew Antoine, who is described as a mulatto in the book, has told Grant, '*I am superior to you. I am superior to any man blacker than me*' (p. 65).

Grant thinks about Mr. Antoine, a frail and defeated man who "*hated himself for the mixture of his blood and the cowardice of his being, and he hated us for daily reminding him of it*" (p. 62). The man had told Grant, '*I told you to go. God has looked after them these past three hundred years without your help* (p. 64).

The data reveals students' diverging opinions about this chapter's focus. Some emphasize Grant's thoughts about teaching, others stress references to the superiority Mr. Antoine claims because of his lighter skin, still others discuss life experiences aligned with the text's description of *'those who had chopped wood here too; then ... were gone. Gone to the fields, to the small towns, to the cities – where they died ... always news coming back to the quarter about someone who had been killed or sent to prison for killing someone else: Snowball, stabbed to death at a nightclub in Port Allen; Claudee, killed by a woman in New Orleans; Smitty, sent to the state penitentiary at Angola for manslaughter. And there were others who did not go anywhere but simply died slower'* (p. 62).

"My cousin ..."

"My brother ..."

"My sister ..."

"My father ..."

"My best friend ..."

The voices in these classrooms are a rambling series of exchanges today:

"He was one a them that was there that night – he got arrested – they took him – and he still in jail waitin' for his trial."

"I be dark enough – you imagine what our children look like, I stay with that man!"

"She the one in our family – our mother – she workin' three jobs – keepin' all a us focus on our education – she pushin' – she be pushin' and pushin' she teachin' all a us to keep goin' no matter what."

"He bitter – he don't know what he doin' - what they all axin' him to do – he thinkin' about what he teachin' them – now he gotta go and teach Jefferson – he don't know – he thinkin' back on his own life and he don't know – he all mixed up – mixed up but not like Mr. Antoine ..."

"Maybe he is mixed up that that –"

"No, that guy, he got his blood all boilin'"

"Grant does too."

"We got racism goin' on between a'selves all the time –"

"What?!"

"He gotta burden – Grant he say, there it says on page 63 *'here is the burden'*.

Private exchanges among pairs of students, sometimes three or more at a time elaborate on these many fragments of expression and it is impossible to clearly hear what is being said sometimes. Students turn to each other and I watch, feeling a bit excluded. I see this is true for some of the students as well. I wait – wait, watching for an opportunity to steer conversation to one or more focal points and feeling like an interloper, a foreign visitor, awkward and somewhat unsure of what will happen as several minutes pass. The conversation is private, the camera and microphone completely forgotten. I pan the room with the camera, trying to capture fragments that can be a focal point for more collective conversation.

Finally I ask, "Is this chapter about teaching? And if it is what do you think the book is saying about teaching? Or is it -"

"You gotta understand," says someone, stopping.

"What?" I ask, feeling vulnerable and unsure about what we were talking about.

"This – this is all real – this stuff – it's Grant yeah – but it's us."

I waited. Many looked away.

"This - they tellin' what the African American people live with – this is then but it's now too."

It's quiet now.

I ask, tentatively, "Is it OK – can I write some things I heard you saying here?" I walk to the charts on the wall and add a few words to the one on 'r-a-c-i-s-m': "among each other", and "darker people" (noting a phrase from p. 66 of the text). Then I moved to the concept map that read 'c-o-m-m-i-t-m-e-n-t' and wrote: "What am I doing? Am I reaching them at all?" and notated p. 62 there. I added the word "education" there as well.

"Let's see," I said, "Where we go from here and what we talk about." The class was ending and we had to move ahead in our reading, to continue exploring the many threads of text and life that were forming the basis for our reading together. I left those classes thinking about teaching. Perhaps the students left thinking about life. I don't know.

Plans were made to read chapters 9 & 10 that night and be prepared to discuss them tomorrow; students were reminded to continue with journal writing.

* * * *

We talked about a lot of things that day – on those days. It seems to me that the national conversation on teaching inexperienced or struggling, or disenfranchised readers has us all focus on the achievement gap. Even if we decry the reductionist nature of the standardized assessments we are forced to use, it's clear that they show that *these readers* are lagging behind, all of them in the lower echelons of those darn scores. But without now turning our backs on the attention that has been paid to reading and literary reading history, to socioculturally-based learning theory, and mediated learning, can we also talk about a variety of perspectives on what it means to teach *these students*? Ladson-Billings has been a key voice in the conversation about teaching African American students. In *Fighting For Our Lives* (2000) she writes that parents cry out for solid teaching for their sons and daughters and that teacher preparation programs need to grapple with the need to prepare teachers to respect the cultural experiences and complementary pedagogical strategies best suited to working with African American students. Her sentiments also speak for disenfranchised others. Lee (1995) offers a teaching approach that relies on signifying (a social discourse skill with which many African American students are familiar) as a scaffold for teaching skills of literary interpretation. Sedlacek (2006) writes that one can learn how to exploit variables that promote success for minority students. But it feels crass somehow to look at such impersonal and objective discussions in light of the growing relationships I was involved in with *my* students. Moving toward more of the literature that helps me articulate this feeling I find Jim Cummins' work (1986). He writes that "legislative and policy reforms [in working with disenfranchised students] may be necessary conditions for effective change, but they are not sufficient" (pp. 18 & 19). He writes that whether students from disenfranchised backgrounds are empowered or disabled rests on 4 interrelated factors:

> These characteristics reflect the extent to which (1) minority students' home language and culture are incorporated into the school program; (2) minority community participation is encouraged as an integral component of children's education; (3) the pedagogy promotes intrinsic motivation on the part of students to use language actively in order to generate their own knowledge; and (4) professionals involved in assessment become advocates for minority students rather then legitimating the location of the "problem" in the students (p. 21).

Despite these "relevant" points, they are brought forth in the genre of argument as most solid academic papers present their points and I don't want to *rationalize* the need to work with my students as though I am formally bringing their home language and culture into the classroom. The classroom has become a shared space that emphasizes these four variables and many more so completely as to make the manifold layers of their experiential dimensions central in style and content to this whole enterprise.

No, it seems much more fitting to borrow the thinking of others for this discussion right now. I want to bring the thoughts of care, ethics, and morality into our story now. Noddings (1983) writes of a feminine aesthetic of care, remarking that a moral education must nurture the ethical ideal of caring. She speaks of commitment, and the "displacement of interest from my own reality to the reality of the others" (p. 14) and that "all caring involves engrossment" (p. 17). We act on behalf of the cared-for, with affection and regard and with actions that are not so much rule-bound as "the sort of behavior that is conditioned not by a host of narrow and rigidly defined principles but by a broad and loosely defined ethic that molds itself in situations and has a proper regard for human affections, weaknesses and anxieties" (p. 25).

Rational objective modes are not preeminent but subjective seeing and feeling is. Moreover, we learn that "[t]he receptivity of the one-caring need not lead to permissiveness nor to an abdication of responsibility for conduct and achievement" (p. 59). And so in teaching with care, "the teacher receives the child and works with him on cooperatively designed projects as she resists the temptation – or the mandate – to manipulate the child, to squeeze him into some mold, she establishes a climate of receptivity" (p. 60). I'll bring Noddings' words again into the text; she writes that "[t]he one-caring reflects reality as she sees it to the child. She accepts him as she hopes he will accept himself – seeing what is there, considering what might be changed, speculating on what might be" (p. 60). Noddings speaks of the teacher's role as one of honest expression that never leaves the child alone, detached or abandoned.

Following Noddings, Owens and Ennis (2005) present an overview of theoretical frameworks focused on further defining care in teaching. They speak of commitment and confirmation, citing Buber (1965) as they also refer to affirmation and encouragement of the one-caring for those cared-for. It is the very essence of caring relationships to be irrational – to be "crazy about that kid" (Bronfenbrenner, 1978, p. 774). Gilligan's work (1982) – in response to Kohlberg (1981) – offers a view of feminine care, the voice of care as a complex understanding of of the relationship between the self and the other. The work of Owens and Ennis (2005) summarizes a body of research that focus on caring relationships between teachers and students. Encapsulating Tarlow's (1996) work, the elements of time, "being there" and talking are decribed as prerequusisites for caring teacher-student relationships. Further, sensitivity and actively promoting students' success are also cited as essential variables. Feeling and doing are referred to as other variables; genuine concern and purposeful actions on behalf of the ones cared-for are part of this framework for caring relationships between students and students and teachers. Other work is summarized by Owens and Ennis (2005) that further delineates key work in the field of caring relationships among students and teachers.

Right now, though, I can't help but think of Jonathon Kozols' book *Fire in the Ashes* (2012). He recounts twenty-five years of his life that were devoted to the poorest children in America and does not develop his story by aligning the sometimes sterile summaries of research-based findings. His work contains all of the essences of the one-caring for those cared-for without once characterizing his work as such. Somehow, at this moment of writing, that work comes across more humbly and genuinely a tale of care than other texts that focally describe care. He seems to be more spinefully aware of the gut-wreching plights of human beings because his work does *not* consciously or focally refer to the qualities that underlie his accounts of their depair. I do not cast aspersion on the work of theory and research at all – not at all. That body of scholarship is as sincere in its intentions as Kozol is in his work. At the same time I am sensitive to the fact that life, and research and theory can be sometimes two very different realities. I don't doubt that the findings and coherently presented implications of research and theory have solid ballast and offer us poignant and thought-provoking reading experiences.

What, finally, is the quality that underlies the work I am engaged in? More and more, it feels like a deeply involved relationship. The day-to-day classroom story and the aligned research story feel related. Yes, each chapter comes through my heart and mind and hands as an entwined set of tendrils – one that follows a story unfolding with each day's newly visited videotaped memories, and the other part suggested by that preeminent chord. Over the first year of the writing of this book, the first parts of each chapter are told, and now in this second year the research and theoretical flavors are admixed. That I cared about the students, the reader will see. That ingredient seems to flow more strongly in each chapter. That the research and theoretical scholarship complements the classroom story, I feel less sure of – not unsure, just less sure of.

9

DESPAIR

There are some issues that can be discussed openly within the public space of a classroom, and others that cannot. The literary text bespeaks the experience of previous generations black of people -- through Grant Wiggins voice -- but it resonates in the present lives of most of the students reading it 'now' in our current world. The various mini-presentations have brought forth unvarnished truths about complexities of living in a racist world, allowing almost all students to engage such challenges as speakers and/or listeners. The presentations elicited feelings and realizations that, in this public forum, are consciously featured with varying ranges of comfort among the students. Some become very quiet, some comfortable and highly verbal, and others not quite sure what to make of the highly charged fabric of classroom tone. These few comments characterize a setting within which we were looking into a past and present world, focusing on core concepts therein, and learning how to construct such a discourse setting in what was a first-time experience for most of these students. What we have read and responded to so far in the novel has established a beginning: we have seen many of the major characters and core precepts and have framed exploratory processes that will be elaborated as we continue. Today we move into a differing location within the novel — one that takes us to a new setting there. We see Grant visit Jefferson in jail for the first time, and I wonder how the work of our first several days together will be expanded.

It is a Thursday – on this day we talk about chapters nine and ten of the novel. But, in this chapter I focus only on chapter 9, so that we can continue to entertain the novel a chapter at a time and also to present a separately focused discussion related to the phenomenology of teaching and co-experiencing literature in a multicultural setting.

I begin: "Over today and tomorrow, and maybe over this weekend, I think we might – we should begin to think about what you are going to choose for your synthesis projects. So maybe we can talk about that for a little bit of time today and then move into some work related to chapters nine and ten of *A Lesson*."

"We have to write something to do these projects?"

"Yeah – maybe we can – can you get out your syllabi – the project descriptions. We should have a look and talk about that for a little while today."

Some have their syllabi – some don't. I hand out extra copies.

"Has anyone looked at these at all – we went over them briefly during our first day together but we haven't talked about them much since then. You've just - with the mini-presentations you've done over the past few days, you have seen – you have done small parts of these projects," I explain.

I ask them to read the projects now to themselves and then pick one that they think they might want to complete as a final project choice: "If you have just presented a film segment and want to do the film project, you can include the film you have already shown us along with segments of three others," I tell them. I go on to point out that those who have shown visuals should keep the images they have shown and if they want to complete a visual collage can add another thirty-ish images and/or small objects within their completed poster board collage. Similarly, those who have played a music segment can keep the one they have played for their mini-presentation and choose three others for their final project presentation. These instructions generate a lot of questions.

"This don't make no sense - "

"What we gonna do – do a big picture – I'll do that!"

"Character map! That sounds like a lotta roads and streets."

And so on.

I laugh and let them continue with teasing remonstrations for a few minutes, then call one of the regular 'camera-men' to take over for me as I walk to one of the poster charts taped to the wall. At the same time, I grab another sheet of chart paper.

"This thing that some of you have been calling a Grant-flower is actually an example of a project that might eventually become a character map," I explain.

"Also – does anyone have any of the visual images that - "

"You mean them pictures?"

"Yeah – does anyone – there -, " I call out as one hand is raised.

"Can I borrow that for a minute?" I ask, then, "Anyone else?"

A few images are held up and I ask if I can tape them to the chart paper, do so, and then stand back.

"This is the beginning of what might become a visual collage – and any one of these," I point to the charts featuring the beginning of our explorations on r-a-c-i-s-m, n-e-e-d,

c-o-m-m-i-t-m-e-n-t, l-o-v-e, and c-o-m-m-u-n-i-c-a-t-i-o-n, "Might become a poster-board project that we are calling a CONCEPT MAP". I wait.

"Let's look at one of the project descriptions – maybe let's look at the visual collage project first. That one - if we look at that one, we can see that some of what we have – we have been doing over the past few days forms the basis for that project – look," I tell them holding up an image that depicts a clock.

"Someone had this image and connected it to time – they read a passage about – where is it?" I ask the student whose image I am holding up.

"That? That was – where was it," she questions herself, paging through chapter 8, "There, page 64 where it says *When you see that those five and a half months you spend in that church are just a waste of your time, you will. You will. You'll see that it'll take more than five and a half months to wipe away – peel - scrape away the blanket of ignorance that has been plastered and replastered over those brains in the past three hundred years',"* the student read.

"So," I ask them, holding up the picture of a clock (and suspecting that many of the other students' visual images that were presented reflect superficially considered details from the text), "What is this?"

"A clock."

"Right. But what is the idea that this image might represent?" I question.

"What you mean, represent?"

"What is an underlying idea or what we have been calling key concept related to this image - this picture of a clock – is this story about a clock?"

"No."

"What then? What might the clock represent - we hear in that passage that five and a half months is a waste of time, and read about – it's the author writing through Grant that ignorance has been plastered over three hundred years, right – that's what that book is saying, right?"

"Yeah."

"So what might the clock represent?"

"Time"

"Maybe – what else?"

"It's been like that – like since way back – it's been – it's always been - they have been oppressed since – like forever".

"So, the clock is not just a clock, is it – it can be representative of an idea that might be central – might be a key concept – a broad foundational concept in this novel, right?" I ask, realizing that my phraseology is now formal.

No one says anything, so I continue, "Let's look now at this character map we have begun of Grant – right now we have characterized him as angry, disrespectful, resentful, unwilling, preoccupied, confused, nostalgic," I say, reading from the chart paper.

"That's all we gotta do – put words all around him like that?"

"Well first we have to have a look at the project description – we have to decide if Grant, or Jefferson, or Miss Emma for that matter, really does reflect a core idea of this text – we have to choose a character who is fundamentally central to the theme of the text – in your opinion," I add.

"Someone might choose Grant, or another person Jefferson or someone else – the point is they are chosen because in that student's opinion he or she is somehow reflecting a key idea – a thematically central idea of the book". I pause, sensing that although my phraseology may be formal, they are following me – they may not express the ideas I am conveying in the terms I am using but they are receptively clear about what I am explaining.

They wait. Right now, during these twenty or more minutes of explanation, I have taken over the direction of the class – I am teacher now as director, orchestrator, and authority figure. I am attempting to work within the material of the students' touchpoints with the text and their presentations. But I am also now attempting to make clear that as we continue with our reading, we will be making decisions about central ideas that will be represented in student projects.

"So," I continue, "Am I saying that your final project right now has to be clear in your mind – no. Am I saying that you should know now what your final project choice might be – no. Can you change your mind about what you think the underlying idea might be – yes".

"Maybe you will decide to complete a CONCEPT MAP project, or a MUSIC PROJECT, or FILM PROJECT, or maybe a VISUAL COLLAGE and so on," I say to them flipping through the range of projects choices in the syllabus.

"It's up to you – the thing is as we continue we should start to think about what that project might be – and we should all be thinking as we read and talk in class – we should be thinking now and then about our impressions of the novel's foundational concepts – in our own opinions – and there may be many differing opinions of what that idea is."

They are listening.

"In one of our classes," I say, "Someone showed a film clip about communication, another showed one about teaching, and another one about - I'm thinking of that scene from *Rosewood* and it seemed like it was featuring the – the film seemed to be – what we saw – exposing rampant racism, right?" They nod.

"So maybe, you will change your minds, maybe some of you did not reflect at all about overall concepts of the text – maybe you did somewhat – the point is that we should begin to read and plan on some decisions related to project selection and key concepts, OK?

"What about – what it say here, a 7-to-10 page paper."

"That's a lot."

"Right, we can talk more about that as we continue and some of our writing and project work will be completed in class, but yes, we will be writing - "

"What like we describing the projects?" someone demands, squinting with incomprehension.

"Not exactly – no – you will begin by explaining why you chose a particular project, then explain what you feel the novel is saying for you – to you – what the key idea of the novel is for you – it's key concept – what the novel meant to you." I wince, thinking that this is not a good explanation.

"Then you'll – OK," I stop, pause and start again.

"We are going to be discovering how to write the paper that goes along with this project over the next few weeks we have together – for now, let me explain it this way – you'll refer to your project – either your music or film or collage or map or whatever project you choose and describe specific details in it that you connect to the main idea of a *A Lesson Before Dying*," I stopped again. That explanation was still too vague. How could I offer them definite guidance without scripting their papers for them?

"I'm not being very helpful right now about this paper," I paused, then went to the white board and began, it seemed, to sketch the idea onto the white board, becoming clearer about it as I went. I felt that I needed to design a framework for them and worry that this idea would come across as stifling to their own evolving thoughts and creativity.

Students take some time to read over the projects, talk among small groups about a project they might complete and prepare a few comments. They have been asked to articulate some thoughts about project choices, ideas that seem prominent in the book so far to them, and further questions they might have about the synthesis projects. We have limited time to explore chapter 9 and with the time remaining in this class, the students seem somewhat matter of fact about this chapter – almost as if what happens here is a foregone conclusion. I try to emphasize that this is the first time in the novel we are finding out more about Jefferson – the first time we have seen him since the first chapter. Grant is about to visit them in the jail for the first time.

"What are you seeing there?" I ask them.

"Grant's still upset."

"What makes you say that?" I ask.

"It says, there – he talkin' about his aunt *She knew how I felt about the whole thing* and *'she knew how much I hated all this'*, and *'I didn't want Miss Emma to think for a moment that my mood had changed'* there on page 68".

"What else – what else do you see here – what are you noticing now that he is here at the jail for the first time?"

"More of the same," said a young man's voice sardonically.

"What do you mean?"

"They get searched and hear the rules about what they can and can't do – all that."

He doesn't want to say any more about it. OK.

"What are you - ?

"It don't matter," says a young man quietly. I am fearful now that all of our discussion about synthesis projects has derailed our connection with the novel.

"What? Why?"

"Naw, - that's what it's sayin' – he – he just want to know when they gonna do it."

"What?" I ask again, seeming to forget some of the details of this chapter momentarily. This was a genuine absence of mind.

"There," says someone, "There – *It don't matter – nothin' don't matter – chicken dirt, it don't' matter – when they gonna do it? Tomorrow?'* "(p. 73).

"OK, a few minutes ago someone said they thought they might complete a character map about Grant Wiggins – they said – who was it – Lee Ann said that – she thought Grant – she thinks so far that Grant's the - he represents one of the key ideas in the book – so – we can explore more about him as we continue – but let me ask you all this – is there anything that shows any sign of Grant - his character evolving in any way in this chapter? Anything?"

"Yeah."

"Where – what are you seeing – what's going on with him – remember he is the one that's telling the story."

"There it say, *'The deputy and I exchanged glances. With his eyes and a mod, he told me to put my arms around her. Which I did'* "(p. 74).

"Who is he putting his arms around – why?"

"You know who – you know why," says someone else, another young lady.

"What's going on with Grant?" I ask. "Why is he putting his arms around Miss Emma like that?" I ask them pointedly.

Then I continue: "First the chapter emphasizes that – Grant says - we heard him sayin' *'I didn't want Miss Emma to think for a moment that my mood had changed'* (p. 68) and then we read that - it's Jefferson that Grant is talking about there on p. 73 – he's saying *'He looked at her* [Miss Emma] *as though he did not know who she was, or what she was doing there. Then he looked at me. You know what I'm talking about don't you? His eyes said. They were big brown eyes, the whites too reddish. You know don't you? His eyes said again. I looked back at him. My eyes would not dare answer. But his eyes knew that my eyes knew.'* That's what I'm noticing – you think – you might think I know – that I have the answers but I am not so sure really and when we talk – it changes – I notice – I notice and I have to say – I wonder about it all. I'm just sayin'".

It was time to go.

* * * *

Many significant moments have transpired over the past two-hour classroom segments that are presented in this chapter. Students reveal that they are not completely comfortable – not so familiar with the phenomenon of metaphoric thinking. They have asked me what is meant by a representational structure; we have talked about how a clock might represent time. This has been a bridge for them toward what is hoped would be an appreciation for metaphoric thought in general. In asking the students to complete a synthesis project I have more fully realized that while it has been natural for them to choose the media of their world as a way to make connections to the literary elements of *A Lesson Before Dying* that may not mean that they have come to have *conscious metacognitive awareness* about how to deliberately proceed. That is, though they been playfully and intuitively facile in aligning media, film, music, self-written poetry, dramatic readings, and images with the novel, now the vastness of intentionally creating a project that represents the whole of the thematic essence of the novel is teetering their confidence and comfort.

This phenomenological research project must be seen both as an exploration and experience of a novel as well as the experience of learning to think with thematically conceptual attention. The students reveal yet a little more uncertainty as they are heard to ask about their writing projects, what a character map is, what representation means, and even when some of them don't have project handouts available they have been guided to refer to them. In previous chapters, we have heard students raising questions that reveal a certain lack of familiarity with reading processes, questioning routines, and most certainly literary reading experience. As we continue with this project many will see these threads of the students' engagements revealed time and again. The multiplicity of dynamics seems more and more complex and vast, as does the theoretical and scholarly terrain that unfolds as we proceed. One thing is certain: as much as anything else we are within the throes of multicultural teaching and might focus on that premise a moment before moving along.

Sonia Nieto (2000) helps us to appreciate the manifold layers encountered in a multicultural classroom. Her account of students who are English Language Learners or those not at all attuned to the Academic English demands of secondary and post-secondary classrooms complements that of the students whom we hear reading and talking here. Throughout their time in school many have been involved in classrooms that emphasized test scores on assessments that did not at all complement their sociolinguistic background and cultural experiences. Many such contexts manifested racial bias. Educational policy, even, dictated that they be schooled with materials and methods that were limited and constraining – they emphasized decontextualized skills-based items that that measured finite processes. The case studies in the Nieto (2000) text emphasize the need for a multicultural education approach that recognizes and affirms the diversity of the students as rich, dynamic, and multifaceted; we see many of those principles highlighted in the ongoing transactions of the students in our study. Banks' (1994; 1995) ideas about transformation of the school curriculum set the stage for other work related to the impetus to reform schools to base their teaching approaches on multicultural methods and recognitions.

In Sleeter's (2005) work we encounter a clear acknowledgement of the damage done to students when curricular pathways block and impede student progress – how a standards and assessment-based school diet disenfranchises a majority of students whose backgrounds are sociolinguistically and culturally diverse. She writes, "[a]s a society we do not collectively seem to know how to educate a diverse population well. Nor do we collectively seem to know how to approach many other challenges that relate directly to equity and diversity …" (p. 5). Her words echo those of many others as she also writes, "[a]llowing for development of diversity in expertise can serve as an intellectual resource for constructive participation in a multicultural democracy and diverse world" (p. 7). So many others join the strain of these words as they also write about how our current mono-cultural approaches stigmatize student's linguistic and cultural identities by levering a uniform curriculum and assessment system that asks students to reproduce facts devoid of the life vibrance of the minds and voices of a diverse society (Apple, 1999, 2004; Aronowitz, 2000; Ayers, 2004; Cummins, 1986; Darling-Hammond, 1994; Howard, 2003).

Friere's work (1998; 2005; 1970) is now legion in the power and influence it has had. Of course, I refer to his notions of what he termed a "banking education" and which he contrasted with a "problem-posing" curriculum. Sleeter's work was influenced a great deal by Friere as so many others have been as well. Friere (1970) writes that those who are marginalized by politically imposed educational structures are oppressed in very much the same way that totalitarian governments oppress their people. Oppressers of a disenfranchised educational populace deem their citizens as there and yet not there. Grant Wiggins knows this feeling and political reality. So do many students whose lives and core identities are eclipsed by school politics. Where bell hooks (1994), influenced by Friere, wrote about teaching to oppose and transgress oppressive educational dictums, Fiere wrote about liberation of those oppressed. He championed the work of those who would help the oppressed to critically perceive the forces of their existence and transform their consciouness and their lives in that process.

It is the poor who are most often those disenfranchised – robbed of an education that allows them to bring the riches of their language and culture into the classroom and see themselves in the literature there and in other curricular materials (Berliner, 2006). Far more so, these students are passively roboticized by teachers' "narration sickness", by their reciting of facts to be merely regurgitated on state-asigned assessments and never to be engaged in a dialogically critical relational dynamic with ideas through texts and real-world issues. Exploration of the world's complexities through authentic dialogue and keenly felt ideas is never a method but an imperative which liberating teachers understand at the core. Friere (1970) speaks of epistemological curiosity – an urge toward knowing that links a theoretical understanding of dialogue with a practical application of this phenomenon. He terms this union "praxis". We intensely engage in urgent conversation because we believe in its ideological roots, its imperatives toward exploring ideas and realities with one another, and its practical complement, the act of co-investigation and collaboration with one another in this pursuit. It is mostly the poor, the sociolinguistically other, the culturally disenfranchised, and the special needs students who find political boulders in the way of such an education.

Where Sleeter (2005) discusses organizing the curriculum around big ideas and goes on to provide concrete hints about what she means by this, Friere (1970) writes of the enforced lethargy of the dispossessed and claims it is the ontological vocation of teachers to act upon and transform the world with their students. Critical consciousness (or *conscientização*) is achieved when classroom praxis (conjoined theory and practice) mobilizes the dialogic intensity and commitment needed to create change in the world fueled by a fundamental change of consciousness of the self. It is not necessarily easy work. Grant Wiggins resisted it. He did not consider it his ontological vocation to take on the project of transforming Jefferson toward personal dignity before his death. Others embrace it. Sleeter writes (2005) of differing stages along a continuum of teacher's complexity of beliefs about adopting a "multicultural curriculum". She suggests that teachers' views about such work are emerging, developing, and/or accomplished. Friere himself wrote that humanization and liberation are, at essence, what is at stake. He says, "[the oppressed] will not gain this liberation by chance but through the praxis of their quest for it, through their recognition of the necessity to fight for it" (1970, p. 45). Friere's words and ideas lay the foundation for the work of so many who write about multicultural education, transformative leadership (McLaren, 2014; Shields, 2013) and critical literacy.

My students are engaged in critical dialogue about a book that mirrors the world – they are reading the world through the words (Friere and Macedo, 1987) of *A Lesson Before Dying*. In their 1987 work Friere and Macedo write that a reading of the world precedes a reading of the word – that "[t]he understanding attained by critical reading of a text implies perceiving the relationship between text and context" (p. 29). As though knowing about today's current assessment dictums, they also say that "reading a text as pure description of an object (like a syntactical rule) and undertaking to memorize the description, is neither real reading nor does it result in knowledge of the object to which the text refers" (p. 33). Rather, they write:

> Reading the world always precedes reading the word,
> and reading the word implies continually reading the
> world. ... this movement from the word to the world
> is always present; even the spoken word flows from

> our reading of the world. In a way, however, we can go
> further and say that reading the word is not preceded
> merely by reading the world, but by a certain form of
> *writing* it or *rewriting* it, that is, of transforming it by
> means of conscious practical work. … this dynamic
> movement is central to the literacy process (p. 35).

I bring Friere's and Macedo's words into this book to highlight the word-world nature of the reading that my students were doing without necessarily knowing if their reading would produce a liberating action in the world. I do know that the novel they read mirrors the world in the way that Friere and Macedo, again, comment. They write, "[we] have always insisted that words used in organizing a literacy program come from what [we] call the "word universe" of people who are learning, expressing their actual language, their anxieties, fears, demands, and dreams" (p. 35). For the most part this is true of the work being explored here as students read and engage in ideas represented within the transactional connections students made between themselves and the universe of *A Lesson Before Dying*; the students' worlds are those represented in the book. Of those for whom this was not true, both the teaching context and the compelling nature of the story engrossed them.

Through the words and dynamic of *these students* we are privileged to share in the experience of a multicultural, literary-teaching scenario that shows us some of the flesh and blood realities related to many of the theorists spoken about here. We also get a sense of why Friere is one of the heroes of this book though he would agree with me that the students must be considered the true heroes as they are front and center of the work we are now exploring. About teachers Friere (2005) writes these words:

> We must scream loudly that, in addition to the activism
> of unions, the scientific preparation of teachers, a
> preparation informed by political clarity, by the capacity
> of teachers by the teachers' desire to learn, and by
> their constant and open curiosity, represents the best

political tool in the defense of their interests and their rights. ... Empowerment includes, for example, teacher's refusal to blindly follow prepackaged educational materials produced by some experts in their offices to unequivocally demonstrate their authoritarianism (p. 15).

Our work as multicultural teachers must always be sensitive to the challenging realities of embracing students' diversities with mindful awareness that our work is made more vibrant and more challenging when we realize the calls to mindfulness that Friere and others set before us.

10

LOOKING BACK AND LOOKING AHEAD

It may be seen as ironic that each of the chapters in this book is thematically oriented: a word or phrase signals my conceptual focus for the chapters. That is, on the one hand I am working hard to restrain myself from teaching my students what the novel is about, insisting that they shape this interpretive process for themselves, and then now from a distanced perspective I am quite deliberately framing each of these chapters, probably making it seem as though the teaching experience evolved quite snugly from one moment, one day, one phase to the next. Nothing could be farther from the truth. Moreover, I also realize that the focal characterization I signal with each chapter's title may run against what others see as a central focus therein. We proceed through these teaching and writing experiences rather at odds with the reality of time's logic; day-to-day teaching runs its often-rambling course and then we write it onto the page and make the process tidy and packaged, shaped and delivered, delineated and smartly defined.

Now, I see resistance, despair, running, and media stories that jibed with the text and the lives of my students. *Now*, I see inside and outside the pages, thinking about things, the beginnings of synthesis, and phases related to learning to trust as the chapter headings point to such phenomenon. We must be reminded that our clearest visions are usually retrospective – now I see clear phases in the work being described and must admit in all humility that, then, I did not. I was figuring it out one day at a time, often unsure of our direction, yet believing in the fidelity of the evolving process and its goals.

It is Friday. I have not satisfactorily explained the writing projects; the weekend looms; reading and interpretation of the novel must be forwarded; students are tired and somewhat listless.

I ask them, "What are you doing in your other classes?"

"Nuthin' like this!" says one young man.

"That is for sure," says another.

"What do you mean?" I ask.

"We got all this talkin' goin' on here – you askin' us all these questions - puttin' that microphone – listenin' to us and then we talkin' and talkin' to each other – all the time … just talkin'".

"Yeah? What are you doin' in your other classes?"

"Not talkin' – that's what we doin' – not talkin'." Some of them laugh, all in agreement.

"What do you mean, 'not talkin'?" I am curious.

"That's what we sayin' – we ain't doin' not talkin' – we – he thinks – he the one doin' all the talkin' – we ain't doin' nuthin'". They look back and forth at one another, snickering.

A discussion ensues led by my curiosity about the teaching methods ongoing in other 'remedial' classes. I ask them what they are reading, writing, what they do in these classes. I ask them, in particular, about their history class, thinking that content would elicit opinions, questions, ranges of interested engagement from them.

"No one's ever - " a young man looks down and stops. He looks at others in the class and says, "We do not discuss *anything*. We write down the notes, we listen - "

"When we aren't sleepin' from boredom!" comments another, prompting gasps of laughter.

"This class – this class – this is the only time I've ever bin asked my opinion of *anything!*"

"Me too." Others nod emphatically.

I ask about teaching and learning experiences they have had in high school; the tenor of their responses -- for all but a few of the seventy-seven students – suggests that they have not been involved with any literacy experiences resembling this one. This impression becomes starkly enlarged over the next few weeks; it is much further elaborated on in subsequent chapters.

"So," I say, "We don't have any time left to say much about chapter ten. Can you work within groups of three over the next ten minutes and get ready to read one critical segment from this chapter – do it – find places where people are talking here – and prepare to offer us a dramatic reading of one of these sections?"

A hand goes up from the back of the room, very tentatively.

"Miss, can I – is it – I don't know but – like – when we – can we - if we don't know one part – is it like cheatin' to read it again – like more than once?"

"What do you mean? Do you mean read it more than once – like reread some sections?" I am dumbfounded and try not to show it.

"Yeah – like can we read it like over and over in places – that's not cheatin?"

"That's a great question," I respond. "That's what I'm trying to have us all do." I realize quite suddenly that this is a core assumption on my part – one that I have not clarified, or even explained as yet. The students feel they have read chapters one through ten (or further) and many may have no notion at all that they will be rereading, referring back to, checking through varying core elements of these chapters repeatedly over the next three weeks as they complete their projects, particularly the written paper. I sit back against the desk and once again ask for one of the students to film me as I offer them a renewed explanation of the synthesis project completion process.

"You know, I'm realizing that I have - that we can – I should say something about what you just asked. It is not – at all – not ever – wrong – we are *supposed* to be rereading these chapters and probably – you probably find yourselves automatically sometimes just rereading – going back over certain places again and again. Is that true?"

Several nod but no one says anything.

"I find every time I look in this book I go back to that first page you know – *I was there yet I was not there* – I must have read that first page ten times by now – I still read it every time I pick up this book."

Still, silence.

"So when we do these projects – when you're reading the chapters – the book by yourselves at night - "

"I awready finish it. I could not - like put it down."

"Really? Well – the thing is – what I want to emphasize here – is that we'll all be reading whole sections, certain places, words, chapters – we will be looking through it all again and again as we begin to work on the syntheis projects – we will be - I think it's maybe even fair to say that you can't – we aren't – you're not even reading it at all if you read it once - this kind of book – maybe all literature is something you read again and again – the rereading is when you really maybe are reading it for the first time – you know what I'm saying?"

"You mean we got to read it again?" asks someone, seemingly dismayed.

"Maybe not the whole thing - I'm not saying that we're just gonna read it then read it again – not like that – no – we still have to make decisions about the project we will do – so we will be finding details – words – checking – reviewing here and there over the book to see what aspects of it - what places we want to you know – we will for example refer to specific quotes from the book – descriptions of people you know – places – things like that details that will be emphasized for the projects once we get started on them – that means that you will want to look back over the novel many times probably for particular elements – details – segments that can be represented in your project and your writing." I continue, realizing that we will have to spend much classroom time working on the projects and, therefore, we have to move the reading forward so that each class will have explored it at least once collaboratively.

"What about chapter ten – I have to move us there – can you work with two other people and get ready to offer us a short dramatic reading of one critical place within this chapter – find a place where the characters are talking to each other – then read it as though you *are* that character – maybe groups of three would work best for this chapter - it will give us a chance to try out the feeling of the drama project a little bit." I explain briefly how, in offering a brief dramatic reading, we are exploring the synthesis project based on a dramatic reading of the novel, saying more about that project briefly.

Here are the dialogue segments that are most frequently read aloud from this chapter, with students assuming the identities of Miss Emma, and Grant's aunt, Tante Lou:

[Miss Emma]: *'Don't force him ... when I am able to get on my feet - God willing – I'll get somebody else to take me up there. I don't want to be a burden on nobody ... he don't have to go'* (p. 78).

[Grant]: *'Maybe I'll go halfway ... maybe I'll dump the food out there in the river. Fishes don't get much to eat in the winter. Maybe they like fried chicken'* (p. 79)

[Tante Lou]: *'You better get that food and get out of here if you know what's good for you'*

[Grant]: *'Everything you sent me to school for, you're stripping me of it ... The humiliation I had to go through going into that man's kitchen. The hours I had to wait while they ate and drank and socialized before they would even see me. Now going up to that jail. To watch them put their dirty hands on that food. To search my body each time as if I'm some kind of common criminal. Maybe today they'll want to look into my mouth, or my nostrils, or make me strip. Anything to humiliate me. All the things you wanted me to escape by going to school. Years ago, Professor Antoine told me that if I stayed here, they were going to break me down to the nigger I was born to be. But he didn't tell me that my aunt would help them to do it'* (p. 79).

[Tante Lou]: *I'm sorry Mr. Grant, I'm helping them white people to humiliate you. I'm so sorry. And I wished they had somebody else we could turn to. But they ain't nobody else'* (p. 79).

With the above words, we have reached the end of chapter ten. I ask students to read chapters 11, 12, and 13 over the weekend and come in on Monday prepared to (a) offer a 1 to 2-minute comment about which project they might choose, (b) refer briefly to five segments from differing chapters of the novel they might try to incorporate within their project, and (c) to possibly offer some tentative thoughts about some key concepts they might organize a project around. I spend some time talking to them about the value of this exercise; they should bring notes, I tell them, yet think through this brief mini-presentation as a way to try out their thinking so far.

* * * *

We have talked about the role of the arts and media in teaching literature. Encouraging students to represent their thoughts through visual, musical, media, drama and self-written poetry venues seemed to liberate elements of their mind and being. We could talk about this through theoretical language to be sure and have done so in an earlier chapter. But first, let's reflect on the plain phenomenon of what arts and media-based appeared to do for the students. It was as though they had been offered a language – their own special language system through which they could relate with this novel. That felt surreptitious to them at first it seemed. They looked to the left and right of each other not quite believing it. When it really dawned on them that they could access arts and media-based language systems to express some of their thoughts about our book it was as though a chord had been liberated within them. They were allowed to bring aspects of their being into a room that had not ever invited such elements of self. And that transformed the classroom into a place that became theirs. They were being asked to do something meaningful and deliberate with a symbol system that placed them in a position of authority to align that system with an aspect of the text that surfaced for them as thematically central. They were also being listened to by one another and by me as they presented their thoughts through a medium of their choice. All these factors brought the students' words and thoughts to center stage.

That they could orchestrate their thinking through the semiotic of their media-oriented world made them fully – cognitively, emotively and aesthetically - involved in what we were doing and moving toward.

The theoretical and research scholarship lends another perspective which I hope won't douse the vibrancy of the students' words and actions. Arnheim (1969) tells us that visual thinking intersects with almost all aspects of human intercourse and many others write about the essential connections between thinking and the visual. For example the New London Group (1996) writes that multiliteracies afford opportunities for students to think through aspects of work processes, that to most fully engage students we have to respect that multiple literacies of their worlds. Moje, Readance & Moore (2000) write that adolescent literacy entails "new" literacies such as visual and multi-media and that bringing such semiotics into classrooms offers students the chance to align their worlds with those of the secondary school classroom. Alvermann, Hinchman, Moore, Phelps & Waff (2006) speak of reconceptualizing the literacies in the lives of adolescents and follow this same tenor of thought. Several others offer related thoughts (Callow, 2003; Clagget & Brown, 1992; Flood, Heath & Lapp, 1997; and Richards, 2002).

Others write of how the use of visual images facilitates students' writing saying that image making aids writers' production of coherent texts, helping their writing processes and leading students toward far more fluid generation of thought (Olshansky, 1998; Walsh-Piper, 2002). Wilhelm (1995) speaks directly about how the use of visual response aids the reading responses of reluctant readers. Cowan & Albers (2006) present work focused on how complex literacy processes can be aided through arts-based integration.

All of these thoughts lend theoretical and practical credence to the work in which these adolescents were engaged. They saw the projects as a medium to express themselves; they allowed the students to shape thinking and to formulate ideas that would eventually be expressed through the writing that accompanied the final version of the projects. Also, bearing in mind that their literary reading represented the first book they had read, they had a great deal of aesthetic and cognitive processing ongoing as has been revealed in certain instances. For these students the arts-based and media projects allowed a medium that was second nature to them. They shaped a great deal of thinking through the graphic organizers, and these projects in a manner that was confortable for them. Given that the students had about as much familiarity with written language as they did with literary reading, expecting them to produce a formal written document without much intermediary processing would have been unrealistic. It would have toppled the aesthetic phenomenon of their reading engagement.

PART II

DECIDING ON THE SHAPE OF THINGS

11

LOOKING BACK, HEADING FORTH

Now, on this Monday of our third week together, it feels as though we are moving together into the deeper waters of this exploratory voyage. I have guided a wobbly reading and interpretive process away from the safe harbor of correct answers or uniform direction. Even more, I am now asking students to formulate ideas about a framework, and point of view through which their ongoing reading might now be oriented. Yes, all the while I have assured them they can change their minds, go in other directions, and revise this thought process. I am asking them, though, to entertain two possibly conflicting mindsets simultaneously: to begin to deliberately assimilate the unfolding elements of the plot of this novel from a thematic perspective *and* be prepared to change their minds about this conceptual orientation as their reading unfolds. Even further, I am asking this of students who are not experienced readers of any genre of literature, or other genres of text for that matter.

These dual expectations are risky. At least two scenarios may be related to this risk: one, that students, in trusting me and feeling compelled by this novel, will forge ahead and move along through this messy process despite ambiguities related to this level of challenge, or, two, that frustrations may arise that will shortchange the interpretive process I am nudging. These considerations are mentioned because they were genuine worries that created uncertainty for this particular set of circumstances, and because they are likely to generally apply in situations similar to this one. The teacher at this point of the process must be a skilled guide, one who is attuned to each student's interpretive voyage, ready to sometimes help with steering, yet always prepared to stand back and let the reader proceed toward his and her own interpretive destination.

Further, it must be noted that the collaborative context established to this point in these courses is the best insurance that students are likely to be receptive to varying -- perhaps divergent -- thematic underpinnings. As they listen and respond to one another (as they have been doing) they are conversationally touching on possible thematic avenues for themselves. They are also being led to consider and reconsider elements of the text they may have overlooked or forgotten about. They are thus structuring possibilities, perspectives, angles of vision, and structures of thought that enrich their range of perspective. The assimilation process happens in all of its unpredictable messiness because of the dynamism of the context, because there are twenty-five or more relatively invested talkers in the room willing to focus, willing to forage within the literary territory we have created with this novel. At this point of the novel -- and at a certain point within all novels -- we are encountering redundancies, revisiting of pathways and plotlines that have been previously established in earlier chapters. I am hoping to somehow highlight these points as they are inevitably referred to while also raising questions about how these elements will be resolved as we continue with our reading. I am reading backwards and forwards at the same time and hoping to instill the same directional imperatives with all of these students. My questions and responses must come forth with sensitive familiarity with the text as I try to energize this interpretive sculptural process, yet not impinge on it overly.

We begin: I draw a series of concentric circles on the white board. There is a central circle with five bands around it, appearing like the rings of Jupiter (see p. 110).

I ask, "Maybe there's someone that can start this off for us this morning – someone that – maybe that – has – does anyone kind of have – you know - "

"What are we talkin' about?"

"Oh - oh yeah – I'm thinking about what I was asking you on Friday – remember – how many of you have – do – did you think about what I asked you on Friday?" I put a list of numbers, 1 to 3 on the board and ask them what they remember about their 1-minute presentation for today.

One of the more able readers puts up his hand; he has not spoken much at all to this point of the class. Something similar happens during the second, class meeting.

"So, what - let's – what's the first thing we are going to mention?"

"The project we picked."

"And we may change our minds, right, but for now we are going to mention the project we might think about working on for our synthesis project."

"Yeah."

"That's the first thing – number 1 right here, right?"

"OK, then - number 2 – maybe - ". I pause then just leap right into it: "What is a word or phrase that might represent a key idea you see going on so far in the book – to this point?" I wait. Then I write "possible key concept" and leave a blank beside that phrase, knowing that I will write many words and phrases as each class proceeds. A hand is raised - as I am being video-recorded by one who has been at the ready each time I am not recording – this seems to ensure his attentiveness to our proceedings.

"Hang on – just let me - I'll mark - what about number three?" I ask them, hurrying to notate TS_1, TS_2, TS_3 TS_4 and TS_5 in a series of bullets beside point 3.

"What's that?!"

"What?" I respond, now confusing myself as much as them.

"That," someone says pointing to the rings.

"No, *that*!" someone else points to the notations I have written out beside point 3.

"OK, hold on," I say, looking back at them. "I am referring to your "TS" text segments 1 through 5 here," pointing to the 3rd bullet point, "And here, " I say, pointing to the embedded concentric circles, "I'm going to make note – put in the details – the points you mention from the 5 chapters."

"I only got three chapters - "

"Me too."

"So I'll sketch the 3 or 4 or 5 chapters – the points from the chapters you mention once you refer to a key idea you're thinking about for your project." I turn, "Make sense?"

No answer. In truth, no one has any idea of what I am talking about at this point. The process will have to be exemplified for them many times over the next hour or more, and probably over the next several days.

"OK, we'll see," I say, nodding as Steve is ready to say something.

"I – we -," he looks at two members of the class with whom he has most frequently worked as a threesome. He continues.

"So, first," he says, "I – I'm gonna do the music project – that's what we – I chose - from the first time we - I saw it – I – that's what I'm choosin'".

"OK, you keep saying 'we' – who else is choosing this project?" Two others raise their hands – a young man and woman who are always quiet.

"Why do I have the feeling the three of you want to work together on this project?"

"Can we do that?" one asks timidly.

"How many of you would like to work with one – with someone else on this project?" Almost everyone raises a hand.

"OK, let's figure out a way for that to work – but for now - "

"We *can* do that – you shoulda said so from the start!" says one young lady effusively.

"OK, let me – can we - let's just – let's see if we can set up some focus for our discussion for today – I want to hear about your project choices and see – and see – let's hear what you have identified from at least five chapters to go along with what you are presenting today." Several students begin paging through the text now. Some have post it notes, some highlighters.

"So, Steve," I turn to him, "Number 1 – the first thing for you for now is your – you have focused on a music – a music project, right?"

"Yeah," he says closely watching the white board where I sketch the following set of notes:

1. Music project;
2. Circus – (In response to my question about a key concept emerging for him at this point of the text, he has commented that, "The whole thing – it's a big circus with everyone – they're all - everyone's got somethin' different goin' on –);
3. TS_1: The courtroom (chapter 1)
    TS_2: The classroom (Chapter 5)
    TS_3: Sheriff Guidry's house (Chapter 6)
    TS_4: Superintendent's visit (Chapter 7)
    TS_5: Jail House (Chapter 9)

The classroom dialogue leading to the identification of the TS's (the Text Segments) for point 3 is as follows:

"OK, for point 2 – for the – you're saying that the overall idea right now for you is 'circus'," I point to number 2, "Circus." I wait; a student works the camera at this point.

"Circus, "I repeat. "What are you – what is it about this word – what idea are you getting at with this word?" No answer.

"We're not sure, right?" Steve nods imperceptibly.

"That makes sense – we're not exactly sure at this point. "So let's do this – let's look at point 3 – you've mentioned 5 different chapters – and we see them there right?" I look around at everyone, and pass the camera-man's book to him from its closed and static place on his desk.

"So let's do this – let's work this idea a bit - no one's sure – what's – what we - what Steve might mean by circus but he's pinpointed certain chapters – so – we have some time today – let's see if there's a place in chapter 1 to start with that goes along with what you're thinking Steven, when you talk about a circus – and we're all going to look at the same time. Take 2 minutes and find what might align – fit with – go along with this notion of a circus." It's Steve's point, yes, but calling on everyone to focus on this detail for a moment or two will draw them into textual review with a conceptual goal in mind. They will become yet more familiar with details of this text.

"Circus," I repeat. "What might be some specific text segments from chapter 1 that go along with - that complement this idea of a circus?" Over the next several minutes or more, I intend to unearth -- or try to unearth – a more fundamental concept. I want to uncover, if possible, the underlying idea represented by the word 'circus' .

I ask the class, "Do you have details from this chapter – places – sentences, paragraphs - segments – that - "

Fortuitously, Steve claims, "I got -," he raises his hand, "There – it's everywhere – there's not one place – but – like on the first page where it's talkin' about the trial – like – but there – on page 7 where it says – where it's takin' about – what this defense attorney is sayin' – callin' him a fool and a - like - on the next page – a hog ." Steve is embarrassed.

"OK – so it's a circus there because … ?" I tonally imply a question. No one says anything.

"So let's look further – you're …," I look to Steve, "Referring us to chapter five as well, yes?" I ask him and refer all of them to the white board, TS$_2$: The classroom (Chapter 5). This conversational exchange is beginning to feel like solving an abstract puzzle.

"Go there," I say. Reviewing the video data now makes me realize just how bossy I may have sounded to the students. But they flip to this chapter and I ask them, "Are there places that seem circus-like to you there in this chapter? Can you try and work with this idea and find places - details – that might fit with the notion of circus?" I ask them. "Two minutes – go!" I say.

Again, they comply. A hand is raised. I raise a finger, suggesting, 'Wait – let everyone have some time to look quietly.'

We wait and I ask again, "What is it – what are the details that might relate to the notion of a circus – what's Steve getting at?"

"Different grades in the class."

"What else?"

Steve again: "He's hittin' one student for –"

"Where," I ask.

"There on page 35, and he's complaining about them usin' too much chalk – like," he pauses. "Like here on page 36 and they won't write – like right – and – on page 37, and then he's thinkin' about all the students and he tells – them -," Steve looks up from his now frantic paging of the chapter, "He tells them about Jefferson – that Jefferson's gonna be electrocuted – and his cousin is cryin' and ... ".

"OK," I point to the white board again, "What about chapters 6, 7, and 9 – what are the text segments – or the details there – that might go along with a circus – what's Steve getting at?"

We review those chapters – details are called out about Grant kept waiting at Mr. Guidry's house and his expressed reluctance for the mission that has been set for him by his Aunt, and Miss Emma (Chapter 6); about the superintendent's humiliations (Chapter 7); and about Jefferson's despondence (chapter 9).

I ask, "What are we really getting at?" I wait.

"Are we talking about a circus? Or are we talking about something else – what are we getting at when - do you really mean circus or something else?' I ask them all, wishing to encourage a thought process for everyone without isolating Steve.

"Lot of stuff goin' on," says someone, who I suspect feels somewhat overwhelmed by the barrage of questions and text reference I am prodding them toward.

"I don't know who this book about!" exclaims another.

"It's confusin'!" another voice chimes in.

"Well maybe we really might be talking about confusion," I say. "Maybe that's the thing going on – when we say circus – maybe we are saying confusion – maybe that's the idea we are looking for right now."

"What?! You sayin' that – you sayin' that -," the student stops, not quite able to articulate her thoughts. I have slightly overwhelmed everyone.

"OK, maybe, - " I stop, now a little worried that the level of thought I am trying to elicit in the students is hampered by my own inabilities as a teacher.

"Maybe – what I think is – Steve you tell me – I'm not so sure that you are saying that this book is about a circus – that that's the basic underlying idea of the book – maybe but I don't think so – but here," I point to the board again, "Here in point 2, where we have written circus – I think that's a great way to play around with – I mean – that's a starting point - that it might have led us to think about the idea of confusion – all the levels of confusion that are going on in the book." I stop and look around – no one is saying anything.

Then, "You're sayin' that the basic idea of this book – it's like about confusion?" someone asks dubiously.

"Well, I'm sayin' that if we play around like this and start with one idea like we did here – that it may lead us to another - that by - look," I direct them, "Look here at what we're building," I say walking over to the concentric circles and quickly sketch a series of ideas reflective of what we have just discussed via Steve's idea structures:

"The classroom irritations
"The trial"

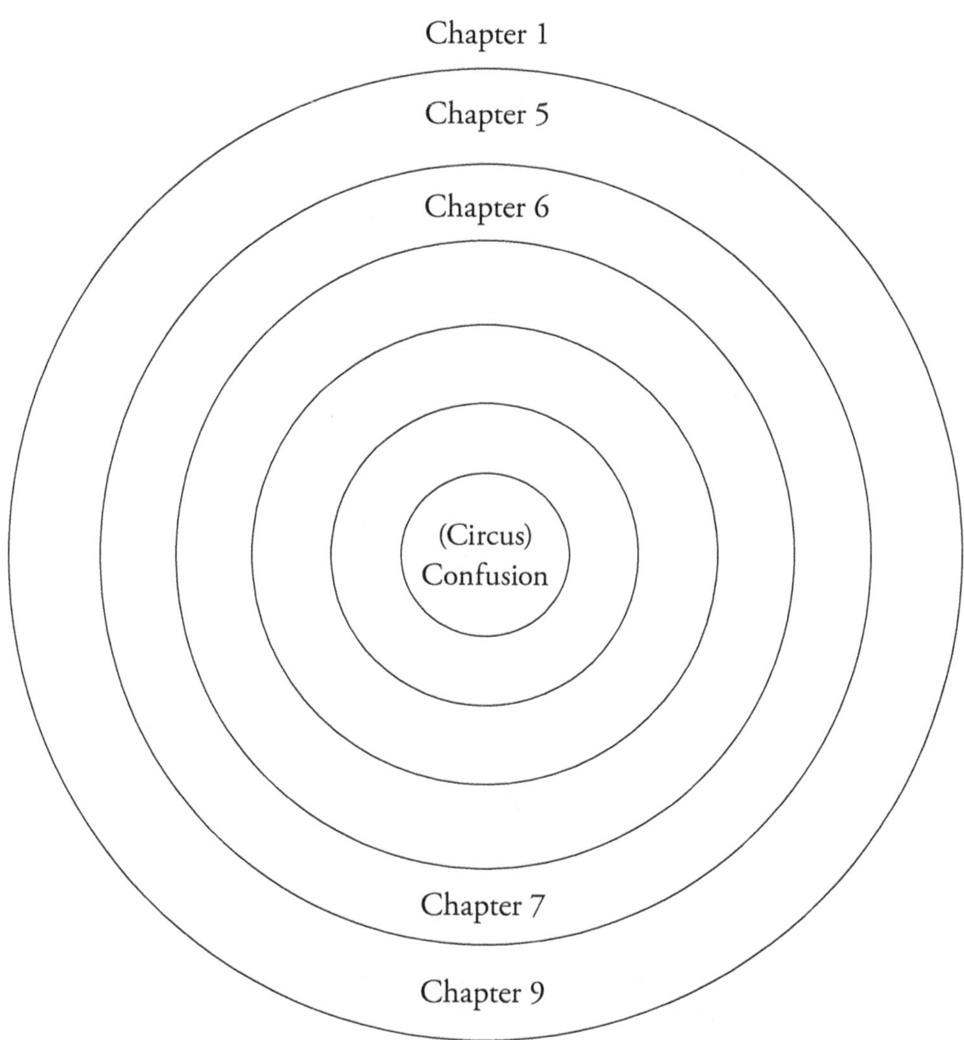

"Jefferson's despair"
"Superintendent's humiliations"
"Mr. Guidry's prejudice"

"What I am saying is, once we start sketching things out a little bit, we might find that the idea you started with might grow a little bit – it might change once you start looking at things – at specific details – you know from the book – like what we did here," I say, trying to sound convincing.

"Right?" I ask them, hopefully.

"Steve started out by saying that he thought the overall idea so far was kind of like a circus. But once we got going – once we began to really look closely at the details – I don't know – maybe I'm wrong – but it seemed like we were not talking exactly about a circus – we're looking for some idea I think – and this concrete thing – this circus – maybe it changes to be more like what we're looking for – more like an idea - an underlying concept – that's what I've been trying to get at." Everyone is overwhelmed and I risk losing them altogether.

I swallow, then forge ahead as though into a blind tunnel, holding my breath and crossing my fingers, "Can we try – do you want to maybe work with a partner for about 10 minutes or so and try out what we did with someone else before we present more of these ideas to the class? I wait.

"Why not try sketching it out like this," I offer a quick framework on the board, then suggest each person copies it onto a sheet of paper:

1. Project Choice:_______________________________________;
2. Possible Key Concept:_____________________________;
3. TS_1: chapter _____________p._________, p._________, p._________
   TS_2: chapter _____________p._________, p._________, p._________
   TS_3: chapter _____________p._________, p._________, p._________
   TS_4: chapter _____________p._________, p._________, p._________
   TS_5: chapter _____________p._________, p._________, p._________

I am getting dubious glances – even resentment. 'Why didn't you create such a framework in the first place,' their eyes seem to ask me, not without a certain sullen quality. Or, perhaps I imagine this.

Someone asks: "Can we do the circles instead?"

"Sure!" I respond, with a sense of relief. It seems that general acquiescence is settling around the activities I have proposed.

I should have offered these frameworks in the first place I think. But no, maybe not. These idea structures evolve out of a context and conversation that is alive. They encapsulate the tenor of a dynamic moment in time. Now, *after* the classroom dialogue has evolved to a certain point, it has become prudent to offer a concretizing template. When directions for this work were offered on the previous Friday, students appeared to be satisfactorily focused; now, under the bright gaze of presentational scrutiny, it seems that the students' approximation of what was asked for is somewhat murky. All seem focused on a synthesis-project choice. But their articulation of a core concept to be represented by the project is just beginning to be expressed as a conceptual focus. Now, it has become clear, after much guided exploration, that it might be worthwhile to have time to possibly refine focal ideas and further explore related textual elements.

Giving them a prepared framework on Friday afternoon might have better elicited develop thinking, *or* it might have served to concretize thought, perhaps conferring on students the assumption that completion of such a neat and tidy page signified work that was done and complete. It might, in fact, have stymied further refinement, expansion, or revision of their thematic expressions. Having the framework now, with a partner, and having seen it evolve as an organic process breathes life into its completion as a dynamic form: it has evolved through a collaboratively created process. Students have participated in its evolution and may be thus more able to breathe shape into its completion with details that are phenomenologically central to the conceptual and thematic unity they are shaping with their evolving synthesis projects.

As the paired classroom work moves along (taking far longer than ten minutes), I move from one pair, threesome, or individual student to the next asking about the forthcoming details – those now being eked onto the pages of their notebooks. This time allows some students to more consciously express conceptual foci and it allows others to fumble with this foreign idea of imagining what is actually meant by thematic focus. Some students listen to conversational partners who have approximated the presentational details quite well in the first place. Others page through the text looking for more chapter details. Various students question one another, much like I have in leading the previous conversation related to Steve's work.

They ask me, "Is this right?"

I respond, "Let' see – can you talk about what you're thinking – what are you seeing in all of the chapters so far?"

They answer in various ways: "It's about commitment".

"It's – like – it's resistance – Grant – he's resisting everything."

"I have no idea – I can pick one of the ideas we got there - " pointing to chart paper taped to the wall in previous classes, "But like – I have no idea."

This process is working for some and not for others I realize.

"Say that then," I respond to the last statement – when you present what you have so far for this work today – that's the right thing to do right now – you see where we're going with this – this work – right? Eventually?"

"Yeah."

"Then leave your thematic focus blank for now – see what others are saying and let's see where we end up by the end of this week and next week".

The next hour or more is a – well, a bit of a circus: varying student voices overlap as page numbers are referred to, the text is read from again and again.

"Tell us where you are," I repeat over and over again, "At the top, the middle or the bottom of that page – tell us – and wait until we find where you are," I insist.

Groups are formed – some automatically, others at my suggestion, as I ask if one young man working on a film project would want to work with two others. Yes. Affinities for a visual project and two separate presentations focused on "Time" as a central concept bring two students together.

"OK," I respond to several people at once, "Yes you can work together as long as there are no more than three people in a group – no exceptions."

Someone asks, "Can we – like – can we – put all these projects together in - like one - one big project?"

"What do you mean?"

"Like we wanna – we wanna – do like the drama project – but we want to bring in some music and some film and - also maybe -," Chris turns to his team members.

One of them elaborates: "Yeah - like he says – we wanna – like combine pieces of them all in one project. Can we do that?"

"Yeah, I guess so – do you know what the overall idea is – your thematic focus?"

"We're figurin' that out – but we know where we're goin' we got the feel for what you're talkin' about."

"OK."

"It's like complicated – it depends on what happens – we don't know yet."

"Yeah."

The work proceeds. Two students have identified Grant as the main focus for a "Character Map" project. Others have pinpointed Miss Emma and Tante Lou as "a" main character for another character project. That evolves through some questioning on my part: African American women are seen as focal to this project, then Vivian becomes involved. Three young women will identify characteristics of these three women (Vivian, Miss Emma and Tante Lou) as they -- for now at least – define their key concept as "strength of African American women". I continue moving from one group to the next, conversing with a pair who feature "resistance" as conceptually central, another pair who discuss "teaching" as thematically vital, and a trio who discuss "transformation". I suspect that members of this latter group have read the book in its entirety at this point; their work is fluid and they are completely comfortable with where they are in their evolving process. I realize we have not discussed particular details related to chapter eleven and call the group together for the latter fifteen to twenty minutes of today's time frame; this applies, variously, to all three of the twenty-five(ish) student groups over the two differing summers.

"We haven't talked about chapter eleven – does – has anyone - does anyone have details for this work that have anything to do with chapter eleven? Can we all go there for the last bit of time we have together today?" I wait.

I ask again, phrasing another question: "Can we find details in this chapter that might fit with some of the projects you are – we are working on? I wait again.

"Just take a look for a minute. Chapter eleven starts on page 80 – do you – does anyone - have any of you included details from today's work – or what you prepared over the weekend from this chapter – and if you haven't, can you have a look and find something now that might fit with how your ideas are evolving?" At this point the camera is pointing to a static image of the rings I have drawn onto the white board and, I hear myself speaking these words from the video recording.

I have to push a bit: "So what's basically happening in this chapter? It's a short chapter, right? What's happening here – where are we?"

"He – Grant's at the prison by his self with Jefferson."

No one says anything else. I have momentarily forgotten what the details are for this chapter as I ask them, "Are there details here that are critical for the work we are doing – where we are going?"

"Yeah."

"What?"

Nothing is said. We all wait. There is a lot of tension in the room now.

"What?" I ask again.

A hand is raised – one hand: "It fits with – what happens here – it – it's – it goes with what were doin'".

"What?" I ask again. "What is your focus for now – with your project?"

"Sacrifice," she says.

"What are you seeing here that aligns with this overall concept?"

"What he does – what Grant says."

"What do you mean? Can we focus on something in particular?"

"There on page 83 - there in the - sort of just above the middle of the page."

There is a long, quiet pause.

I ask her, "Can you read it – what you're seeing there?"

She does: *"I'm an old hog,'"* the student reads. She stops and says, "It's Jefferson talkin' and Grant too." She continues: *"I'm an old hog they fattening up to kill'".*

"'That would hurt your nannan if she heard you say that. You want me to tell her you said that?'"

"'Old hog don't care what people say.'"

"'She cares,' I said, 'And I care too Jefferson'".

"'Y'all youmans,' he said.

"'You're a human being Jefferson. You're a man.'"

'He kept his eyes on me as he got up from the bunk.'

"'I'm go'n show you how a old hog eat,' he said".

"He knelt down on the floor and put his head inside the bag and started eating, without using his hands. He even sounded like a hog.'" The student's soft voice was piercing the silence in the classroom like that of a resolute child; she continued to read seemingly certain how these text segments aligned with her project work, yet not quite conscious of the public shame that might be discomforting.

The student stopped, then said, "On the next page, it's Grant talking - there kind of near - just – sort of above the middle of the page: *"'That man out there doesn't want me up here either,' I told him. 'He said I will never be able to make you understand anything. He said I'm just wasting my time coming up here now. But you nannan doesn't think so. She wants me to come up here. She wants us to talk. What do you want? You want me to stay away and let him win? The white man? You want him to win?'"*

She didn't read anything else. Neither did I. Nor did anyone else say anything. We all waited.

Seemingly unaware of the voluble silence in the room, the young lady continued, clearly following the pattern she had noticed during the first part of today's work and the conversations I had maintained in my visits to pairs and small groups of students.

"So it's like Grant is starting to realize that he has to make a sacrifice to be there – he is fighting – he can't let the Sheriff and the white people win – and Jefferson know's – he kind of – he's gonna have to work with

Grant so – to I don't know – to redeem his godmother's love – even though he is there – and it's not his fault."

"So we have a lot of ideas right now," I say. "Some of your ideas will grow and change. Some of them may become completely transformed – others will be elaborated as we continue reading."

* * * *

Another of the essential features of this ongoing phenomenological literary reading experience is the power of the dialogic process within the classroom. We have heard students say that what they aren't doing in other classrooms is talking – they are doing a lot of listening and notetaking but they aren't talking. Their bodies yawn when they describe such teaching contexts. It does not overstate things to suggest that the range and depth of the classroom conversation animates their focus and interest in continued pursuit of our activities. This point is made well by Nagda and Gurin (2007); they focus on the power of inter-group dialogue (IGD) to "build relationships across cultural and power differences in experiences across identity groups" (p. 35). This work aims to "promote feelings of unity, tolerance, and acceptance *within the exisiting societal structure* (p. 35, original italics). Though our work was not focally aimed at sponsoring relationships or acceptance, the substantive dimensions of inter-group dialogue were present in the classroom. Also, the core traits of IGD came to bear in that we were, through virtue of the book being read, touching on difference and dominance, and engaging in community building and conflict engagement related to the dynamics between characters in the book. In these ways the work of IGD had relevance to our shared time in the classroom over these weeks.

Students' conscientization (as per Friere, 1970) is expanded – here they are reading the word and world simultaneously and thus exploring the interconnections between the life of the novel and the lives of their worlds. In these efforts, they are embroiled in life and societal issues; their phenomenological experience of the novel is akin to a phenomenological experience of the world. IDG emphasizes some of the very processes of collaboration we see unfolding day by day. For example, its focus on increasing critical and social awareness, collaborative activities, affective expression and empathic relations is evident. Also, this process emphasizes contextualization in larger social systems, as well as a search for collaborative possibilities in its goal of searching for social justice. The choice of our novel provided a real-world context and certainly students did discuss justice issues! It must be emphasized through that I was not intent on pursuing social justice – not deliberately so. Our focus was on the students' collective experience of a literary reading journey. It was as though the novel created the context through which many of the features of IGD took place.

Dialogic processes are a core compoent of everything we did together in our work from day-to-day. In a publication of some years ago Driver et al (1994) express ideas that are akin to Friere's notion of a problem-posing educational context. This work was in connection with science teaching but its underlying premises support notions that we have visited in reference to a liberatory education versus a banking education. Driver et al write, "the core commitment of a constructivist position, that knowledge is not transmitted directly from one knower to another, but is actively built up by the learner, is shared by a wide range of different research traditions ..." (p. 5). As has been previously asserted, I was not studying the acquisition of knowledge but a phenomenological process. However, that dialogic constructivist position offers an important layer of realization about the ongoing work in which we were engaged.

Yet more fundamentally, the work of dialogic processes as understood in connection with phenomenological research is yet more promising. Husserl's work (1931) along with Moustakas' (1994) brings us to a direct appreciation about the role of language in phenomenological experience, in this case literary experience. We are possessed by language; in the case of the research being undertaken it was primarily through language that the experience of this literary text could be known from the persons who had the experience and were able to provide the words that revealed their comprehensive description of it. These words unfolded over the 25 days of their reading of *A Lesson Before Dying*. As I reveal their language in the manner ongoing here, I am providing the core elements of the students' experience of the novel as I seek in an ongoing manner to understand the nature of that experience. My words evolve out of shared pursuit with the students; we are experiencing the phenomenon together. Also, as per Mosutakass (1994) I am uncovering the qualitative dimensions of their experience through varied language expressions. The research experience has engaged me – both at the time it was conducted and now for some years later as I sift through all of the data of the videotaped research exploration. The vivid recounting and comprehensive descriptions of the research context are also exactly accurate in terms of what was said, by whom, and in response to particularly defined moments.

It may prove worthwhile to assimilate, at this point, core dimenions of the phenomenological research endeavor taking place. Moustakas (1994) is helpful toward this end. He tells us that the first step of empirical phenomenological studies is the delineation of the focus of investigation – the formulation of a comprehensive question appreciable to others. The following set of questions have formed the basis of this study:

> What is the phenomenological experience of oppressed adolescents in their reading of a novel?

> What is the teacher place in the classroom when facilitating a phenomenologically based literary reading experience?

Many variables contextualize these two questions; they include (a) consideration of the arts and media-based projects through which students will ultimately express their thematic vision of the novel, (b) that students wrote journal responses to the novel on most nights during their first reading of the text, that (c) the students collaborated with one another intensively throughout the classroom reading and discussion experience, and that (d) many visual, or graphic representations were used throughout the reading experience as well. These heuristic methods and procedures facilitated the students' engagements and brought focus to many of the discussions especially as the reading became more and more involved, as we moved more deeply into the text. In organizing these varying phenomena and artifacts the transcriptions of the classroom engagements, some interviews, artwork, and visual media were gathered and organized to tell the research story as seen through its evolving pathways from chapter to chapter.

The wholeness of the experience is only gradually seen at this point as the book unfolds. The essence of the experience so far can be characterized according to two poles of experience: the teacher's role and the students' experiences. Systematic efforts have been made to "set aside prejudgements regarding the phenomenon being investigated (known as the epoche process) in order to launch the study as far as possible free of pre-conditions, beliefs, and knowledge" that may impinge on the interpretation of the data thus far (Moustakas, 1994, p. 22). Moustakas' emphasizes that intuition and imagination play a huge role in interpretation of the data. This point is important. I am intuiting and inferring some of the essential characteristics that can be gleaned about the research questions at this point. It is I now, more than the students themselves, who am describing what I perceive, sense and know about the immediate research context. The students have not been interviewed and presented, as such, with a question that has asked them, "What is the essence of your phenomenological experience of *A Lesson Before Dying*, and how, as oppressed students do you experience this novel?" No, rather they are engaged in this reading experience and I, as the researcher, am describing the context that leads me to make inferences about the answer to this question. Later in the study, the students are interviewed about their experiences, but at this point they are still at the point of experiencing the literary reading.

Moustakas says that "[t]he challenge facing the human science researcher is to describe things in themselves, to permit what is before one to enter consciousness and be understood in its meanings and essences in the light of intuition and self-reflection" (1994, p. 27). Intentionality in this light refers to the conscious experience of "something" – that one's act of consciousness is intentionally related to, in this case, the novel that is being experienced. All of the students were intentionally engaged in the unfolding story of the novel as has been seen. The notion of setting aside (i.e. the epoche) the everyday understandings of reading literature so that we can see this particular reading phenomenon from the vantage point of a pure and unmitigated perspective is important. The students are experiencing the phenomenon before they actually reflect on and describe that conscious experience. Thus, at this point, it is I, as researcher, who rely on the classroom activities and voices of the students to, as Moustakas again puts it, "explicate the phenomena in terms of its constituents and possible meanings" (1994, p. 49).

Moustakas tells us that Husserl used the word *act* to "refer to experiences of meaning" (p. 51) and that acts are intentional experiences. With these thoughts in mind we can summarize the core facts of the research project and also then offer some realizations about the students' phenomenological experiences of the literary reading act. We are reminded that phenomenology focuses on "a return to things just as they are" (p. 58) and an examination of an entity "from many sides, angles, and perspectives until a unified vision of the essences of a phenomena or experience is achieved" (p. 58). Further, phenomenology arrives at essences through intuition and reflection on "conscious acts of experience leading to ideas, concepts, judgements and understandings" (p. 58) and is committed to descriptions of experience that retain the "original texture of things, their phenomenal qualities and material properties" (p. 59). We see that these descriptions are to be presented in "vivid and accurate terms, in complete terms, what appears in consciousness and in direct seeing" (p. 59). The question being asked gives a direction and focus to the meaning of the students' experiences of the literary text and, consistent with this line of research, I have a personal and intimate connection in what is an autobiographical rendering of this reading experience in which we all share a vested interest.

What I see of the students' experiences is, so far, a set of the following themes:

- A profound attraction to the literary text;
- Life relevance with the literary text;
- A sense of play;

- An invested collaborative dynamic among class members;
- A sense of voice and ownership as discussion ensues;
- Ongoing and caring teacher interaction;
- Naiveté, or inexperience with literary reading and writing.

Each of these themes can be further characterized with great detail and will be as we continue. For now, it is sufficient to refer to these themes in light of the range of discourse that has transpired. That the text is engaging for the students has been stated explicitly by many members of all three cohorts of students. Also, the students have commented that the text is about their lives and their ongoing involvement in it may derive in large part as a result of this phenomenon. Their play with the text, with me, and with one another is seen in their humour, occasional whimsy and involvement with the many arts and media projects as well as the visual graphics we have used to further depth of exploration as the reading continues. That the students own the text and have a sense of voice has also been stated explicitly in many instances – they have initiated conversational exchanges and are responding to the novel as though to chords within their own life experience. They are also experiencing this novel with me on a constant bais as I provide bridges into the novel by asking them to complete a range of activities from day to day. These have ranged from questions posed, to organizational groupings with the students, to moments of teaching, to the very projects we have engaged and which will become their final statements about the book. That the teacher's presence contributes to the students' phenomenological experience of this novel is definite and must be acknowledge as a key element of their phenomenological aesthetic. And yet further, the students' lack of experience or naiveté with literary reading constitutes yet another essential dimension of their phenomenological experience of the work.

At this point in the proceedings I must acknowledge that I seem to be involved in almost every aspect of the students' reading except their private moments with the text at night and even then their journalling establishes a thread of connection with me as I read and then coordinate discussions about the elements of the text they have pinpointed in those journal records which take pace each evening. I have not stood back and allowed the students to do much of anything without my constant presence in every moment. Exceptions to this take place with small-group conversation as I cannot attend to every one of those discussions; even then, many of the small group engagements see me hovering with camera and microphone often enough. One might ask if the students' experience of the novel would have been very different had I allowed them to read the text and decide each day what to do and even how they might have independently decided on venues through which they'd have expressed their experiences with the reading. But considering that few of the students reported ever having read a book completely before, I felt that offering them concrete things to do and allowing their prerogatives about how to engage those choices offered necessary guidance while yet having their decisions prevail about how they chose to focus on and engage the many options posed for them. As is often evident I constantly fuss about whether or not my facilitations constitute intrusion or offer calibrated support that leads students toward involvement with the novel on their own terms. This worry manifests throughout the work.

12

HEROES AND DEMONS

The twelfth chapter of *A Lesson Before Dying* reveals Grant's inner thoughts, those of a teacher deeply reflective and deeply conflicted. He struggles with what to say to Miss Emma about the recent ugliness of Jefferson's self-degradation. He sits at Claiborne's bar listening to the men talking about Jackie Robinson and he thinks about Joe Louis, a hero from another time before Jackie R. had come along. Then he remembers a little white man from one of his university classes, a man who had talked about James Joyce's *Dubliners* and he recalls finally being able to borrow that book from his teacher. He remembers reading and rereading that book and not understanding what it had to do with America, with his people – not until years later.

Grant realizes, sitting at the bar musing to himself, that he did not understand *Dubliners* until he really began to listen, to really listen to his people talking in bars and barbershops and street corners about their heroes, about their dead and about how great their dead had once been. At that moment, his thoughts return to 'that cold depressing cell uptown'. And immediately, he thinks of Vivian and goes to her classroom asking her, yet again, to run away with him. She cannot, she tells him. She cannot risk losing her children to her ex-husband. Even more, she insists, Grant cannot leave because he loves the people here more than he hates all that living here represents. These are the basic premises that the text lays forth in chapter twelve. Yet in our classroom proceedings for this day, the students' focus is only on the love we see Vivian again professing for Grant, only on the repeated frustrations Grant expresses about being here, about his uncertainty about whether he stays here because of love for his people or because of cowardice; he asks himself if he is just too afraid to take a chance and leave for California where his folks are.

Classroom presentations continue today, yet none of them feature Grant's reflections on heroes. None of the projects speak of heroism as a thematic focus. No one today, a Tuesday, highlights details from the text that reveal Grant's inner thoughts – glimmers of realization about the heroic power of the dead. No one in any of those three classes gravitated toward the text's subtle movements of Grant's character, his burgeoning thoughts about the universality of heroism, and the deepening chasm within him that furrowed as he thought about his people and their need to glorify the memories of their dead heroes.

In our proceedings today the students continued the work of yesterday, needing time again to work with group members, needing time to talk to one another, needing time to sketch maps, complete frameworks, reread, and generally settle the many challenges of this particular literary reading process. Some students shifted the focus of their projects after hearing others present. Some found details from earlier chapters that fit with their evolving work. Some began collecting a list of text segments, intent on incorporating pertinent details thereto related into their visual collages, character maps, or media projects.

As their presentations move along today, I ask them, "Why is Grant thinking about James Joyce and a story about universality? What is going on here in that part of the text?"

"Uni – what?"

"Universality? Is he saying that - look here on page 90 where it says, *"'What had that to do with America, especially with my people? It was not until years later that I saw what it meant,'"* I read to them, *" 'I had gone to bars, to barbershops; I had stood on street corners and I had gone to many suppers there in the quarter. But I had never really listened to what was being said. Then I began to listen, to listen closely to how they talked about their heroes, how they talked about the dead and about how great the dead had once been. I heard it everywhere'".*

They look at me. I wait.

"Why is he saying that – thinking that – we are seeing Grant's thoughts here, right, again in his own words?" Students look back at me with uncertainty.

I ask another question: "Why – here," I flip backwards a page or so, "Why here," I repeat, is he talking about why – how everyone is in mourning when Joe Louis lost the first boxing fight with Max Schmeling, the German?" No one answers.

This focus on heroes and on Grant's specific recounting of his people's heroes is not fitting well with the relative comfort zones we had achieved given the focus of yesterday's work and today's discussions as more thought structures evolve related to synthesis projects. Today's work and tomorrow's, as well, is a rambling, seemingly scattered series of connections, randomly chosen details, and personal anecdotes. Proceedings seem frayed around the edges.

I ask another question: "Then why here," I ask flipping forward in the chapter, "Is Grant talking about his dreams about a young boy's execution in Florida – how the boy kept crying out to Joe Louis to help him – there – here on page ninety one?"

"Why is he thinking about these things now?" I ask them. "Why does he keep dreaming about the cries of the young boy in another cell in Florida?"

"It reminds him of Jefferson."

"What else – why altogether – what does it mean that he is thinking about heroes, and this thing he is calling universality?"

"More of these questions!"

"We got – we got - we don't know!"

"Right," I say, "Well I'm not so sure I know either but I'm wondering – to be honest I don't either – I don't know why he is talking about heroes, but he is – he's talking about heroes, about listening to people talking about heroes and then he wants to go away again – he says that to Vivian and I'm just - I'm – to be honest, I'm really wondering - I guess I'm wondering about who this story is for right now – who is - who is the hero – who are the heroes."

Again. it is quiet.

They are waiting for me to tell them, to close the cycle of this series of questions with answers that they cannot provide. What are those answers? Why are these questions being raised?

"Universality," I say again. "Is this story only about Grant and Jefferson and African American characters – or –"

Someone interjects: "Yeah!"

"Yeah I guess so. I guess so," I repeat. "But why is Grant thinking about an Irish writer – why is he thinking about a universal story – a story that applies to – a story with – that everyone can relate to – that might be about how people – how humble people who may not have a lot of freedom or possessions or opportunities depend on the only heroes they know? Why is he thinking about that now?"

"He's rememberin'".

"Right," I say musingly. Grant is remembering. It may not have been all that clear to him either as the moments ensued – as he was caught up in the day-to-day tensions in which he was embroiled at that time. I ask myself now, 'Should I have led the students toward the idea that Grant as a teacher, as an African American teacher in a rural and racially segregated time was heavily burdened by the plight of his position as the only hero they could turn to at that time? That that burden is one he shared with heroes from literature and history and that this struggle signals a universal story – one that resonates for all people at certain times?' Should I have offered the students then an account of those possible interpretations? Would doing this have toppled the inchoate structures of thought that were being created by students who had never read and really owned a literary interpretive process before? I was asking questions about some of the concepts that were signaled by this chapter, yet not quite marching students to the precipices of my own interpretive realizations about the metaphoric position of Grant Wiggins as a character enfolded within the cataclysms of history – of black history in America in particular. Was it enough – is it ever enough – to raise possible avenues of exploration and yet stand aside as students' own imperatives leave out some of the subtleties *we* might see and realize as unexpressed in their own interpretative edifices?

I wondered then and I wonder now.

I did ask this question: "Does this book connect with – does it remind you of any other books you have read?" I wanted to expand students' regard for Grant -- and for other characters within the novel as well. I was trying to subtly pose the notion of intertextuality so that they might see that this text was one singular voice within a chorus of other voices – other texts that spoke of related themes. Was it possible, I wondered, to nudge the students toward realization of this text as a deliberately constructed linguistic structure that was united with multiple other texts that explored related themes? Or, again, did such intentions undermine the phenomenological nature of the ongoing work? Can students' literary interpretations be aroused toward broader conceptual frames without trouncing their own defined boundaries?

The answer to my question was answered by one young man – one lone hand extended into the air and waiting for me to answer it.

I said, "OK, one of you – anyone else?" I asked again: "Does this book remind you of any others you have read? Can you compare this book we are reading with any others you have read?" I acknowledge the young man waiting with a nod.

"Think about it," I ask, "Any books like this one – any at all?"

"Marcus?" I ask, "Which one?"

"Malcolm X," he said.

"OK, Malcolm X," I respond. "In what way might *A Lesson Before Dying* and *Malcolm X* be compared – are there similarities?"

"Well like," says Marcus, "I saw the movie – is that what you mean – like stories that are the same?"

"Sort of," I respond, now appreciating that by setting up synthesis project choices (such as the 'Film Project'), I have opened the door to this response. It is not the answer I had hoped for but it was a logical answer given the pathways I had invited from students since our work had begun. Yes, this movie and this novel featured male protagonists who were seen as leaders for their chosen people – one far more willingly than the other. Now I was more curious and posed the question again.

"Anyone else?"

No one else in any of the classes spoke about a literary text that reminded them of this one. I did not pursue any of the themes I had been ruminating about. It was my voice that had spoken of the key elements of this chapter, not the students'. In foregrounding these details about heroism and universality, I realized that a subtle shift had taken place – my thoughts had become dominant. If that pattern continued, the research project and the literary reading process would be undermined; this text, and the students' evolving experiential expression of it could not be thwarted by my domination over what they saw and felt and were willing to say about this ongoing process. Yet we had over half of the book remaining – several new threads were yet to be explored. The process was beginning to feel like a house of cards that might come down at any moment.

* * * *

It is time to talk more about heroes. Bahktin tells us that "[o]ne of the basic internal themes of the novel is precisely the theme of the hero's inadequacy to his fate or situation. The individual is either greater than his fate, or less than his condition as a man" (1981, p. 37). The hero has always an unrealized potential, we are told, as an "incongruity of a man with himself. There always remains in him unrealized potential and unrealized demands" (p. 37). But our students are not seeing Grant Wiggins as a hero. They are not focused on this element of the text nor on the reflections Grant speaks of when he talks about those who are heroic and what that quality has meant to him or to those who revere such champions. They are preoccupied, it would seem, with other discussions.

Moustaka (1994) explains a process of "horizonalization" whereby "we can never exhaust completely our experience of things no matter how many times we consider them or view them (p. 95). It may be, with this thought in mind, that students might begin to reflect on the concept of heroism, the notion that Grant and possibly even Jefferson embody these traits. In the chapter just read by the students, the text offers them poignant testament that heroism is at least on Grant's mind. He thinks about this phenomenon a great deal, ruminating about how he had listened to people talk about their heroes, "how they talked about the dead and about how great the dead had once been" (Gaines, 1993, p. 90). But within the horizons of the students these thoughts do not register and I must not press them about it. It may be that as we continue they will return to this thought but as Moustakas also tells us, "we experience things that exist in the world from the vantage point of self-awareness, self-reflection, and self-knowledge" and that "we consider each of the horizons and the textural qualities that enable us to understand an experience" (p. 95). Perhaps because students have not experienced a great range of African American literature (or any other literature for that matter) they cannot align Grant or the concepts of heroism and universality with the tropes of such horizons. It must be postulated that the students' reading histories may not allow them to see Grant in kinship with other stories – ones that tell the allegorical tales of a people and its literary heroes.

13

INCREASING PRESSURES

Forestalled in my attempts to infuse our conversation with intertextual referents, or focus on the narrator's (Grant's) somewhat involved reflections on heroism, I urged us to focus on chapter thirteen. There remains another half hour or so in this Tuesday class and it seems obvious (yet only to me) that the text continues here in this next chapter to develop in keeping with Grant's perspective, his recounting of the events surrounding the assignment put upon him by his aunt. Perhaps one simple question would elicit continued exploration of the intense dynamics surrounding this narrator's expanding web of complications. If we could not see Grant as a composite symbol whose centrifugal literary universe enfolded hundreds of characters whose burdens were also heavy, then focusing on specific elements of his perceptions and memories might at least reveal differing layers of Grant and, through him, core essences of this novel. This was borne out in varying ways.

I asked the students, "What is the most significant thing that Grant is saying and thinking in this chapter?"

"What do you mean, like - 'sayin'?"

"Well, he's the one telling the story, right?"

"Yeah." This answer comes forth somewhat uncertainly.

"So he's - so everything - everything here in this chapter is what he sees and hears, and says and does, right?"

"Yeah." There is still an implied tone of questioning evident in this response.

"So, what do each of you think is the most significant thing he is saying and/or thinking in this chapter?" I resisted asking anything more about their projects or asking them to make references to other chapters. The process of linking related key details across chapters had been ongoing and working with varying degrees of effectiveness for students. Perhaps narrowing our focus for the latter portion of time for this day would allow a refreshing glance at our shared experience of the story's unfolding.

"He's sayin' he ain't religious!"

"That is foh shuh!"

Suddenly the room feels like a musical chorus, voices skipping across one another like a series of punctuated notes in the air. For the time being, I resist asking them to pinpoint textual details. They are looking into their books but right now the text seems like a script that facilitates back and forth banter. I listen, and watch as the microphone is held by one young man who crisscrosses the room as quickly as he can. It is clear he relishes this role; it's as though we are all together within a studio for a reality TV show.

"His aunt – she religious – she - "

"She don't want him to go so she don't say nuthin' when he – when Grant won't go to church no more."

"Um hmmm."

"That's right – she don't want him to go."

"He there thinkin' - "

"He got a guilty conscience - "

"No – he don't know what to think!"

"They all sittin' there givin' him – like - the third degree."

"That's right."

I glanced into the chapter and realized they were referring to the conversation Grant had had with Reverend Ambrose, his aunt and Miss Emma. They had wanted to know how Jefferson had been. They had been waiting for him for a long time.

"He don't know what to say."

"That's what I'm sayin'".

"He got to think of lies to tell them."

"He don't want to tell them the truth – how he ate on the floor like a hog"

"He shoulda just told them the truth!"

"He can't do that, fool!"

"That minister he there – they're gonna figure out that Grant is lyin' – they all starin' at him with mean eyes!"

"It's not mean – they don't know – he the only one they got to tell them what's goin' on!"

"They should be a lot nicer to him – they pressurin' him – he don't want to be there!"

"But he ain't goin' nowhere – he ain't goin' to leave Vivian."

"That is foh shuh!"

"What he's sayin' to them – it's the truth but it ain't the truth at the same time."

"That's all he *can* say!"

"They don't believe him – they askin' him how come he was there for five hours and he don't remember anythin' else – they onto him."

"He ain't been there five hours – he just go for an hour then sneak away somewhere to think about what to say to them - his head is gonna explode!"

"His aunt – she be givin' him the mean eye!"

"That minister – what's his name?"

"Reverend Ambrose!" someone calls out.

"Yeah – that Rev – Reverend Ambrose – he keep askin' Grant what's deep in him."

"What?"

"Yeah – he – he – he sayin' what's – he askin' what Jefferson be thinkin' – what he thinkin' - "

Someone else interjected: "Deep in him – what he really - how he's really like, doin'".

"Yeah!"

"They want to know about his soul!"

"They want to know - the Reverend – he want to know did they talk about God".

"Grant he don't – he say he don't know about God".

"No, he say – he didn't get round to God!" someone corrects.

"They all upset about that!"

"That's true – they don't like that – that – the - Reverend Ambrose – they askin' him about *God*!" There is a triumphant tone in the voice of one young student as this utterance is expressed and then a lot of laughter.

"It ain't fair!"

"They - they all goin' there and bringin' him the bible!"

"He'll still die!"

This conversational exchange reflects one that took place in one classroom. Others focused on music that could be heard floating over the plantation as Grant sat reflecting. Some fixated on Reverend Ambrose's preoccupation with whether or not Grant should be imparting God's wisdom to Jefferson. Some noted that the song that could be heard in the background was the Determination song, "Were You There When They Crucified My Lord?" Still other details related to whether or not Grant should be lying about Jefferson's well being.

Despite my uncertainties about the wisdom of it – for fear of capsizing lively exchanges, I asked them in the final few minutes, "Is there one passage – one segment - just one in this chapter that might capture something important about Grant – what he's thinking – the pressures – the situation in which he finds himself? Can you work with one other person – with a partner and come up and write just maybe one or two sentences that seem the most critical about what's up with Grant in this one chapter?"

Here are the most frequently represented examples of what was written onto the board and captured by the camera:

'I couldn't think of another lie so I shifted to something else' [p. 99]
'My aunt still wanted to put me on the rack' [p. 99]
'Reverend Ambrose … was a simple devoted believer' [p. 101]
'He stared at me as though I was one of the worst sinners' [p. 101]

'I cared less and less about the church' [p. 102]
'I had been running in place ever since, unable to accept what used to be my life, unable to leave it' [p. 102]

I want to ask them to pinpoint particularly salient elements of this chapter, the thirteenth, but the class ended. I am constantly monitoring the fine divide between sharing this literary reading experience with the students and channeling their appreciation toward some of the structural and extra-textual residues offered within it. I asked them to write three of the statements that seemed most important into their notebooks. This was done hurriedly as they left the room.

In Grant we see an image of a teacher who is deeply conflicted about the work that has been visited upon him by his aunt. We see him struggling here as varying demands press upon him. Grant may not willingly have taken upon himself the responsibility of redeeming in Jefferson a sense of wholeness. Nonetheless he is embroiled in the day-to-day pressures seemingly forced upon him by the circumstances of his life as the only black educated person there, surrounded by a white racist world that impinges on him and restricts his work with his students.

Similarly, teachers in the present-day reality of their work are conflicted by external exigencies. Most strive to engage their students in meaningful activities while at the same time juggling multiple agendas brought upon them by external, often stated-mandated exigencies that often relate to testing protocols and standardized curriculum. Grant could not rely on a proscribed answer to reach Jefferson, try through Reverend Ambrose might to convince him of that. He asked Grant what he felt deep within himself and it was a deeply felt constant struggle for him (Grant) to eventually find an answer to that question.

Reaching students who are disenfranchised is hard work and often entails much soul searching on behalf of teachers and researchers. Finding ready-made answers to this phenomenon often results in teachers thinking outside the packaged boxes of packaged curriculum. Tatum writes, in fact, that "lower reading achievement is associated with practices that accompany test-driven instruction" (2000, p. 52).

He speaks of a culturally relevant approach to teaching saying that "culturally relevant literature is key to a culturally relevant approach" (p. 53) and that "[t]here is a fundamental tension between a basic skills approach to meet standards and a culturally relevant approach" (p. 53). His work focused on teaching grade 9 students a range of skills within an emphasis on "literacy instruction to help sustain them" (p. 54) given that they lived in what Tatum characterizes as "the racial dehumanizing of inner-city urban youth" (p. 54).

Grant is a teacher who has no easy answers. He faces the daily realities of his life without sure solutions and when confronted by those who would seem to present answers for him, cannot accept them. As we continue watching the unfolding story of engagement of *these students* we are more and more conscious of the parallel stories of *A Lesson Before Dying* and the teaching and learning saga that unfolds one day at a time. Grant is more embroiled in the assignment given him by both fate and his Aunt while I become more densely entwined with the teaching dynamics of the students' life in the novel.

14

PASTORAL REFLECTIONS

Today is a quiet day. We left yesterday – in all classes – without specifically outlining assigned reading for Tuesday night. Since the pace of reading for the first class of twenty five students was followed for all other classes, this meant that everyone began this day without having read any further into the novel. This was true of all but a very few students; most followed specified expectations set forth for each of their classes and did no more (and sometimes less) reading than what was assigned. Their personal and collective level of involvement in the characters and events of the novel appeared consistently involved and yet at this point, perhaps due to demands of academic work and pacing in other classes, the rate of what was read from it each night depended on what I assigned for the most part. On this day, a Wednesday, it seems that we each needed to nestle within the books privately so I suggest we read and raise thoughts, questions, ideas and responses within journals, noting page numbers and particular details quietly, each with our own selves over a span of our time. I am also aware that we must talk about the writing demands set forth in the projects but I do not want to do that until we have had more time for aesthetic exploration of the varying threads of the novel.

As we begin, I sit at my desk reading and writing within my own journal notebook, but then I move ever so silently to the camera, which has become a permanent fixture in all of the classes. Its presence, at this point, is like that of any other piece of furniture in the room: barely noticed, walked past, virtually ignored. I hit the record button and slide a chair softly behind it where I can sit. One student looks up. I hope that my unassuming manner will impart the casual sense that our work should simply continue. I wait. He resumes his reading. There is a deep feeling of calm in the room. It is very quiet. We are comfortable with one another and there is the sensation of a collective sigh having been well fed, then released as everyone is immersed in chapter 14. I have learned to use the many levers on this overly sophisticated tripod onto which the camera is locked and so can now easily and lazily sweep the lens across the faces in the room.

Their varying postures have one thing in common: unselfconscious absorption in this story. I am slightly nervous as I realize this, feeling intrusive, like a furtive interloper watching an intensely intimate moment. In that sense, it is somewhat like watching my infant and very young toddler sleep at night. The students' faces are completely relaxed, eyes riveted on the page, flitting from word, phrase, and sentence, trusting the absorption and being carried along by it, all the while unaware that I am watching them through a camera lens. I have pulled the lens into very close focus on each face, then even more closely focused now, only on the eyes of one person. They are lit up, absorbing the mind's translation of the black marks on the page to spectacle and images, all the while registering involvement in the experiential reel that is ongoing. A page is turned. No one is writing anything down at all. I enlarge the camera's lens to a wider range. Still, everyone is reading. I wonder what they are seeing, what the qualitative dimensions are as these private moments pass by.

I leave the camera now after twenty-five minutes have passed and tip toe closer to one group of students who sit quietly reading in one larger group. I want to see what pages they are on – to see if they have moved beyond this chapter and into the next.

In a voice that surprises me with its soothing tones, I remind them, "See if you can write down some of your thoughts, feelings, ideas, and responses as you go along". Many students have now moved on into chapter 15.

It is time: "Can we talk about chapter 14?" I ask, rousing them from the solvency of their tranquil, inner thoughts. They stretch, then blink as though they've been transported here from another place.

"What are you seeing there? What are you thinking about what you've read here today?" I ask. I am curious. I have read this chapter too, and once more, again, just prior to my secretive gazes at their facial and eye postures through the camera. What have they noticed? What has aroused their attention in these same pages?

I wait as I so often do after asking these questions. I wait and I wonder.

"Anything?" I ask them.

There are subtle giggles. Oh, I realize, remembering now some of the particular details that will have caught their urgent attention. I smile, waiting for their words.

"Yeah …" says a voice a shy young woman's voice.

"Yeah?" I ask.

"They still praying!" says a male voice. It is followed by laughter.

"Still prayin'," he repeats.

"Lot more than prayin' goin' on in this chapter – this one – this one is chapter fourteen right?" anxious now for confirmation that he has read the correct chapter.

"*Lot* more than prayin'," says someone else suggestively.

I say nothing.

"He ain't never goin' leave the plantation *now*." Raucous laughter ensues.

Still, I am quiet. That last remark seems to have loosened their tongues and words bubble out of them.

"She better watch out, goin' off like that with him."

"Yeah but they're in love!"

"Still … ".

"Ummm …"

"What?"

"They shoulda just stayed at the – at house."

"His aunt gonna come back - "

"She's at the church".

"Vivian say Grant should be there too".

"They be sayin' somethin' else after that!"

"She gonna have a baby!"

"What are you sayin'?"

"That's what it say".

"Where – where is it sayin that?" someone asks demandingly.

"That's what they're talkin' about – what do you think they're talkin' about?"

"I am not followin' you all – at all."

"She's pregnant girl".

"She thinks she's pregnant – she – that's why they're talkin' about names."

All conversations among all classes contain some traces of judgment about Vivian's morals – whether she is a loose woman, a good mother to leave her children as she does and go off with Grant from time to time, a religious person, a loyal person and so on.

Genuinely curious I ask, "How do you see this chapter connecting to anything else we have read before – anything going on with Grant or what's going on with anyone else in the novel?" Almost all of the students – or those directing the conversation at least - seem particularly preoccupied by Vivian's character and the very particular love scene that has been described in this chapter. I really do want to know how they might situate the gently erotic tenderness that has been described with the levels of other tensions across the novel to this point. I wonder if the shared carnal embrace might be viewed as a moment of genuine bliss in the midst of the mounting and continuous strain for Grant that has been described throughout the novel to this point.

I ask another question: "I mean – why is this scene seeming to come after - right in the middle of the book – after all of Grant's – the narrator's - the key character's descriptions we talked about a little yesterday – you know running in place, unable to accept his life and yet unable to leave? You know?" I entreat them, wondering about this aloud in a pondering tone.

"Right?" I invite them to wonder along with me, to situate the intimate details with a thematic banner that suspends many of the individual strands in the story, such as this one is: particularly evocative, and yet related to an overall coherent literary universe within as well as beyond this novel.

"I mean," I ask them, continuing, "We read about this scene after – you know after – after everything too - everything about Grant thinkin' about people's heroes and - "

"Grant got his hero now!" says a young man's voice salaciously. Collective mirth washes over the room.

"Right but there is love here right – there is love - on this quiet plantation on a Sunday, on a day that - look at page 107 – what are they describing there – can you read something that describes where they are now?" A few of them do. One is below:

> 'The entire plantation was deadly quiet except for the
> singing coming from the church up the quarter behind us'
> [p. 107)

"Something else from there – what else?" I ask them.

> 'Left of the weighing scales and the derrick was the
> plantation cemetery, where my ancestors had been buried
> for the past century'.

The voice stopped.

I said, "Can you read just a little more from there – from – a few more sentences right after that?"

> 'The cemetery had lots of trees in it, pecans and oaks, and
> it was weedy too, and since there were so few gravestones,
> it was pretty hard to see many graves from the road. Just
> before we came to the cemetery, we turned left on a road
> that would take us father into the field. This was Vivian's
> first time back here, and I told her that my people had
> worked these fields ever since slavery, and many of them
> were buried in the cemetery behind us.' [p. 107]

"Right," I say stopping the young man's reading.

"So there they are in the middle of a deeply quiet and private place and Grant is remembering – it's his story right – he is remembering that time and that place and his people – and this is all happening after these previous chapters about running in place, right, and about heroes and now he is with Vivian and it seems like - someone said it seems like they may be having a baby and planning a future and so I'm just wondering why is this happening now at this point in the story, that's all".

"He's happy right now."

"Yeah, he's happy and he got – he got like you said – he got some peace and quiet for a change." They look at me.

"OK. OK" I say to them, "I'm just wondering you know. I'm just wondering, you know?"

"Where are we going with this story – why are we reading about this now – why is the author telling us this now."

"I guess we'll see," says a young lady quietly.

"I guess we'll see," I respond leaving it at that, and knowing that right away at the very beginning of the next chapter, Vivian asks Grant when he will see Jefferson again. I do wonder if the intensity of the love affair between Vivian and Grant is somehow entwined with the agonies of Grant's involvement with Jefferson, with his deeply rooted soul searching about heroes, and his ambivalent connections to this deeply racist world in which he is seemingly immobilized. I also wonder just how much of this possible interrelatedness I should be questioning the students about. Where would their own path of connection with this work travel without my constant questions? Am I intruding?

I write a question onto the board and they sit quietly watching me do so; I turn and peek at them, pointedly after each few words, theatrically suggesting that this question might be one worth thinking about: 'Are there connections - between Vivian and Grant's love affair - and references to commitment – and heroes - and the situation with Jefferson?'

If we begin to notice more carefully the deliberate structural evolution of the novel's elements, will the students be facilitated toward a more refined relative coherence of their projects and its written components?

This thought also asserts itself as we work our way father into the work, and thus closer to focused construction of their varying syntheses.

I wait, as I so very often do. I reread the question out loud and then I ask them to write it into their notebooks, realizing as I do so that we should have been - all along - taking note of the many questions that I have asked. We should have constantly recorded these many questions and referred back to them from time to time. It's a shame that we have not consciously written and highlighted them in journals with an asterisk so that we could revisit them. I realize yet more consciously that the questions I have asked over the past several days are often thematically oriented. I wonder if it will facilitate the students' creative syntheses if we look back into our notes and sometimes discuss these prompts that emphasize possible core premises of the novel. This I resolve to do and as the work of assembling the projects becomes more and more intense, it proves a worthwhile teaching idea, as later chapters will reveal. I feel it important to help students engage the ideas of each chapter as threads within the overall fabric of the text and not, as they have been wont to do with this fourteenth chapter, as a scene that is, in and of itself, seductive to them. They have become so immersed in the details of this chapter that they may have foreclosed on its relatedness to the prevailing current and direction of the story.

I repeat the question out loud in a playfully dramatic tone: 'Are there connections - between Vivian and Grant's love affair - and references to commitment – and heroes - and the situation with Jefferson?'

"Are there?" I ask them.

"Why is everything gotta be - like – have to - we gotta go over the same things every time – like all the time! We just wanna read the story!"

"OK," I quickly acquiesce. "But let me say this – let me just say that we might be coming back to this – I know I keep asking these questions – these pesky questions – and I'm gonna probably keep doing that – and we can leave it all alone for now if you want to – we can come back to it. Do you want to spend some more time reading for today – we have to make a plan for completing the novel so that we have time to work on our projects and write our papers – do you want me to talk about that for awhile instead today?"

"No!"

"OK," I laugh out loud with great amusement. They do not want to work at some of these ideas. They are tired and many of my questions have caused them stress here and there. I have often raised questions that have been discomforting and now they are beginning to let me know that.

"Let's do this, then," I say to them. "Let's spend some more time reading – we'll read chapter 15 for now. I think we will have time to finish chapter 15 and talk about that. Now when you read it, can you peek back a bit and see if – see if there are - are there topics or ideas or – you know – are there details in this chapter that remind you of other related or similar things in previous chapters?" I pause then ask again, "Can you make note – can you kind of make some notes – just quick notes you know – about any other details from previous chapters that this chapter reminds you about? Can we do that?" Again I wait.

"Can I get a solemn declaration that you will with your utmost abilities be aware of anything in this chapter that reminds you about details from another chapter?" This mock legality causes some of them to smile and I realize that some of them will. I plan to create student groupings in about 20 minutes or so, asking those who have made such connections to work with those who have not. All the while I am bearing the upcoming project constructions and writing in mind. Also, I know that there is little risk at this point that they will become dissuaded from their interest in the story; my job will be to depend on their attraction to it as an insurance against resistance to the work of the writing elements. Even further, I know now that the assembly of their various projects will also provide yet more grist that will counter the struggle they will have with their writing. I have come to realize all of this in the course of our time together and now am thinking actively about timing of work related to the writing. It will be a challenge.

* * * *

Many have written about the work entailed in teaching students to write. Casey (2009) refers to the work of engaging students in active reading and writing events and says that, "untangling the struggling adolecent learner's frustrations with reading and writing is a complex process of understanding ability, considering engagement, and providing access to appropriate materials" (p. 285). Like earlier work I have cited, Casey's is situated within sociocultural views of learning. She writes that "mapping adolescents' literacy development involves understanding the larger community in which the school is situated, recognizing the nultiple social systems that exist within the classroom, and understanding the unique needs and interests of the individual students" (p. 285). She discusses learning clubs, commenting that "teachers guide the process by deciding areas of inquiry available available for students to select from, how groups will be structured, the nature of students involvement, and the formats available for response" (p. 285).

Students involved in such learning clubs meet with success due to the chance to be motivated by material, use a range of strategies, engage transactionally with the novel and interact with others as they build a comprehensive appreciation for the texts they are reading and writing. Negotiating resistances to this approach to reading and writing is not unusual: "it is a lot of work to encourage students to assume ownership of literacy events" (Casey, 2009, p. 290). The students are often characterized as lazy and unmotivated (Biancarosa & Snow, 2004; Long et al, 2007). These are the very same students who, like mine, have not much – if ever – been fully involved in reading and writing events at school. I have often commented that it's not that *these students* can't read and write, it's that they don't do it. By that I mean simply that their abilities have not been tapped into. It has been assumed that involving them in rote worksheets will somehow result in their being able to produce interpretations and coherent writing. They've been robbed of the opportunity to do other than respond desultorily and so when offered the opportunity they sometimes apply standard responses to school "work".

I found that my students had more resistance to writing than to reading. We will hear them saying so.

15

THE POWER OF LOVE

I sit watching them again, still on this 13th day, a Wednesday, and worry that the risk I am taking in pushing along with their synthesis projects and writing, as planned, might derail our growing relationship – the deep connection I am forming with *these students*. Can I provide sufficient direction and support for the work I have outlined for them? Will I let them down? Am I able to strike a fitting tone – one that marries them productively to the vision they would shape with their arts and media-based projects and accompanying written text, as well as one that will more fully articulate this expression of their various synthetically unifying themes? It will never be enough - never, never – to simply provide idea frameworks and writing templates. Depending on point-by-point struts such as these will only reinforce a mechanical paint-by-number approach. The work that is being invited will be best energized by a depth of involvement verging at least in part on intrinsic intent to gather a nest of fulsome details. They will create a coherent home for their ideas if they feel some level of passionate investment in their edifice. It has to matter to them. I am more and more seeing myself as the architect of influence with such a happening.

I wonder what they will see. By now, the students know that I am interested in what they say; our conversations have become spirited and genuine. Despite the constancy of assigned work, journal prompts for classroom reading, reminders about project deadlines, regularly forthcoming sketches of new frameworks, and a deluge of questions, not to mention a prevailing climate of expectation on my part, it seems that we have moved through our time together respectfully. I like them tremendously and they know it. Our engagements with one another and with this book are deep and real.

As they seem to be emerging from their reading of chapter 15, I suggest that partnerships be formed between those who have found details in this chapter that can be related with those of earlier chapters. As shuffling ensues related to this proposal, I also move from one pair to the next, listening in on their exchanges. Sometimes it is clear that I am too close but, in most cases, they are accustomed to my "eavesdropping" persona and simply continue chatting. Here are some of the snippets of what was recorded:

"What are we supposed to be doin'? She got that microphone goin'"

I overhear this and wait a few minutes before reminding them to work together to share elements from this chapter that remind them of similar details in previous ones. I continue to stroll, then turn and suddenly it occurs to me to offer a more particularly directed suggestion:

"Why don't you read to each other," I suggest. "Why not read passages to one another from this chapter, then see if your partner can guess the idea you are thinking about that relates to one from a previous chapter. Start with the person who has found something that connects to something else – some other key point from another chapter, then ..."

Another idea springs to mind: "Why not see if this works – if it does - that's great – if it doesn't then don't worry about it:

Quickly I sketch the following frame onto yet another sheet of chart paper, wishing to provide possibly needed structure yet also shrinking from the reluctance to too stringently define interpretive direction:

3rd Related detail from one <u>previous</u> chapter	2nd Related detail from one <u>previous</u> chapter	1st **START HERE** **CHAPTER** _____	4th Related detail from one <u>subsequent</u> chapter	5th Related detail from one <u>subsequent</u> chapter
p._____ I am noticing:	p. _____ I am noticing:	p. #, significant element from this chapter:	p. _____ I am noticing:	p. _____ I am noticing:

"Look, start here," I tell them, pointing to the middle column of this quickly improvised framework, "And move backwards, to the 2nd column, and then the 1st one," I say, becoming quite pleased with the assimilation support that I assume this response framework might offer - without stifling variant interpretive directions. I look back at them after taping the sheet of paper to the wall. I look at them and they wait for me to say something else.

"Does this make sense?" I ask them.

"Like - what are we supposed to do?"

"Well, do you want to try one together first?"

No answer.

Someone else asks, "You want us to draw that – like – in our books – and -," her voice trails off.

"Well," now I am uncertain of – no – very certain that I have offered too many directions without first clarifying one of them. Quickly I ask, "Can anyone refer to something that they have noticed from this chapter that connects in some way to a previous one?"

"Natasha?"

"When they talkin' about – like when Vivian is there - and Grant's rememberin' – like – how they're all prejudiced."

"Can you read that for us?"

"Yeah – where is it – yeah there - on – at the bottom – there on page 111 and it like – it carries over."

"OK."

She starts to read, and then looks up to say, "It's – like he's – Grant's - it says she married a guy with – like darker skin – and - " she begins, "*Everything turned out as she had feared. Her family had nothing to say to her husband and hardly anything to say to her. He never went back. When her first child was born, she took the baby to visit. No one held the child or gave it a present or any attention*'".

The student looked up – I had written a few words into the center column of the chart:

3rd Related detail from one previous chapter	2nd Related detail from one previous chapter	1st START HERE CHAPTER _______	4th Related detail from one subsequent chapter	5th Related detail from one subsequent chapter
p. ___________ I am noticing: ___________ ___________ ___________ ___________	p. ___________ I am noticing: ___________ ___________ ___________ ___________	p. 112, significant element from this chapter: *Vivian's family are unfriendly to her dark-skinned husband and baby*	p. ___________ I am noticing: ___________ ___________ ___________ ___________	p. ___________ I am noticing: ___________ ___________ ___________ ___________

"Does this seem like a fair summary of what was read?" I ask them.

"Yeah."

"OK," I continue, "Has there been any other such - any other references to similar incidents, or related details anywhere else."

"Yeah!"

"Where?" I ask them, "Can you find it?"

"It's there where – that teacher – what's his name?" asks one young man, looking up at me.

"Tell us what you mean and we'll help you find it," I say.

"Yeah," he says, "You know - you know – where that man – that - "

"Mr. Antoine – yeah!"

"He say he's better than any man blacker than him."

"There it is – chapter 8," says someone else, "There on page 65 – we read that before!"

I write another statement into the framework, in the second column:

3rd Related detail from one previous chapter	2nd Related detail from one previous chapter	1st START HERE CHAPTER	4th Related detail from one subsequent chapter	5th Related detail from one subsequent chapter
p. ___________ I am noticing: ___________ ___________ ___________ ___________	p. 65 I am noticing: *Mr. Antoine's claims about being superior to any man blacker than him.*	p. 112, significant element from this chapter: *Vivian's family are unfriendly to her dark-skinned husband and baby*	p. ___________ I am noticing: ___________ ___________ ___________ ___________	p. ___________ I am noticing: ___________ ___________ ___________ ___________

"Is that – does that seem – is that accurate or should I write it another way?"

"That's – what you got is right."

"OK, so … "

"What are we supposed to do in the other columns?"

"Well we can't do anything yet in the last two columns because we haven't read any further than this one – this chapter 15, right - where we are today, right?"

"Yeah."

"And, I don't know if you have anything else – if Natasha and Sylvia have anything - if there is anything else from another chapter before that related to this idea – or not."

I wait.

Then I say, "But you can't have their ideas – I am just showing you – this is what *they* notice and how *they* make connections – how they see a connection to – between - "

"There's something else!" someone calls out.

"What do you mean?"

"There – they say – it says - there in that same chapter that – his – that teacher – his relative." She reads from the page, "*he was being looked after by a relative who did not care too much for anyone visiting him, and especially darker people'"* (p. 66).

I have found the spot and quickly make another notation on the chart:

3rd Related detail from one previous chapter	2nd Related detail from one previous chapter	1ST START HERE CHAPTER _______	4th Related detail from one subsequent chapter	5th Related detail from one subsequent chapter
p. 66 I am noticing: *Mr. Antoine's relative does not like darker people visiting him*	p. 65 I am noticing: *Mr. Antoine's claims about being superior to any man blacker than him.*	p. 112, significant element from this chapter: *Vivian's family are unfriendly to her dark-skinned husband and baby*	p._______ I am noticing: _______ _______ _______ _______	p. _______ I am noticing: _______ _______ _______ _______

"OK, so," I say to them, "There may be all sorts of different ideas that you find – like this – the way – that these chapters – these ideas – this idea from chapter 15 here where we started," I point to the middle column of the chart. I stop, then continue, "We don't have much time left today but see if you can all - with your partner - find something important – something that seems significant from this chapter 15 and make a connection – see if there's a connection to other related details from a previous chapter or two – if there are three, even better." I stop and wait.

"Can you try that?"

The conversations that take place with our remaining time in this day link varying details across chapters. Sometimes (quite often) students complete linkages of ideas from chapter 15 to a previous one without specifying the chapter and page number details. In other cases, (less often) some students are quite particular about completing neat sets of notes that outline a framework much like the one I have spontaneously sketched onto chart paper. Sometimes as pairs of students offer comments to the class after working together for fifteen minutes, their ideas are offered without the neat textual referencing that I have modeled. Some samples of these exchanges follow:

"Here – like she – Vivian – like it says she has quality and in other places, like she loves Grant, and she supports him goin' to be with Jefferson – and it said before she wants him to go – she told him he loves them – he can't leave."

Another:

"It's talkin' about his aunt – she – like here it says she's a boulder in the road – and before - like she made him go to the jail – and before that she tells him she's sorry she's humil – humilatin' him but they got no one else and – another time she - it was his aunt that forced him to go and be with Jefferson."

Of course, my intent had been to offer a supportive bridge that would smooth the progress of connecting related ideas – ones that figured as central in the student's experience of them as their reading progressed. This work today has grown out of the previous days' engagements, and a continued building of a classroom context that attempts to nourish students' interpretive prerogatives while also affording them support for an enriched, integral structure among ideas. We are soon to begin intensive work on projects that are to express varying thematic syntheses. I wonder if this work today is successful. Does it intrude on the reading experience of some students? Or is it helpful in allowing them to begin deliberately amassing coherent thought configurations? It may be too soon to tell. We have no more time for me to ask them to articulate underlying themes that tie their observations together. It seems sufficient for some to have engaged this thought process without further prodding to elucidate it any further than that. Would this passage of experience with Vivian with Grant and his aunt at their house, sensitize the students to more fully notice the succeeding ideas – ones that seem to emerge from the hearth of this time on the plantation as recounted by Grant over these past few chapters? Are the students becoming more aware of the integrated nature of the text's growing convergence on "an" experience? I don't know. We leave today with plans to read chapters 16 and 17 for tomorrow. I ask them to be prepared to talk about details in these chapters that may figure prominently in their projects.

* * * *

My role as a practitioner researcher has been framed in a paradoxical manner – I have been facilitating certain directions of student reading by offering interpretive frames, by posing questions and certainly by assigning the synthesis projects in the first place. I am thus determining the broader contours of this aesthetic literary reading and research process. At the same time, I consistently invite students to define the contours of meaning and detail that shape their particular interpretive feelings and direction. Thus, I am both facilitator of the broader macrostructure of the classroom climate, yet always stand aside as each student's interpretation of scenes and growing synthesis of collective meaning are variously defined. As a practitioner researcher thus engaging in collaborative action inquiry our work was developing toward final form with young adults in an emergent social setting. This work was ongoing in the face of challenges for these students: they had never participated in such work before having been socialized into traditional schooling patterns. They had never collaborated in a project such as this, having throughout almost all of their schooling years been in traditional teacher dominated classrooms where non-exploratory, correct answers had been the norm. In my role as co-inquirer I was holistically engaged with them in creating a learning space as a full learning partner in their interpretive creation process. Such approaches for adult learners are described by Yorks (2005) and others as of growing interest in the field of adult learning in resting on a participatory worldview drawing from practitioner-based action research related to generative learning (Heron, 1996; Dickens & Watkins, 1999; Nowotny, Scott & Gibbons, 2001). This action research is discussed by Jacobson (1998) in particular connection with adult learning. The age of the students – all eighteen or older – places them within these discussions in the scholarly literature though they are young adults to be sure. The work was focused on a transformative experience for these young adults; they spoke of it in emancipatory terms though used non-scholarly terms to express this idea. Certainly, as will be seen in the next chapter, the words they used to describe the work they did in reading and variously responding to *A Lesson Before Dying* fall in line with such a liberating context. Mezirow (1991) emphasizes trust and security as needed ingredients for transformative learning. I believe these conditions are met in the various day-to-day classroom research settings. The interactions among us are characterized by shared interpretation within a trusting context characterized by intense dialogue. As we worked toward eventual expression of their arts and media-based structures we were co-producing knowledge of the self within an academic setting and within the world as well given the contents of the book we were reading. The relationship among all of the participants changed positively; repetitive cycles of action and reflection were ongoing as we progressed through the book via classroom discussion, group work, mapping structures and frequent whole-class discussion.

In keeping with the contours of this work we were involved in a co-inquiry with one another that had the goal of producing a structure of their interpretive aesthetic of this literary text. The reading of the book was directly related to their actions and experiences in the world and was intended as an educationally useful and developmental experience for the participants. This particular practitioner-based collaborative action inquiry involved, as has been specifically shown through exact dialogue among participants, doing research *with* these young adults rather than *on* them or *about* them. The work rested on an epistemology of participation in which I as both teacher and researcher was engaged in authentic experience. I was inside of that experience as it unfolded, engaging the students to be self-directing as they defined meaningful patterns of the text within the social space of the classrooms. The political dimensions of work insisted on the students' rights to participate and express their own thoughts, feelings and opinions and thus were empowered by the experience. We were peers in co-producing the reading of this literary text.

The students' final projects, as will be much more discussed, represented the actions they took as the final statement about their work. These actions varied among them as film projects, visual collages, sculptures, character maps, drama projects, and interior monlogues expressed their view of a text that, for everyone, was a statement about the world in which they lived. Thus in producing and presenting their syntheis projects, they were creating an action statement about the world in which they lived. They identified the characters as real persons in their worlds and were making statements about their relationship to them as such. The dialectical relationship between their reflections and actions represent yet another example of a central pillar of learning from experience much along the lines of the work of Dewey (1910).

Even further, the educative process for all of the seventy-seven participants resulted in profound changes in how they viewed themselves as readers, writers, collaborators and presenters. They became far more confident in their abilities to express opinions, refer to textual support, produce elaborated discourse in connection with the literary text, and create synthetic structures of details in connection with a governing point. They learned new cognitive strategies and gained a sense of intellectual perspective on themselves as active creators of coherent knowledge. They were validated to think of their opinions as mattering and, given that, they came to be quite careful about how they developed their points of view. These learning changes were quite significant to almost all of the students, and accorded with Bateson's (1972) view of the notion of learning as change.

16

TAKING RESPONSIBILITY

My role as a teacher and research in this setting is complicated. On the one hand I sincerely want to explore – as researcher – the students' phenomenological experience with this novel. At the same time, my influence as a teacher is surely affecting this experience, perhaps variously heightening, forestalling, and otherwise altering what it would have been on its own terms, what it would be if the text were not being read in a particular academic context. As both arbiter of this context, and self-appointed researcher within it, my dual presence there tempers both of these roles. Fearful that the teaching influence in general, and the teaching strategies in particular may now have infringed on paths of literary interpretation students may have undertaken independently, I approach today's work determined to stand back and listen, hopeful that there will be sufficient conversational imperative.

In truth, I am also hopeful that yesterday's prompt will be productive. Specifically, I wait to see if students will, in fact, have read chapters 16 and 17 with a thematically-oriented eye. I have suggested that they identify details in these chapters that might feature in their projects and wonder if this will sufficiently arouse ancillary thoughts about the core conceptual premises to be represented therein. I am hopeful, in light of these reflections, that students' comments today will reflect simultaneous insight into their continued experiential trajectory with the novel, and that they might interweave their insights today with the whole of it over our time together. I want to be able to stand back as a researcher and see what comes of the teaching prerogatives that have accompanied the literary reading experience thus far.

I ask them, "What are we talking about today?" They look at me and I back at them. I pass the microphone to a student.

"What do you want me to say?"

"What are we talking about today?" I ask them all, speaking not to the young man, but calling on the class as a whole to remember our direction for today's discussions.

They are quiet.

"Does any - anyone remember?"

"We – we readin' - we read two chapters las' night."

"OK, which ones?"

"Chapter 16 an' 17."

"OK, what else?" I ask them.

"Ah … ah – like – we're – we – you said to see if there are details – things in this chapter – in chapter 16 that we can put in our projects."

"OK, so - so can we talk about that now or do you want to work with group members for ten minutes or so first?"

"Can we work together for a little while?"

"OK, you know that I'll be – can I listen in – you know come around and listen in a little bit?"

"Yeah."

The room quickly becomes a broth of voices. I interrupt them.

"You know in - in – in about – in a little while I am going to see if we can talk about what you're all talking about in your groups - so that we can share some thoughts together, OK?

I leave the camera at the front of the room as the students' groupings assemble into a raggedy U-shape formation on either side of it. I walk around with the microphone in hand and as I hear fragments of focus on one detail and the next, I hand the microphone into the group members, one takes it, and then I return to the camera and point it toward these respective interactions. I hear varying references to elements of chapter 16:

"He's in a good mood today."

"They getting ready for the Christmas play."

"He say he want them to remember Jefferson - "

"Yeah …"

"I wanna – I wanna know like – do they think – they keep up pressurin' him – they back from the prison and they know he lied to them before – they - "

"Yeah."

"Was he there?"

"What?"

"How does he know – they talkin' about Jefferson and - "

"It was one a their friends, Miss Eloise – she came and he – he heard her tell – no the aunt was tellin' that friend a hers."

"Oh."

"It was the same - like – when Grant went there – he done the same thing – and now she – now Miss Emma knows he was lyin' about it before!"

"She – they got Grant there – but she cryin' now - "

I listen in here and there and remind them with a question, "What are you seeing here that you will need – that you will represent in your projects? What are the details here that may fit with your sense of the key concept of this book?" I listen some more:

"She keep sayin' – she keep axin' who gonna do somethin' for her before she die?"

"Yeah."

"His aunt tellin' him the same thing – he's goin' and that's that – he still don't want to go and she tellin' him he's goin'".

I walk back and forth in the various classrooms, then call everyone together after twenty minutes have passed. They have not been talking about projects at all.

"What do we need to notice about what's going on here?" I ask them, first. Then, "What is happening here that seems important maybe in various places in the novel?"

"They talkin'"

"OK, who's talking?"

"They all there at Miss Emma's talkin' to him - ".

"Who's there?"

"Grant and his aunt, and Miss Emma, and that Reverend – what's his name?"

"Reverend Ambrose".

"Yeah."

"So what's happening there?"

"Same thing that's been happening since the first."

"What do you mean?"

"They keep pressurin' him – he gotta go back there 'cept now they madder at him than ever."

"Why?"

"Miss Emma was there – Jefferson won't talk to her and he actin' like a hog."

"No, he feel like that – he's depressed!"

"OK, so when you say that it's the same thing that's been happening before, what do you mean exactly – can you read something from the book that shows that?"

"Yeah."

"Go ahead."

"There she says - "

"Where?"

"There on page – where is that what she say to him?" says a young lady, turning into the pages.

"What you lookin' for?"

"When his aunt tell him, he goin' back and that's that!"

"There it is."

"Where?"

"There on page 123, she say *'you're going back ... you aint' going to run away from this Grant'*"

I look into the book and see something else above that and ask, "Is there anything else on that same page – something about what Miss Emma says to him as well?" They look at the same page.

"Yeah – she say go back!"

"What else?" I ask.

Someone else says, "She say someone got to do somethin' for her before she dies."

"She said the same thing to Mr. Guidry when she went to his house."

"But he still don't want to go – he sayin' that Jefferson wants him to feel guilty and he don't want to feel guilty – he don't want to go!"

"Right," I say, and then, "look at the bottom of page 123 – look there – can someone read what it says there?"

"He say he want to take her face and maybe be gentle with her 'cause it ain't goin' to work to scream and be angry," comments a student, paraphrasing from the text.

"OK," I say, "And then look – what are you noticing on the last page of this chapter?"

"Nuthin' goin' to change!"

"OK so nothing is going to change – it's the same thing, right?"

"Yep."

"So what exactly is the same – what's the same thing that's been going on?

"They got Grant in the middle of everything!"

"They got Grant in the middle of everything," I repeat, going to the board again.

I draw a circle – a simple concept circle, and turn to them after writing Grant's name in the middle of it, "What is the 'everything' you're talking about – what do you mean by everything?" I wait.

"What's everything?" I ask them again.

"Just – like – all the stuff goin' on with Jefferson – and him with Vivian and everything."

"So let's do this," I decide quickly. "Let's – I'll - there are 16 chapters we have read so far and there are twenty-five of us – I'm going to give - I'm going to put some pairs of people with certain chapters, and some of you will be all alone working on - with one chapter – just for 3 minutes."

"What do you mean?"

"I'll show you," I tell them. Quickly I point to a pair of students and say, "Chapter 1," then another pair and call out "Chapter 2", and another pair, calling out "Chapter 3" and so on, until everyone was assigned to look over one chapter, either singly or with a partner.

Then I said, "Now find something in your chapter – that fits with – when we said that Grant was in the middle of everything, find one specific thing from your chapter – if possible – see if in your chapter – the one you were just assigned to – see if there is something there that – you know about – that connects Grant to specific things going on - then we'll work with your ideas a bit - it will become clear once we start – just each of you – can you find something from your assigned chapter that seems most importantly connected to Grant."

I draw a large concept map onto the board (next page) to represent the 16 chapters we have read and discussed so far – space limitations prevent me from fully representing there all of the details students volunteered about the chapter each rescanned. The whole-class discussion that follows reveals each chapter's focal element related to the point about "Grant in the middle of everything!" After about ten minutes (and some reminders from me in the midst of camera and microphone balancing), we began to discuss details from each chapter that might be most relevant to this phrase.

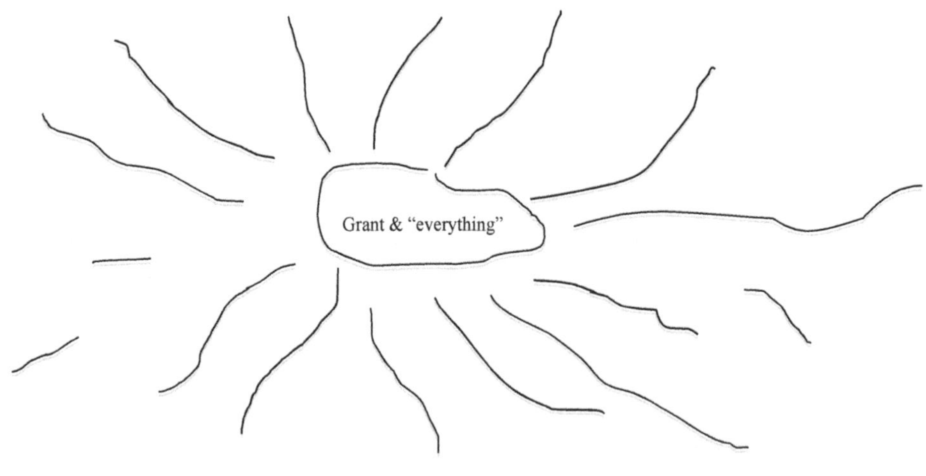

At the end of each of these sixteen tentacles is a small circle related to chapters 1 through 16. As the varying configurations of student-chapter focus wind down I motion for our replacement camera-man to step in as I orchestrate conversation and mapping on the board. This is what the conversation looked like:

"So, what have you found in chapter one – who worked on chapter one – OK – what should we note here on our map about this chapter – can we all look there as we go along here today and see if may be we are missing something?"

"Like he was there – but he was not there – he knew what would happen – and he heard everything – it was like he was sitting beside his aunt and Miss Emma and he knew- he knew what was goin' on the whole time – even though he was not there – he knew the whole story – he knew it would be death – that was the sentence."

"Why – what should I put here?" I refer to the notation I have made beside chapter one on the map.

"It's like – it's – the same thing that's been goin' on all over time – since - in that community – in all the black communities – it's the same – it's been goin' on – it's still goin' on – he's sick of it – he's like – he's sayin' – it's sayin' it's the same old story – all the racism and twelve white men – they got the power – and he – they can't they – we – it just – it's the way it's always been."

"OK – so for now, should I put, *'I was not there, yet I was there'*?"
"Yeah."

"OK, now I'm wondering if we should go chapter by chapter – or - "
"I got somethin' that connects with that."
"What chapter?"

"It's – what – it' s – chapter 13 – that part about him runnin' in place – kinda like what he said about bein' there and not bein' there."

I walk to the placeholder I have drawn for chapter 13 and quickly write "Running in place" then decide we'd better build a renewed sense of the text by proceeding through the text chapter-by-chapter as I also respond to what has just been said.

"So he's - he's what – what would you say – we hear him say he's there – he isn't there and we have kind of got a sense of what he means by that and then this – this – he says – it's his words still here in this chapter 13, right?"

"Yeah."

"He's what – what did you say from that – about that chapter?"

"Runnin' in place."

"What – how arc – what's the sense you have about these phrases?"

"He's – they - he tryin' to hold everything together and the only person he got is Vivian and - "

Another voice chimes in: "She pressurin' him too – really – we got – we found something from chapter 4 – where she sayin' to him – remindin' him that he left before – and then she say - she wants him to go to Jefferson – and that - she say she'll marry him after that as long as he responsible for what he do there."

"Ok – so," I skip to my chapter 4 location on the map and look back at this group, "Should I write 'Vivian: support and pressure'?"

"Yeah maybe."

"What about chapter 2?"

"Pain in Miss Emma's face, and running in place again on p. 15, and how he wanted to scream, and he teachin' what he told to teach and - "

I notate these four details and ask about the next and the next and the next chapter, all the while notating, questioning, and attempting to draw out reflections about how these emerging details, seen like this all in one place, and being revisited now, might spark realizations about a unifying vibrancy that courses through the universe of this novel. It is not -- not -- a reduction of the novel's elements to a core frame that was being invited, no, rather a personalized vision of its live moments that might be assembled as a whole expression – one that would reflect a deep exploration and even, yes, an invested struggle with how to shape this coherently. The work is inviting a deeply involved participation, and reminding students, now, of the possibilities that might arise within the conceptions and renderings of their own synthesis projects.

"Chapter 3?"

"We got that – his aunt's eyes on the back of his neck, and bein' tolerated at Mr. Henri's house, and too educated – and - he - they say let the teacha' go to him – to Jefferson."

"Chapter 4? No we have details there – what about 5?"

"Problems at home with his aunt – and he's irritated at school – it's about some of his students – how they always there – it's always been the same."

And when we were done, we had a ring of phrases encircling the one that read "Grant in the middle of everything!" All of the previous days' references had been reflected upon, and chewed over, and now a panoply of phrases resonant of the students' gazes were swimming around this one axiom.

Then I asked them, "But what is the 'everything'?"

"Just everything – all of it – all the - everything that they livin' there – all of it –everything – all the stuff you – we put there – all pressure and ... everything!"

"Yeah," I said, realizing that they would be shaping expressions of the "everything", and working further on their evolving visions of the "everything" as we moved forward.

I realize that we have now spent much time on the activity just described, and have not addressed anything that happens in chapter 17 as we have done so. Why have we not focused on this chapter here today? It is the first time that Grant and Jefferson have a genuine interaction. What will students see in this exchange, and will they see it as pivotal that the two men have actually talked? How will they speak about Miss Emma's request that the future visits now take place in another room so that they can all sit down together? Where will this story of literary reading go from here?

* * * *

Galda and Beach (2001) tell us that research on response to literature features work that looks at either the role of the text, and subjective and psychoanalytic dimensions of readers (as per Bleich, 1978 & Holland, 1975), or the influence of context. But as we have seen in previous discussions and in the classroom engagements heard, this research explores the phenomenological dimensions of a transactional engagement as per Rosenblatt (1978) who refuses to parse attention to any one of these triadic dimensions of the literary reading experience, rather emphasizing the interrelating dynamics of all three. She writes that, "the various strands of response are often simultaneous, often interwoven, and often interrelating. The dynamics of the literary experience include, then, first the dialogue of the reader with the text as he creates the world of the work and that … aesthetic pleasure consists in satisfaction derived from the varied kinds of activity … " (p. 69). It becomes impossible in this research project to separately focus on the reader, the text, or the context, as each variable is so essentially a part of the students' reading experience. Readers in this particular context are engaged with this particular text and evoking a personally unique experience of the work. While it may be true that some readers' experiences rather dominate the text and for others the text more influentially determines the response, it must be kept in mind that the focal direction of this work was on a collective phenomenological aesthetic experience; therefore, reader, text and context become a triadic event.

In fact, Galda and Beach (2001) acknowledge that researchers began to "focus increasingly on response not simply as a transaction between texts and readers but as a construction of text meaning and reader stances and identities within larger sociocultural contexts" (p. 66). Further they say, "[r]eaders, texts, and contexts are studied as constituted by culture and history" (p. 66), referring to a sociocultural theory of learning that regards engagement as an activity that arises from the cultural identities of, in all cases, specific readers. These students are learning to engage a literary text through explorations that are new for them; they are tentatively acquiring discourse processes of reading, writing, speaking, and listening, along with visual and media practices. Their connection to the book comes through these mediums, yes, but is largely moored in their sociocultural and ideological oneness with the book. Their lives reflect the very social forces or systems, so they say, of the book they are reading. The students, then, are navigating the very new-to-them context of reading and discussing a novel even as they are bringing their own life-in-the-world social and identity systems in alignment with the novel. Most of the young adults are in the Frierian (1970) sense very much reading the word as world – reading the text as a microcosm of the world in which they live. Many of these ideas are further expounded by others (Beach, 2000; Hynds, 1997; Gee & Crawford, 1998; and Bruner, 1990).

The influence of context and sociocultural influence in transactional aesthetic reading bears special mention as it applies to all readers – more, *or* less experienced ones. Gee's work (2000a, 2000b; 2001, 2002) helps us to realize that context is a variable that shapes readers from birth – from the time they are born within certain sociolinguistic and economic circumstances and throughout their years of schooling. Triplett (2007) discusses how students' struggles with reading are socially constructed - greatly influenced by teachers' reactions, particular school contexts, curricular variables and relationships. This premise is widely accepted and developed by many theorists and researchers who often claim contextual variables as the overarching influence in most teaching and research situations. As this book unfolds, the influence of context remains paramount; the work of Gruenewald (2003a, 2003b) establishes its crucial role in all educational and/or research settings as he emphasizes "place-based education" and "critical pedagogy". The related work of Valdeboncoeur (2006) also stresses the influential role that learning contexts play in shaping participants' degree of involvement in, and reactions to the activities of varied contexts. Alvermann (2001; 2006) suggests that schools may, in fact, may be creating struggling or inexperienced readers due to contextual variables. Readers then may *be* their context – they come to school embedded with linguistic, cultural and economic influences as Heath (1983) has shown us and they conjoin with texts, seeing in them what is relevant to and connected with their beings. As was the case with the reading of *A Lesson Before Dying* the eighteen-year-old young adults saw the text as a reflection of their own lives.

I resist delving too deeply into the well-established literature on "struggling" or "resistant readers" here as I wish to explore theoretical and pragmatic terrains of multicultural issues in subsequent chapters, discussing these students from that perspective even more fully. But to fully acknowledge the work that has been done I want to mention Franzak's (2006) work. She summarizes reader-response, strategic reading, and critical literacy approaches, with varying emphases being undertaken within each of these three paradigms. Also, her work on policy issues reminds us of the importance of the prevailing contexts influencing young aults, once again. Then again, so does the work of Luke & Freebody (1997) and that of Moje (2002) who urged the American field of adolescent literacy research to pay more attention to adolescent literacy as a complex phenomenon that considers the social contexts and realities of adolescents as they constructed multiple identities within school, *and* also through the multiple, hybrid realities of their complex lives outside of school. Alvermann's (2006) work responds to this plea. Assembled in her book is a multi-pronged attempt to reconceptualize the literacies in adolescents' lives; consideration is dedicated to their cultural capitol, democratic citizenry, critical literacy, and how changing policies affect their literate identities in and out of school contexts. *A Lesson Before Dying* became a vehicle that seemed to elicit vibrances of the students' lives along all of these dimenions so much so that the students considered the book non-fiction as some students were heard to discuss. This book was about their lives as they saw it! Thus, rather than allow theory to obstruct and overly burden the voices of the young adults, I wish to align the theory with the major chords of the students' engagements. The theory fits because it complements the classroom transactions; it characterizes the prevailing centrality of the phenomenological literary essences of this collective reading experience.

17

SHACKLED FOR LIFE

Still, we are together today on this fourth day of the school week.

I ask them, "Are you seeing anything here in chapter 17 that seems - that captures your attention? Anything going on here that we can fit with what we've just done with our map here?"

"They all still there!"

"Yeah but what are - what's happening – what are you seeing that might – that - "

"Jefferson – he bad mouthing Vivian! Grant gonna hit him but he stopped."

"At first there – at the beginning it say he ain't so mad any more, then when Jefferson say that, he mad."

"She want - she gonna want – there on the first page – you know – it say, '*I could never stay angry long over anything. But I could never believe in anything either*' – there on the first page, and then Jefferson – he call Vivian – he talk about her -"

"That's nasty – you can't say that!"

"But that's what it say – he call her – he say her - he call her that yellow woman and she – she no good," says a student, not quite using the coarse language of the text to refer to Jefferson's description of Vivian.

"Grant's talkin' to one of the deputies – one of the ones – the decent one – he askin' about his day?"

"What's - what might be – is there anything different going on here – anything that's different from the other times?"

"There," I say, "There on page 127, Grant's talking to that deputy, Paul right?"

"Yeah."

I wait.

"Is anything changing?" I ask them and turn and make more room on our map for chapter 17.

"He never asked about him before."

"He never had a chance before – this is first time anyone speak to him about it."

"OK, then what?" I ask them. I wonder if they have noticed that the last thing mentioned in chapter 16 is that his aunt and Miss Emma continue in their insistence on him being there – that nothing he said was going to change that.

"What else?" I ask, urging them forward, I hope, through these non-committal directives.

"They talkin'.

"Who's talking?"

"Grant and Jefferson."

"Why? Why have they started to talk now – they haven't talked before, right?"

"Yeah, but Grant – he say they got to talk 'cause a Miss Emma".

"Grant's tellin' him that she was cryin' and Jefferson says everybody cry – and Grant keeps vexin' him – that he - he goin' to walk out of there – and Grant's tellin' him he got to think of Miss Emma – and then Jefferson he – that's when he say – he call Vivian an old yellow woman and Grant says she the only reason he keeps comin'".

"And he called his bluff - Jefferson say he'll scream and Grant say go ahead and then – that's when he realize that Jefferson need him there just so he got – so he can be angry."

"They both angry – they both don't want to be there – they both trapped – and Grant tell him – he say, *If I didn't have Vivian I wouldn't be in this damn hole'* and that's when Grant sees – Jefferson is cryin'".

"So, you know – we have this – we have Grant in the middle of everything, right? So I'm wondering if we can say anything else about the 'everything' – I don't know."

"They in it together now – they stuck together."

"They two black men stuck in the same mess."

"They trapped together and only one of them gettin' out."

"Which one?" I ask.

"Grant!"

"No, Jefferson – he be – he – his pain soon be over."

"That – that makes things worse."

"Are they trapped together?" I ask.

"Yeah!"

"Is it – are they the same person?"

"Same person?"

"It's another one of those - one of my questions – I don't know – I - ".

"They both black men trapped there – they in the same place and they got the same – they both - one a them got more chances – he's got more pressure to fix everything – to make it right- and he say he can't make it right but they still pressurin' him to try so - ".

"So – like they are not the same person but they are in the same place – they got to - one of them got to help the other – like - ".

"They are tied together – they are all tied together – they got to help each other- ain't no one else gonna help them."

"It's about the whole black race! There's – they show backstabbin' and Grant – they makin' him – they makin' him step up – and he got to – he's the – he's the - "

"This book – it's like a lesson for Grant, a lesson for the reader, a lesson for everybody – like – this book – I don't know – I never woulda got this much out of this book if I read it myself - "

"I – I- it's like this book it's way more than you think – it's like – it's like – everything – they got the whole black race in this book."

"Yeah. It's deep."

This is not the right time for me to insert a question that probes for a defined view – a possibly reductionist view – or expression of a banner phrase that conveys a simplistically uttered thematic phrase. Now I worry that some aspects of the teaching situation and the project work may have actually preempted deeper recognitions at times. Now the students' comments reflect realizations about the novel's representations of their lives and present-day realities. They have often cited convergences between this novel and their personal and community lives. But today the comments come forth with a deeper resonance of the place of the text within this life. It is as though at this point of their acquaintance with this book, they are becoming aware of it as an expression of how the plight of these literary figures presents an age-old story that speaks of a profound pathos and struggle. But they, of course, are not putting it in such terms. I am characterizing their discussion as such, and I am realizing as I listen that this is not the time to press for a phrase that neatly assimilates their insights to this point. More than ever, I hope and believe that the creative synergy inspired by their project constructions will express the vision of felt unity among the many elements of the story. It seems that an accumulated essence of this novel is beginning to be expressed by the students now. Some of their further comments, across classes, fuel my impressions.

"This story – this story is like – it's like about everyone – not just black people – but – it's black people's lives – but it's our whole society – like black people and white people together and - "

"We ain't together – the white people got the power – they always got the power - "

"Yeah but it's sayin' like – it's showin' how she – Miss Emma – and his aunt like – they the ones – they do somethin' – it's not Grant - "

"Yeah but is - is Grant – he the one that got to go – "

"Yeah but he don't want to go."

"Yeah but he is there - "

"He is there and yet he is not there," says a voice clearly poking fun at the many times we have referred to this phrase over the course of our discussions. The room cascades with laughter.

"But – no – I'm serious!"

"He – it's serious."

"Yeah."

"He like – they pushin' him!"

"They pushin' him and he's goin'".

"Yeah, he's there – and y'all – Dr. Sullivan we gotta look - you axin' us what happen in this chapter and we ain't like – this is for real – they are doin' it here!"

"Doin' it! What are you talkin' about girl?!" Again, a chorus of rambunctious laughter crowds out any discussion for several moments.

"I'm sayin' – like I said I'm like sayin'," the young lady insists.

I resist pushing their noses into the pages of this chapter. I wait and the chattering cadences of their discussion carry on like an incessantly bubbling brook.

Then they are called to order, as it were, by the young lady who has meant, earlier, that Grant and Jefferson are engaging one another deeply as they talk for the first time.

She says, "I gotta - I gotta point – you all like – I'm sayin' that they are - they are like – they're for real here – he sayin like – he sayin – they're sayin'," she stops and looks at me.

I wonder what I should do. Articulate for the class what I think she is trying to say? No, I would be phrasing in my words what I suspect she is feeling and thinking.

I'd say, 'It seems as though, for he first time a realization is coming to Grant. For the first time, he may be beginning to recognize that he is there to help another human being to come to an awareness of his own dignity as a human being.'

I'd say, 'Grant is realizing that he may be one of the common heroes upon whose lives he reflected in previous chapters. He may be finally listening and as he sees – really sees Jefferson's pain for the first time, he is coming to terms with his own humanity.'

I'd say, 'Grant and Jefferson, together, and the women who support these men, are wringing dignity and immense strength and pride out of a horrendous wrong, one that has been ongoing throughout the time of their people in this country.'

I'd say all this and more but in those words I would be expressing my reading of this text. Instead, I ask them to do something I have asked them to do many times before.

"Can we look here and see if there are places - you know — are there places in this chapter that kind of get at what you're sayin' – what your point is here."

"Yeah – yeah."

"Let's just take a minute and find those places – can we all do that?"

"*'I would have hit any other man for saying that. But I recognized his grin for what it was – the expression of the most heartrending pain I had ever seen on anyone's face'* and then on that same page - "

"What page are we on?"

"There, page 132, - there at the bottom like it says, *'I saw tears on those big reddened eyes'* and like - "

Someone else comments, "Yeah that but it's the women – it's the women – look there they at the sheriff's wife's house again and – she – she they're in the living room and getting' coffee and they ask her if she can get the sheriff to let them have a bigger room – it's the women – that's what I'm sayin'".

"OK so – we don't have much time left – so we have different things going on – what would I write for a chapter 17 if we had room ..." I look with some doubt at the range of phrases we have scribbled onto the board.

"Grant and Jefferson ah – they – ah – they talkin' and - "

"Maybe they gonna make some – make some – like – they getting' somewhere – the women – it's the women – the white women and the black women - "

"No, the black women – they the ones – they the ones – they doin' it again."

We have to go and in the end I do not write anything else onto the board for chapter 17.

I say, "We really have to talk about our projects and our writing for a while tomorrow and – can you read chapters 18 and 19 for tonight?"

"That's a lot of reading – we got – we got - "

"It's about ten pages."

"Yeah, we can."

"OK."

They shuffle out until tomorrow, a Friday, with only two more full weeks remaining until the course ends.

* * * *

As I struggled with the degree of my influence on this particular learning moment among the students, I am led to reflect on the work of various writers who discuss culturally responsive teaching and the importance of critical race theory (Gay, 2002, Ladson-Billings, 1994; 1995; 2000; 2006; 2009a; 2009b; and Banks & Banks, 1995). Gay convinces us that we can improve the school success of ethnically diverse students by acquainting ourselves as teachers with explicit knowledge about cultural diversity, designing culturally relevant curricula (including societal curriculm), demonstrating cultural caring and building a learning community. That the novel read was culturally relevant has been stated by students. Also demonstrated has been an evolving learning community; the small-group and whole-class interactions have evidenced a cohesive community day-by-day. Readers can surely infer the degree of care present in the ongoing classroom dynamic. Gay (2000) tells us that culturally-responsive caring entails teaching "in an ethical, emotional, and academic partnership with ethnically diverse students, a partnership that that is anchored in respect, honor, integrity, resource sharing, and a deep belief in the possibility of transcendence" (p.52) that also includes expectations for the highest academic achievement for such students. The students' phenomenological aesthetic is shaped within the contextual parameters discussed.

Moreover, the teaching proceeded bearing in mind Ladson-Billings and Tate's remarks about theorizing race as a topic of scholarly inquiry - namely that it is highly significant, a huge factor to be used "as an analytic tool for understanding school inequity" (2009, p.167), a view that has come to be known as critical race theory. We have to consider these words alongside the reality that most of these students had not ever read a book before and at the same time wonder if that was because most of them had existed throughout their school lives in fetid contexts.

In an article about teaching for social responsibility with adolescent literature, Wolk (2009) restates what school meant to him as he refers to what it meant to the adolescent young men interviewed by Smith & Wilhelm (2003): "[s]chool just kept having me read and write year after year to torture me in the name of ... nothing" (p. 664). This sentiment is not unusual; most teachers who work with struggling young adults, in particular, lament their lackadaisical involvement with school reading, calling it apathy, disinterest, laziness, or any of a number of terms generally akin with disengagement. Yet many claim that adolescents are teeming with multiple literacies, rich with complex and multilayered significance (Moje, 2002). With Gay's (2000) and Ladson-Billings' (2009) throughts in mind we have to wonder if the students' uncertainty about how to phrase their inchoate realizations about the novels' amassing thematic elements was due to inexperience and if that inexperience was due to school contexts which had them tracked as "underachieving" from early in their school years and thus did not offer them a curricular path that included the opportunity to read and discuss literature – at all. Berliner's (2006) claims about the role of poverty, too, may pertain here; his work forwards a view that it "affects particularly ... urban minorities [and] is associated with academic performance that is well below international means on a number of different international assessments" (p. 949). I propose that if most of *these students* had been engaged in richly stimulating, challenging and supportive contexts throughout their schooling years they would not now be in a 'remedial' class over these two summers. Also, I consider it a tragedy akin to that of Jefferson's life that these young adults had not been nourished appropriately; their place in my life came about because of a lack of opportunity not unwillingess or inability to engage academic settings.

18

REALIZING TRUE BEGINNINGS

Today there is an accident. And as a result of it, I begin to realize the magnitude of the interpretive journey that has been ongoing over the past few weeks. They straggle in appearing tired; they have been participating in six hours of classes every day for the past three weeks. Before we leave for the weekend it is crucial that time be focused on their projects, the assigned writing elements in particular. In preparation for this work, I ask students to assemble with at least one other person. Most students work in two or three-person collaborative groups. Those who plan to complete a project individually are asked to pair with another who may have a different project in mind but with whom ideas can be comfortably shared. These arrangements formed, I suggest that they focus on chapters eighteen and nineteen and pinpoint details there that can be connected with a concept that will be central to their still-emerging project constructions. Of course, I remind them, I will listen in and sometimes interrupt to ask questions, or be available for questions they may pose to me. Thus oriented for the next half hour or more, the room begins to settle into yet another conversational focus.

Within minutes I am inserting myself within these tired pairs and trios. One group of young men appears absorbed in errant chatter about the upcoming weekend's plans. I stand near them; they listlessly open their books and one asks the other, "What are we supposed to be doin?"

"She listenin' to everything you're sayin'."

"Dr. Sullivan, are you listenin' to us."

"Well I'm - "

"Tell the truth now Dr. Sullivan."

"Well I'm – I'm - I am curious to know what you thought of these two chapters. You know – I guess I'm wondering how things are coming together for everyone you know. Are you guys working together on a project – is that the plan?"

"Yeah."

"OK, so what are you thinking – what project are you gonna do?"

"We doin' the character map."

"OK – so which character are you focusing on?"

"Which - we're not sure – either Grant or Jefferson – we dunno."

"OK – well is there anything in these two chapters that helps you decide?"

"Ah – that means – she tellin' us we gotta look there and talk about that – that's pretty cool Dr. Sullivan – you know how you gettin' us to - "

"You trickin' us."

"No – I – no – well, I'm nudging you, right? Isn't that right?" I turn and smile at one of the guys. The student to whom I turn is among the least verbal of all seventy-seven of them across the three research scenarios. He shrugs. For him, being a part of a threesome allows verbal involvement and idea exploration through listening; hearing ideas articulated and exchanged has been especially opportune for him. The small-group setting gives him the chance to delve into the idea configurations that emerge, and sometimes offer tentative insights as well as questions. He sits quietly while I am there today.

"I ask him, "Anthony, who do you think you'll focus on for the character map project?"

He is very reluctant to say. I wait. "Jefferson?" he asks me. Clearly he is not sure.

"Well, can we look at what - why don't I just listen – and we – you can talk about the chapters for a minute. Do you want to have a look – maybe compare some details each of you may have spotted as you read last night. Did you all read these chapters?

"Yeah."

Invariably, the assigned chapters are read each evening; this seems to be consistently borne out, suggesting their continued investment in the novel.

"Should I leave you for a few minutes and then maybe I can come back and ask you again about the – how the details of these chapters might fit with your project idea?

"Yeah."

I overhear and record fragments from various groupings:

"They makin' him decide – they sayin' do he want to go and he sayin' if they want him to and the sheriff sayin' no, if he want to – and anyway they there - "

"He in chains – she puttin' – Miss Emma puttin' out the food and they tell him he got to stay in one place and she say he stay put, then Grant come too and they take him to the same place."

"He still don't want to eat."

"No. He still – they both still eyein' each other – they both – they both like – stubborn."

"They – they there together again."

"Yeah."

I resist butting into any other group discussions, despite inclinations to do so, and simply remind them to discuss details in these two chapters that seem to fit with their evolving senses of the essence of this book, given their varying perspectives.

Students refer to various project choices and I strain to hear them articulate how the many details of previous days' discussions, and details from our two focal chapters today might be seen within a unified representation. How might a character map project reveal core elements of a central character in relation to a pivotally vital governing idea of the novel, for example? Are they talking about how respective visual collages, film, drama, and music projects resound textual elements relative to a unifying interpretive focal point? Not in so many words. It seems that the day-to-day dialogue is more and more attuned to significant thematic touch points within each chapter. Formulating an overaching idea that embraces these discretely explored segments is still embryonic. Classroom conversations are supporting their growing awareness that a project expression will shape renderings of coherent interpretive wholeness but it is increasingly clear that the students are negotiating two levels of realized engagement. One is an experiential dynamic; this text resonates with them deeply at a personal, social, and political level. The other is at an academic level; they realize that they are to create a definite statement that orders this literary experience in a particular way. I am realizing that the latter aspect of the students' processing is still very challenging for them when the accident takes place.

I go back to Anthony's group and sit in again, asking, "Are you finding details in these two chapters that seem significant to you – ones that maybe fit with the ideas you want to get across in your project?"

They look at me, one of the young men more pregnantly than the other two. He wants to say something.

I ask, "Are you getting more insights about a key character from these two chapters?"

He waited, "Yeah but … like … ." He looked at the other two guys. "We see what's goin' on like – but – like this is - the - like the first book I ever read. The only other book I ever got close to readin' all the way though was, like, *Catcher in the Rye*, like."

"Really?" I was incredulous. The young man who has made this statement is among the more experienced and articulate of all of students. His statement seems to offer another of the three of them confidence.

"Really?" I ask again, "You have never - "

"I never read one either. This is like the first book I ever read from cover - like almost and I enjoyed – I'm enjoyin'."

The group's third member, Anthony, sits silently, staring at his fingernails.

I bump his arm with my elbow to prompt a response from him and he says, "Same."

"Never? Not in high school – you never read a book – there's not one you ever read and talked about like this."

The three of them simply shake their heads: no, their expressions final and certain.

"What about any other time? Any book ever?"

Again, they sat silently shaking their heads. No.

"OK, well," I pause not sure of how to continue. It suddenly becomes very clear to me that a very complex literary reading and response process is being asked of readers with little background supportive of the endeavor I am asking of them.

"Well," I start again. "So is this project we have been talking about, is it - is it making sense?"

"Sort of," one of them said

I look at another member of this group, "What about for you?"

"Yeah, like when we talk and stuff, and like – like read the book, it all makes sense, and like the project, you're – it's – like when we bin doing stuff like in class – like and talkin' but - "

"But?" I ask them, waiting to see if they will describe the particular nature of the challenges that the synthesis projects represent.

"But like – we keep – when you say about – like about the main like idea of the book - and then writing about it – like ... ." Marcus' voice trails off.

"Yeah," a voice chimes in, suggesting assent.

This is a very difficult project all considered; it has successfully involved students in the act of reading a literary text and gradually assembling related interpretations of its respective chapter elements, given ranges of dialogic classroom support and students' intrinsic attraction for this book. Their mini-presentations of film, music, dramatic readings, visuals, and media of several days past successfully relayed an impressionistic depiction of the novel's import at an early stage of their presence within its pages. But the work being undertaken now asks that students compose a more formal statement through two mediums: project and written text.

As the course moves toward these summative expressions, students are uncertain. They are overwhelmed by the thought of formulating a written text *and* a coherent project reflecting thematic intensity. Even more, I now realize, it is possible that many of them have not ever read a book before! Could this be true? And if so, for how many students is this true? There are far more variables in the mix than I have realized, some of them possibly conflicting with others. Itemizing these many critical factors, it becomes startlingly apparent that (a) vastly inexperienced young adults are (b) considering an array of literary elements, as they are also being initiated into (c) discussion, art-and-media, and writing processes for the first time. It is overwhelming them – some of them at least - as I have just discovered. Without toppling the integral quality of the trust that has evolved and which in a few instances has been hard-won, I now have to find out how students are feeling about the assigned completion projects and how to address their hesitations without destabilizing the whole enterprise.

I continue to chat with them, briefly, before touching base with others, asking them, "Do you think you can talk about these two chapters for a few more minutes while I touch base with other groups?"

"Yeah."

"So what are you looking for – when you talk about these chapters, what are you looking for – what would you – when you think about let's say – let's say Grant – you know we had a big map on the board yesterday about Grant, remember?"

They nod, "Yeah."

"Well, let's say for now, if you were deciding just for now, you know, that you'd create a character map for Grant, what would you look for – what would you try to find in just these two chapters that would help you create a map on Grant - maybe like the one we made together during some of our first classes. Do you remember?"

"Yeah."

"What would you look for in this chapter to build a map like that?"

No one says anything. I wait.

"Maybe like what he doin'?"

"Like maybe what he sayin' to Jefferson?" They are asking me if this is correct.

They are uncertain if this is the answer to my question and they are also nervous about having disclosed to me just how innocent they are in regard to literary reading and with the conceptual orientation of these final course experiences.

"OK," I respond, "Why not see what you can find and we'll talk more about these chapters and our projects and the writing part of things, OK?"

"Yeah."

I leave them and sit in on various other group conversations, finding relatively unobtrusive ways to ask, "How many other books have you read that are like this one?" or "Have you read other books that remind you of this one?" Some of the answers I received, from various members of the seventy-seven students, are as follows:

"I never read a book before."

"Like when I read, I just study for the answers and then I just - like close the book."

"I don't read a lot of books. This is, like, maybe the second book I ever read."

"I hate reading, you know, hate it!"

"I never, ever – ever, ever – read a whole book from cover to cover."

"When I read a book, like – I just skip to the end to find out, like, what's gonna happen – that's it."

"We don't – like – we don't read the books – we just get the Cliff notes."

"No one ever – we never – none a us – we talk - like in the residence at night – none a us have ever read a book before – not like this!"

On it went. As these conversations ensued (some of them over subsequent days) it was revealed that fifty-nine of the seventy-seven students who participated in this literary reading project claimed never to have read a book before. There was no ambiguity about their certainty. Fifty-nine of them revealed without hesitation that they had never read a book nor had they ever been involved in a school reading experience that asked them to engage a text in a manner resembling our discussion and project based approaches. Even fewer of the students are able to bring to mind any extended writing assignments; they refer to short answer exams, fill-in-the-blank tests, and multiple-choice formats. Some comment on the skill sheets they have completed for remedial classes – a high proportion of the students had been "in remediation" for many years of school. They reveal very limited experience in reading or writing-related activities entailing elaborated thought; supporting the acts of synthesis *and* emotively engaged mindsets relative to this enterprise is becoming far more challenging than I had realized.

I stand to myself for a moment, thinking, then call everyone together for whole-class conversation.

"How many of you are – you know – would you say – are struggling – are finding this – these synthesis projects hard to think about?"

No one says anything.

I ask them, "What about the paper that goes with it – does that seem hard – or – are you feeling OK about that?"

"Can you – ah … ."

"We never thought much about it yet really."

"OK, well let's try something – let's divide the class in half, one half of you will focus on Jefferson for this one chapter - for chapter eighteen. The other half of you will focus on Grant. Let's do this – let's - let's work on these two boards," I pointed.

"Focus on chapter eighteen and come up with - first details from the chapter – then adjectives that characterize each of the men. This is familiar right?"

"Yeah but like can we add things from the other chapters?"

"Yes, but make sure you focus on this chapter first – just take about 3 minutes, then we are going to try something else."

I walk back and forth from one side of the room to the other, sweeping the camera in one direction and then another, inserting the microphone into the midst of each cluster of people for one of them to direct toward alternating voices.

"This is the first time they talkin' – you know really talkin'."

"Should we write that down?"

"Not that – not yet – no – wait – what they – what are they sayin' - we should look at that, right?"

"They got the Christmas program goin' at the school – yeah – but - "

"No here, look here it say - Grant axin' him what moral and obligation mean."

"Where?"

"There – look here on page 139 – that's when they gettin' down to it."

"Yeah – Jefferson say – what he mean - he sayin' Grant makin' him – gettin' him wool-gathered – it says – what that mean?"

"He messin' with his head – that's what he thinks."

"Who thinks?"

"Jefferson thinks Grants messin' with his head – there."

"He telling Jefferson to be kind to Miss Emma and – "

"Yeah but Jefferson say he ain't youman – human, like."

"Yeah and then, like - then he goes off with Vivian again and says he will run away – he still don't want to do this – and she sayin' that things are changin' and Grant's not so sure, right?"

"Yeah and," they snicker, "It ain't goin' so good for them lately – you know when they go to Baton Rouge."

"What?" someone asks.

"Here look – right here it says after he visits Jefferson things do not go so well for them in bed."

"Oh yeah!"

The two groups of students review the chapter, some add differing details, yet for the most part noting that the two men have conversed, and that Grant continues to seek Vivian's blessing to drop everything and run away with her.

I interrupt, and ask them to create a quick map for the character each group has focused on. For Jefferson, one group notates 'angry', 'scared', 'resentful', 'innocent', 'sacrifice', and 'depressed'. For Grant, details include 'tries to talk', 'still trying to run away', and 'maybe things changing'.

"OK," I say to them, feeling nervous.

"We've been talking about the chapters and - well – let's suppose we are going to try a little writing – start to create a draft – based on a character map project for example - see if we can kind of get warmed up about the writing parts of this work for the next two weeks."

"OK."

"So," I point back and forth between the two boards, opposite one another on either sides of the room. "We see some details here about Jefferson and about Grant, right?"

"Yeah."

"So, if you were to choose to write your project on, let's say, Grant – let's focus on Grant for a minute, what would you say – what would you write, you know if you were creating a concept map project related to him?"

Silence. No one says a word. The classroom feels hollow, empty, vacant. Everyone is uncomfortable. The harmonious ease of our work over the past three weeks has withered in a vacuum of nervousness and definite fear. It is palpably clear. I feel as though everything we have done to this point has been betrayed – that I have played a trick on all of them. It is as though I have been leading my students toward a point along an exploratory path that is now being foreclosed by the familiar strictures of formula, right and wrong answers, and, even worse, graded criteria that ensure the typically resulting endgame of failure, low grades, and a shaming dead-end void. Possibly I am a fraud and this wholesome literary adventure is a scheme set up to deceive them; I suspect they are thinking, 'it's the same old thing'. If I ask them to explain their feelings right now, they will stare back at me suspiciously and say nothing. So, hurrying forward to the familiar territory of our shared habits, I begin to frame a conversation that might establish a sense of relative comfort toward the process of composing written language that resonates thematically.

"Well," I start, "What's going on just in this one chapter?" No one says anything for a minute.

"Where are we now – who is in this chapter?"

"Miss Emma and Jefferson and – Rev'rend Ambrose, he there and - "

"He got the chains on."

"Yeah."

"OK, now look," I say pointing to the two maps featuring Grant and Jefferson.

"Do you think – is there something going on with them in this chapter? Are they starting to talk?"

"Sorta – yeah."

"OK, mostly where – let's look and focus on – on one page – is there a place in this chapter where they are talking – that we can look at?"

"Page one thirty-nine," someone says in a quick, clear voice.

"Can we – can someone – will – I – will someone read Grant's voice and maybe someone else read what Jefferson says?" Two volunteers raise their hands,

"But I'm sittin' right here."

"OK."

"Where do we start?"

"Well maybe – Jefferson has just asked about Christmas, right? And if that's when Christ was born or died?"

"Yeah."

"So, he's thinking about that and Grant knows it, right?

"Yeah."

"So Jefferson is thinking about when – he's – he seems to be thinking about – you know – he's worried about – he's thinking about Christ's crucifixion – and then – and then - so right there kind of near the top of page one thirty-nine Grant asks him a question, right?

"Yeah."

"So can we start - can you guys read from there for a little bit?"

"It says, *Jefferson do you know what moral means?*'"

"Right – can you - can we hear – can you both read that part of what they say to each other? After that Jefferson doesn't answer him, right? And Grant asks another question, right?"

"He say *Jefferson, do you know what moral means?*'"

"And then, there's another question from Grant right? What is it?"

"'*Do you know what obligation means?*' "

"And Jefferson still can't answer and Grant keeps on talking, right? What does he say?"

"He say, '*No matter how bad off we are, we still owe something. You owe something Jefferson. Not to me. Surely not to that Sheriff out there. But to your godmother. You must show her some understanding, some kind of love.*' "

"Right, and Grant suggests that Jefferson can be kinder to Miss Emma and then on the next page it says Grant talks to him a little more about the Christmas tree they found for the pageant this year, and then he leaves, right, and he goes off to find Vivian and that's when we learn that things are changing for them, and she tells him that things are changing and the chapter ends, right?"

"Yeah."

"So let's say we are going to write about Grant," I continue, hoping to steer us back to the details of their upcoming projects.

I turn to the board and write, 'I have decided to complete a Character Map on _________________ for my project about _____________________________________ . I havedecidedtofocuson_____________________________because__________ seems to be the most important character in this story. Almost everything that happens with this character is connected to the underlying key idea of this book. I think that this key idea is _____________________ in my opinion. I think that this book tells a story about ____ (*two or three sentences here would be appropriate*). My project on _____________________ shows _________________ involved in most/all of the important scenes that are connected to this overall idea, in my opinion. '

I turn and look at the class, with someone else having taken over the camera and microphone yet again. They are transfixed. No one says a word and I continue to scribble sentences onto the board. Quite soon thereafter, a few students pull out notebooks and, thinking they are unnoticed, they secretly begin copying these guidepost sentences.

'In the first few chapters I notice that _____________________ is _____________________, _____________________, and _____________________ . Some examples of these (<u>attitudes</u>), or (<u>behaviors</u>), or (feelings) are seen on page, __________, __________, and __________ . For example on page __________ we see/hear him _____________________________________ .

Then on page __________ we see/hear him, and then finally on page __________ we also see/hear him _____________________ . This is connected to my opinion that this book is about _________________ because ____.

I turn again and look at them, waiting for someone to comment, or ask a question.

"I know," I said to them, "This is about the Character Map project but does this kind of show you a way to start?"

"Yeah," someone says.

They are clearly relieved.

"We can – I can write this in – like that - can say 'I' like that?"

"Write it in the first person, you mean?"

"Yeah."

"Yes. I recommend that we all do it this way at least for the first draft. If we have time to revise it to be more formal than this, that's fine and if we don't – and I suspect we might not have time, then that's OK."

"Really?" This student sounds very dubious.

"Yes. I think it should be OK for each of us to write 5 to 7 pages once we get started."

"Do we each write the pages – like we got three people on our group."

"Yeah …," I pause. "I know you can work together but I'd like us each to try and write out our own thoughts like this. Also," I continue, "I think it might be a good idea for me to meet every day or so with everyone starting on Monday and right through the next week as we finish up and then get ready for our presentations for the following – the final week of class. I think that's going to take all of the last week."

"You know, I just want to see your thinking – you know – the way you are feeling about your own thoughts. It's the same as what we have been doing when we have talked about the book each day, right? You will write out what you are thinking, right, kind of like the way I have maybe given us a start here?"

"No it's not the same!

"It ain't the same *at all*!"

"Well, once you have the project part of things done, it will be easier I think."

"What do you mean?"

"Well you can't do the writing – the writing will be easier once you have done the project – you know, the visual collages, and the films are selected, and the music and you have – you know – you have your segments from the books for the drama projects – once you have done the work you need to do to get this ready, the writing will be much easier."

"Can we work on it in class next week?"

"Let's start sketching out plans next week and then - we should make a plan for next week and maybe that will also get things – things will be more organized and you'll know where you are going – where things are going – does that make sense?"

"Yeah."

"OK – we have to – I think one of the things that is hard is that we are trying to think of what this book might mean to us – what it's about you know, before we have finished it. We need to finish this book – I think we need to finish this book by Wednesday of next week – before the end of next weekend for sure."

We negotiate and agree to (a) complete 5 chapters over the weekend – with relative willingness; (b) bring in plain paper so that sketches can be prepared, plans made; and (c) share drafts of evolving writing with me and with class members occasionally as our work evolves.

"You're really gonna help us with – with the writing?"

"Yeah, I am not going to write it for you but I will read and guide you with feedback and suggestions as we move through next week."

"Also, I have to say this: I am realizing that the writing is kind of throwing us for a loop a bit, right?"

A chorus of voices exclaims agreement!

"Right, but I would like it if we could relax and still – you know – just still explore the book and continue to talk and just take our time a little bit over the days of next week to start getting organized – the projects will help you with the writing – I mean, once you have some thoughts organized and some planning done and work completed on the projects, that will guide your writing. You'll have the concept maps, and the character maps and visual collages, and segments selected for film and music and drama work, and that will be part of the thinking that you'll talk about – you'll have that done first and that will organize your thinking for the writing."

"But we're still getting graded on these writing projects right?"

"Right, but the grades are based on class work, and the projects, and the writing will – the writing is all part of that – if the work is completed and if you are able to write about your thoughts, and present your thoughts for your presentation, then you will receive a solid grade for the course."

"We all gonna pass, right?"

"Its looks that way to me right now for those of you who are here and participating – here - and more or less following what's going on – yes! This whole project is about your experience in this book and how you express that experience through the projects and the writing. I do not want the writing to hold you up – to get in the way of things. Can we leave it at that for now and I will meet with each of you over the days of next week's class and we will move forward from there?"

"What if we can't write anything?"

"You will be able to write something – you are all involved in this book – we have been talking about it for weeks now. You will be able to express an opinion - and I am going to have to help you with that."

Many more questions are forthcoming, but I realize that many of them will be addressed in the subsequent days as I meet with individuals and groups of students. Moreover, we need to spend at least some time discussing chapter 20. I want to be able to draw the elements of this chapter within today's discussion if that is feasible.

* * * *

The great majority of these students have never read a book before and have virtually no experience with the process of expressing thoughts in written language – have rarely completed writing that has asked them to elaborate ideas in the manner requested of them. To be conscious about a thematic idea and develop a series of points leading coherently toward a clear and logical connection to such a thematic focus is asking more of them than is comfortable and clearly moves them outside of any comfortable ranges of experience. Various frames of reference might be aligned with this phenomenon. One of them is found in the literature on working with struggling writers through a sociocognitive basis for learning (Collins, 1997). Collins speaks of writing process and a traditional skills (text-based) approach commenting that "struggling writers ... tend to see text-based rules and structures for writing as unattached to the problems they encounter during the act of writing" (p.3). Rather, he suggests looking at the teaching of writing with inexperienced writers through a sociocognitive lens suggesting that learning to write entails secondary discourses – those that require specialized forms and functions of language. Collins states, "strategic writing instruction takes the view that literacy abilities are acquired and learned through meaningful participation in communities" (p. 8) and that this participation must validate the primary discourse used in students' communities. Students learn to acquire and use specific writing strategies (such as that modelled for them, seen earlier in this chapter) as they also employ sociocognitive process such as learning to see writing as part of their controlled literacy identity, a tall order sometimes. They need to learn specific skills about writing while also having that work connected to their sociocultural identities. Others contribute core ideas about sociocultural approaches and collaboration (John-Steiner and Mann, 1996; Scribner and Cole, 1981; and Vygotsky, 1978). Tatum and Gue (2012) add ballast to the idea that we need to retheorize writing, especially for African American males, realizing that communities of collaborative acts have historically always been formed among African Americans around a meaningful social context; this must be replicated in a teaching environment for them. The work of De La Luz Reyes (2010) stands with this idea as well as does that of Ball (2000; 2008).

Since writing and producing projects are integral to students' phenomenological experience(s) of *A Lesson Before Dying* we need to look closely at both of these topics, with writing being focused on here for now. The National Commission on Writing (2003) found that there were serious limitations in students' writing abilities, while the gap in writing abilities between poor, Black and Hispanic students and white and Asian students remains substantial (Persky, Daane and Jin, 2003). Certainly, the majority of the students involved in this work were Black and Hispanic and the fear and uncertainty with which they greeted the writing process at eighteen or more years of age was noteworthy, born primarily out of inexperience I conjecture. In their discussion of younger writers, Graham, Harris, and Mason (2005) talk about the importance of recognizing the need to improve writing instruction for poor and minority students emphasizing the planning process, much like I tried to do with my students in offering them a beginning frame that they could use as a starting point for their own thoughts. They claim "[a]dvanced planning may be especially advantageous for novice and struggling writers" (p. 209) and also that social (peer) support helps students.

It became clear immediately that in facilitating the writing experiences of the students I had to offer them something concrete – a framework that they would see as helpful and complementing our supportive structures for the reading experience. I had to give them strategic support that would be perceived as supportive and doable right away. Some work in the area of bilingualism offers stances that are helpful in shaping a perspective about the writing struggles of the students. Many of the students' home language was other than English and most of the students' spoken language was non-academic English. This, coupled with their inexperience, aligns them with many of the characteristics of bilingual students in terms of cultural diversity, needs of linguistically diverse students, as well as those who are academically challenged due to schooling contexts and breadth of literacy experiences. The social contexts of such students affect their writing experiences as do relationships, race, ethnicity and class. Throughout their schooling experiences many such students have been subjected to "highly controlled language exercises at the sentence or paragraph level" and "dictation, short answer and writing paragraphs from models" which are "attributable to their education in low ability classes (Harklau, Siegal, and Losey, 1999, p. 10). These writers, along with so many others, emphasize the need for young adult writers to be engaged in instruction that emphasizes a social world – critical literacy that is situated in accordance with students' perspectives and sociocultural idenies, a "socioliterate" approach.

Indeed, in glancing at the history of the evolution of written language from Mesopotamia, China, and Mesoamerica it is clear that the rudiments of written language coincided with specific socioeconomic and cultural purposes directly connected with business, funerary rites, and the impact of the alphabet on ideas, abstract thought, and consciousness all in connection with socially embedded purposes (Schmandt-Besserate and Erard, 2008). In a related sense, our explorations of writing were linked directly to *A Lesson Before Dying*, a text that resonated in socioculturally meaningful ways within an environment that centered the students' responses as central; writing here was thus moored to their identities. But additionally it was used with recognition of the phenomenological effects of writing on the students' thinking and reflection about themselves and the world with respect for the ideas of Ong (1982) and Olson (1994). For example, I knew that their articulation of thought through writing would both consolidate, concretize and possibly enlarge the realizations that they would first express through their arts-based and media projects and that, therefore, their writing was entwined with their formation of personal and critical experience of the book. Ever so briefly now, too (and to be expanded later), I want to plant the thought offered us by Latour (1986). In the evolution of writing as representational marks of purpose and identity and culture, it also came to be realized that drawings, charts, and photos facilitated the ability for individuals to formulate and present thoughts and arguments about phenomena being explored, enabling them to depict kernel ideas and relationships and connections among those ideas. All in all, structured support for writing and arts-based and media projects within a structurally supportive and identity-based context was undertaken with these many frames of thought in mind.

I felt that the context of our work was respectful of the students' sociolinguistic and cultural identities and that the text that influenced the classroom environment also complemented these traits. It was also very clear that simply assigning students to peer groups and fostering collaborative writing would not be sufficiently helpful to them. Thus, in the moment, I tried to jump-start the structure and progress of students' writing by providing them with a structured frame that they could use to elaborate and expand their thinking about a key thematic concept that would form the basis for their synthesis projects. In meeting with each of them privately and among them in writing groups I was able to question and prompt them toward the details that could be written about in connection with their projects. It happened, then, that their reading, discussions, and writing activities were all a fundamental part of their phenomenological experience of the novel.

19

CONTINUED UNCERTAINTY

I t is Friday still. Within the novel the scene shifts to the school Christmas play where Reverend Ambrose prays for the afflicted, for the guilty and the innocent, and for those who do not know God who are also locked in a cold dark cell of their ignorance (Grant feels implicated). The details of the school play are recounted: it was raining outside and all of the community is there. The children have saved their nickels and a package for Jefferson sits under the tree. Christmas carols are sung and the children portray wise men and shepherds who speak of how God works in mysterious ways and for whom the lowest is highest in his eyes. Grant stands alone wondering if things are changing as Vivian has said; he has listened to the same carols, the same play, the same mistakes, prayers, and people for all of his life.

I ask my students, "What are you noticing – what do you see that might fit within your sense of things here," a vague question but one that will elicit, I hope, a train of thought that verges toward their making sense of this phenomenological project we have undertaken.

"They're having their Christmas play."

"Yeah."

"Yeah but you know she lookin' for the particulars." More laughter ensures.

"I am," I admit to them. "What are you seeing here – what are the places – the little you know – the tidbits that – "

"The what?"

Now I laugh, "The tidbits – the - you know – the details that helps us answer this question about what's going on here – what is the author getting at? What's it all about, in your opinion?" I ask them, and stand waiting.

"What's he saying? What's Grant saying and thinking?" I ask them.

"It's still the same," someone calls out in a song-song voice.

"Where is it the same? What is the same? The same as what?" I ask them.

"There she goes!" hollers a young man at the back.

I smile as they giggle and then I ask again, ""Where is it the same? What is the same? The same as what?"

"She wants details!"

"I do! Can you find me details?"

They page through the chapter and no one pinpoints anything in particular; they remain tired today and are listlessly attentive at this point.

I read from the text: "*Vivian said things were changing. But where were they changing?*" I read from the last page of this chapter, page 151.

"What do you make of this?" I ask them.

"He not sure."

"About what?"

"Whether things are changing – or not, like."

"What things is he talking about?"

"Everything – like we said before – everything!"

"OK," I turn and write the word 'everything' on the board, and look back to the students, asking, "Can we think of some specific details related to this word 'everything'?"

"Just everything," says another student.

"Everything like …," I ask, waiting with my marker ready to record their thoughts, then stopping as I have another idea: "Can you write this word in your journal notebooks – just put it at the top of the page, and whatever chapter you focused on a few days ago when we skimmed over the book, can you look at that chapter now for two whole minutes and find something specific from your chapter about this word everything," I ask them. Then I say, "everything like what – find only two, maybe three key ideas – just two or three from the chapter you looked over the other day and tell me what this 'everything' relates to. Three minutes, OK, and I'll time us for that." It took much, much longer than three minutes.

I also say, "Just two or three phrases that get at the essence of things for your chapter – we're going to go fast and not discuss it too much, OK?"

After about forty-five minutes, hands are raised and I say, "Write down these details on a clean page of your notebooks, and put this word 'everything' at the top of the page.

I scribe what is offered one chapter at a time, in strict order of chapter progression:

1. "Blacks gettin' accused without a fair trial."
   "White power in everything."
   "Blacks gettin' murdered."

2. "The pain of black women from many years past."
   "All the screaming and running in place and teachin'"

3. "White people's disrespect."
   "Pressure from those two women."

4. "Racism and segregation."
   "Feeling tired of commitment."
   "Loving Vivian."

Someone argues, "But he ain't tired a lovin' Vivian!"

"No," I respond, "Maybe not, but she is part of the 'everything', right? Can we just make sure we get her here as part of 'everything'?"

"She pressurin' him too," someone argues, "In her own way, she pressurin' him too."

"Let's keep going," I say. "What else? Let's just get two or three key ideas from each chapter and – let's just get them down and move fast – if we can."

5. "Irritations at school."
   "All the people on the plantation – nuthin' changes"
   "Bein' mean to the students."

6. "Bein angry at his Aunt and Miss Emma – at the women."
   "Bowin' down to white people white men."
   "Playin' dumb for white people – white men."

7. "The White superintendent."
   "Black kids getting' inspected by the white - by the superintendent."
   "Not havin' paper and pencils and books."

8. "Same old vicious circle - things aren't changin'"
   "Mr. Antoine tellin' him to run and fight – no freedom there."
   "Mr. Antoine bein' – he superior to any man blacker."

9. "He hates goin' to the filthy jail."
   "Jefferson real bad – depressed – won't eat."
   "Grant sayin' he put his arms around Miss Emma – she so – she so sad."

10. "Miss Emma sick – she ain't goin' to the jail."
    "Grant feelin' humiliated – he the only one they got though."

11. "Jefferson get on the floor and eat like a hog at the jail."
    "Grant say don't let the white man win – but Jefferson won't talk."

12. "Grant at the bar thinkin' about Joe Louis and Jackie Robinson."
    "Grant thinkin' about stories he read – and heroes."
    "Grant talks to Vivian about runnin' away – and she say you came back here."

13. "They at Determination Sunday – and they lookin' at Grant."
    "Rev'rent Ambrose axe him about Jefferson's soul."
    "Grant been runnin' in place all the whole time."

14. "Vivian come to see him at his plantation house."
"They go out on the plantation – they make love."

15. "Vivian tell about her dark husband and the racism for darker blacks."
"They meet with Grant's aunt and talk about religion."
"They say Vivian got quality."

16. "Miss Emma tell Grant that Jefferson say he a hog."
"They say Grant lyin' about Jefferson."
"Miss Emma say someone got to do something for her before she die and Grant say nuthins' changin'."

17. "Grant tryin' to talk to Jefferson and Jefferson ugly about Vivian, and Grant sees Jefferson's pain."
"The women got a plan for meetin' in another room and the sheriff don' like it."
"Grant's thinkin' that nuthin's gonna change.

18. "They all meetin' in the dayroom and Jefferson's in chains."
"Grant axe Jefferson what he want to talk about, and Grant axe Jefferson about moral, and obligation and owing to Miss Emma."
"Grant sees Vivian and he still want to run away and she say things changin'."

19. "They at the Christmas play and the same people there."
"Grant thinks Rev'rent Ambrose sayin' he in a cold cell a ignorance."
"Grant's wonderin' if things changin' like Vivian say."

"OK," I say to them, standing back from the display we have created, "What's all this about?"

"It's a story about black people – about how one a them gets pressured into helpin' another one and all the trouble it's makin' for him with his life and everything."

"We keep talking about this word, 'everything'," I tease them, looking up at the clock.

"Do you remember," I asked them, "When we were first starting to talk about this book and I asked you if Grant was one man or if he was – you know – when I asked you if he represented - if this was the story of one man or the story – a story that represented maybe the lives of black people and maybe - "

"Yeah but - "

"It's about struggling!" says one student triumphantly, as though suddenly realizing how the various synopses stretched in front of her crystallized as a unified realization.

"Is that right?" she asked me.

"It makes sense - there's no right or wrong – that's the thing," I said, looking around the room.

"It will mean different things to different people – what matters is that you create a unified presentation – like what just happened maybe – and be able to express that in your project and your writing."

"I still think it's about the women in the book – that's what we're doin'," says another student.

"We're gonna focus on just one person – we're doin' Grant – so like," this student asks, "We can do him right – if we think it's just about Grant and how he – what he dealin' with – like all those things – we can just like add them up – and show like – show it from like his point of view, like?"

"You can," I respond, "You can – if you think it's about one man and one situation," I answer, realizing that to push further now will surely threaten the moment of clarity that seems to have arisen for some students; they are thinking about an idea that arises from a momentary synthesis – one that encompasses the whole of the text to this point. It seems that this moment of awareness is consciously realized and that the process of arriving at this point is one that might be enlarged by further work over the next week or so.

"Can we all make a commitment to read the next five chapters, pages 152 through ...," I glance at the pages to check when someone says,

"That's too much – we got other stuff we gotta do."

"OK," I realize, "How about to page 186 – that's three chapters and I know you want to find out what's happening here, right?"

"Yeah but – "

"We can do three chapters," another voice agrees.

"Do we gotta do the writing?"

"Yeah, that's takin' too long."

"Well, how about you do for the next three chapters what we just did here on the board – how about that? If you can just do that – maybe get specific page numbers, and specific lines to focus on, we can come right in on Monday and talk about that and then do some more project planning, a little bit - "

"We already know what we're doin'."

"OK, can we get agreement on that - we can come right in on Monday and look over the notes that you get together?" There is assent.

"Yeah, OK, we gotta go - we're over time. You need lunch before your next class, right?"

"Yeah."

* * * *

Quite obviously the students' engagements with reading and writing were continually being led by me. And I continued to worry that the directions I was taking them toward (with writing, arts and media-based projects, and even teacher questions) might be intruding on their independently realized phenomenological experience of the novel. Was my influence distracting from this literary reading experience or leading them deeper into it? I think the latter. I say this because at no point did the students become resistant to the activities, seem deterred from their embrace of the novel, or ever express disaffection for what we were doing – once on their way "into" the core of the various undertakings we engaged, even with writing, eventually.

I believe that the various activities we participated in conjured for the students an active reading process, that being distinguished from passive reading as Ingarden (1973) distinguishes such acts of mind with a literary work. "In purely passive reading," he says, "one does not attempt to apprehend [the meanings of the sentences] or, in particular to constitute them synthetically" (p. 38). He tells us that in passive reading "one does not think the meanings of the sentences by performing the corresponding signitive acts" (p. 38). By contrast an "active reader" performs a "series of complicated and interconnected acts" (p. 39) demanding a "considerable amount of activity and attentiveness" (p. 39) Even further, reading a literary text can engage us in active reading if and when "we project ourselves in a cocreative attitude into the realm of the objects determined by the sentence meanings" (p. 39) and thus enter into the meaning of the text. It is through such active reading, Ingarden explains, that we discover the characteristic fullness of a literary work and thus are co-creators of it.

I submit that the various activities undertaken deepened rather than intruded upon the students' phenomenological experience of *A Lesson Before Dying* which was a text readily seen by students as one that could be entered into variously and deeply, one that our many specific classroom acts of mind enlarged for the students as we moved into discussions, projects, and writing-related syntheses. Where Ingarden would name the active reading of a literary work as "objectification", I am thinking of it as aesthetic reading as per Rosenblatt's (1978) characterization presented in earlier chapters. In reading another segment of Ingarden's work we might conclude that such "objectifications" or "concretizations" and aesthetic reading are closely aligned; Ingarden says "literary works of art or their concretizations can be objects of aesthetic experiences or at least objects of the foundation of which with the proper aesthetic experiences, specific aesthetic objects are constituted, provided the constitution attains a certain conclusion in the experience" (p. 176).

Rosenblatt's work conveys a characterization of aesthetic reading which is situated in the world, and that exists within the reader as s/he moves toward a synthesis of the literary elements within her/himself. Where Ingarden might be perceived to consider the aesthetic experience as a reader's "objectification" or concretization of various stages of reading which "proceed regularly" (p. 180), Rosenblatt says, in referring to Ingarden, that his "whole analogy of strata or layers, because it is too static, falsifies the actual process of [aesthetic] evocation" (1978, p. 108). She also reminds us, again referring to Ingarden, that "[t]he notion of even a hypothetical reader who will make the most "complete" synthesis of the various "levels" brings us back therefore simply to the problem of justifying a single "right" reader" (p. 108).

All of these reflections have relevance for the work of the readers featured in this book. As we have seen in the various responses made to it, *A Lesson Before Dying* was not read uniformly nor objectified, as such, but rather "lived through" as Rosenblatt has characterized her theoretical stance on aesthetic reading. There was, for each individual reader, a highly socioculturally personalized interpretation that became enlarged through collaborative discussion. Though guided to select resonant moments of the text and organize those responses in various ways as we have also seen, they did so with one another after an individual and private engagement with the novel that was then further spotlighted in the classroom activities. Further, they selected segments that were resonant for them in particular social and personal ways. This text elicited a reader-text-world aesthetic transaction that varied from person to person in each one's individual way. Where some have characterized literary reading as determined by the text (Iser, 1980), or by the authority of interpretive communities (Fish, 1980), we hear voices of readers who arrive at a merger of text, self, and world as Rosenblatt describes aesthetic reading: "[w]ith the aesthetic transaction as his fulcrum [readers] can range as far as [they] wish bringing to bear ever wider and richer circles of literary, social, ethical, and philosophical contexts" (p. 174) and "the transactional concept can only reinforce interest in the dynamics of the realtionship between the author, the text, the reader and their cultural environments" (p. 174). This view of aesthetic reading has been adopted by classroom teachers as they strive to infuse their teaching of literature with practical approaches that embed these theoretical premises (Clifford, 1991; Sullivan, 1995; Marshall, 2000; and Rosenblatt, 2005). Altogether considered, both the choice of socioculturally relevant text and the range of classroom activities are seen to have facilitated the active aesthetic synthesizing entailed in the reading, writing, and process of construction of the thematic projects.

20

NO MATTER HOW EDUCATED

Monday comes and ten days remain in this literary journey. We continue our work. We arrived at a moment on Friday where phenomenological experience of the novel clashed with formulating an organized expression thereof. What happened then and on previous days, too, from a teaching perspective, might be compared with conducting a complex symphony. But, I have been *both* teaching students how to hold and 'sound' the instrument of their minds and feelings *as well as* assemble a final performative synthesis using the novel as a basis for this arrangement. It feels as though I have been infusing the energies of thought construction and emotive order for all of the students then leaving them to decide on the final determinant form of their interpretive manifestation. Guiding students to gather the raw elements of their transactional embrace of the novel is like orchestrating energy, attention, and interpretive synergy for an elucidation that is ultimately not mine to determine. It is a paradoxical situation.

Like Grant, in some ways, I felt 'there' yet not fully able to influence the complete range of circumstances that prevail; in the final analysis many factors are beyond my control. Unlike him, I am able to facilitate a relative range of freedom in shaping a context that helps students learn how to apply, focus and organize their minds and feelings. I can - and do - try to nudge students into a genuinely thoughtful involvement with *A Lesson Before Dying*, and I have come to realize that most students' previous history of such work is absent. For both Grant and I, the final presentation of circumstances is not of our making. Jefferson has not ever had the freedom to define any aspect of his existence nor have my students ever been asked to articulate and order a literary journey of this magnitude. For all of us, events have moved along with a moment-to-moment involvement in circumstances that are dependent on the realizations and willingness of those closest to us in these respective enterprises.

As we move toward the concluding moments of this encompassing journey, details about the students' reading of each of the chapters are presented differently. In this chapter, for example, I present particulars about their work with Chapters 20, 21 and 22 of the novel. The same pattern applies for the next chapter as we move into the third section of this book; there, chapters 23, 24, & 25 of the novel are discussed by students, and their classroom activities are presented. During this fourth week of the course, three chapters a day from the novel are discussed in class, they work on final project constructions, and meet with me for interviews and consultation about the whole of their involvement with this course.

"Let's start right in," I announce as students stream in and we get settled.

"Everybody have a good weekend?"

"Too much work to do!"

"That's too much readin'," says another.

"And we got all these final assignments," another adds menacingly.

I laugh and ask them, "What's happening with your reading of our book – our novel? What's goin' on with that? Did you get to it?

"Yeah," they answer, "We got to it."

"OK, before we get too comfortable, let's get everyone up – I've got more markers – let's write out some of what you found," I suggest. I have the camera at the back of the room and ask one of the regular guys to keep it focused as I walk with the microphone to the front of the room, then each side of it where the boards are. I write chapter 20 on one board surface, then chapter, 21 on another, chapter 22 on the last one.

"Let's count off," I suggest, asking students to number 1, 2, 3 and repeat that until each student is organized in one of three groups according to these three numbers.

"Did you really read and do you have notes?" I ask them, then add, "Can I peek at your notes before we get going?"

Everyone opens their notebooks and I move among them glancing at what they have documented.

"OK, if you are a number 1, you'll go here, "I point to one board, "and record all of the details that you agree are important to chapter 20. Number 2's go here and come up with details about chapter 21, and number three's here for chapter 22, and then we'll talk, OK? You'll all have different details and it's likely many of you will have the same details but let's do that first, OK, and then we'll talk." They move toward the boards with the novel and notebooks and begin to decide what will be recorded.

"Don't forget the page numbers, if you can - if you have them – and if you don't - can you find them for the quotes you may have?"

Here is a range of phrases – some literally recorded from the text and some paraphrases of it - for chapter 20:

> 'They come and tell Grant that the date is set for the execution."

> 'Rev'rend Ambrose is there and they go in the front room of Mr. Pichot's house and the sheriff tells them the date.'

> 'The execution is April 8th and Grant asks, why that date, and Mr. Guidry does not like his question.'

> 'The sheriff asks if Miss Emma will need a doctor.'

Many students have noted the following phrases exactly from the text for chapter 20:

> *'Twelve white men say a black man must die, and another white man sets the date and time without consulting one black person. Justice?' p. 157.*

> *'We, us, white folks all, have decided its time for you to die because this is the convenient time and date' p. 158.*

> *'And on Friday too. Always on Friday. Same time as he died, between twelve and three' p. 158.*

> *'I wanted to see nothing but miles and miles of clear, blue water, then an island where I could be alone. Or Vivian and me, just the two of us, and absolutely no one else' p. 159.*

"OK," I announce after about fifteen minutes have elapsed, "Move to your right – if you've been recording details for chapter 20, move to the board for chapter 21 and add to what's there. Chapter 21 folks move to chapter 22, and if you are working right now on chapter 22, move to chapter 20 and add to what is there – if there are details there now that you have in your notes, add a check mark beside those phrases – for everyone that has the same phrases that are already there, add one check mark, OK?"

This shift takes place; here is an arrangement of phrases for chapter 21:

> *'Miss Emma lay under a quilt – her eyes were looking at something that was not in the room' pp. 160 & 161.*

> *'Rev. Ambrose gave me a long hard look to let me know what he thought of me but I already knew what he thought of me' p. 161.*

> *'Vivian came – we were holding hands, lying very close together with all of our clothes on' p. 162.*

'Vivian goes to see Miss Emma and Miss Emma tells Grant it's in his hands and she wants Grant and Rev'rend Ambrose to work together.'

'Vivian thinks Irene [one of Grant's most responsible students] is in love with Grant.'

'The rest of them love me, too, and don't want an outsider taking me away from them. They want me for their own. Isn't that how it is everywhere' p. 165.

'Miss Emma needs a memory. Rev'rend Ambrose and I should get along and together – together – we should try to reach Jefferson. Why not only Reverend Ambrose? Why not only the soul? No, she wants memories, memories of him standing like a man' p. 166.

'We black men have failed to protect our women since the time of slavery. We stay here in the South and are broken, or we run away and leave them to look after the children and themselves. So each time a male child is born they hope he will be the one to change this vicious circle which he never does' p. 167.

'Because even though he wants to change it, and maybe even tries to change it is too heavy a burden because of all the others who have run away and left their burdens behind. So he, too, must run away if he to hold onto his sanity and have a life of his own' p. 167.

'What she wants is for him, Jefferson, and me to change everything that has been going on for three hundred years' p. 167.

'What she wants to hear first is that he did not crawl to that white man, that he stood at the last moment and walked.

Because if he does not, she knows that she will never get another chance to see a black man stand for her' p. 167.

'I can give them something that neither a husband, a father, nor a grandfather ever did, so they want to hold on for as long as they can not realizing that their holding on will break me too.' P. 167.

Grant says it's all up to Jefferson.

Again, we break from a focus on one chapter and move to another so that each group of about 8 students has been able to focus on each chapter and talk with others about which of the notes they have recorded ought to be represented on the board. Their negotiations and discussions also yield the details that are recorded for chapter 22. Again, some notes are paraphrased generalizations, some are direct quotations and, in those instances, I continue to remind them to note page numbers for quoted phrases from the novel:

'Grant goes to visit Jefferson again at the jail.'

'Grant asks Jefferson what he wants and he says a whole gallon of ice cream.'

'He looked at me with an inner calmness now' p. 171.

'Grant tells Jefferson about a baby born on the plantation.'

'Grant buys Jefferson a radio.'

"The white woman wants to sell him an older radio but he wants a brand new one.'

'Grant gets the money from people at the bar.'

'Grant takes the radio to Jefferson.'

"OK," I say after students have spent about forty-five minutes recording these textual elements, discussing them, arguing about them, deciding who should write on the board, who should hold the microphone (as I pass it into their midst and aim the camera at them yet again), and why certain details should not be written onto the board. Their instinctive attention to salient elements of this novel seems consistently attuned, as it has been from the beginning of this venture. Desks are shuffled back into place, most yawning has abated, and we are ready to consider how all of what we have done over the past weekend, and Friday before that, and the weeks before that – how all of that will now be formally organized and expressed within projects and their written language.

"OK," I say again, "Can we look – can we – can we – can we - ". I stop and wait, as their murmurings are *not* easily subsiding this morning.

"OK," I say, again, this time more pointedly.

"Waiting …," I say somewhat more suggestively. "Still waiting."

Finally: "This is great! It's great! Look at what you have done. It's great!" I effuse sweeping my hand toward the board.

"OK, pull out your notes from Friday and then let's talk." Once ready, I ask, "What's going on?! What are you seeing?"

"They talkin'."

"Who?"

"Jefferson and Grant – they - "

"Yeah but mostly it's Grant talkin' from what we got there -"

"Where?"

"There - " the student's voice stops. We all wait. An awkward moment passes.

"Here is my question for you this morning," I begin, in an attempt to bring us to a moment of focused synthesis. I think for a moment about how to compose the question.

"All these notes from Friday," I begin, "And what we have here now all over the board in front of us from these chapters – from chapters 20 and 21 and 22 – and everything that – "

Someone interrupts: "You be usin' that word again Dr. Sullivan!" Some giggle.

"What word?" I ask, uncertain about the joke.

"That 'everything' word – you doin' it now too!" Others smile.

"Yeah!" I smile back, "I am, aren't I." I stop and think some more. Then I say, "Speaking of everything – and – and - look at what we have here and what you have there in our work from Friday – you know – and all the other days," I point to the various charts of our idea generation and arrangement of phrases from earlier days of work in the course and I ask them, "If I had – if you had to say - if you could point to one chapter that seemed to present, you know – one chapter that seems to be the one that kind of – kind of – seems most significant or important – you know one that kind of ties everything together – is there one – you know so far – from what we've read so far – is there one chapter that does that – kind of brings everything together?"

Several voices answer at once and it is difficult to discern all of the individual responses but here are a few of them:

"Yeah."

"It's what Grant sayin'."

"It's him and Vivian."

"It's what he sayin' there," someone points to one of the three boards where phrases are recorded about the three chapters we have worked on thus far this morning.

I watch and wait, uncertain about how to encourage a collective moment of awareness related to a synthesis of literary elements – one I can spring from to support realizations related to their projects and its incumbent processes. But I do not want to push this aspect of the conversation before we have solidified a secure footing in connection with the question I have asked.

"OK," I say to them, "Can we talk about that question – you are saying yes - I think you are saying yes - that there is one place so far in this book that kind of brings everything together – is that right?"

Many answer: "Yeah!"

"Where? Look at your notes from Friday and look at the notes we have for today for the three chapters we are focusing on – where is it that things come together – do you want to talk about it in groups for a few minutes and – ”

“No it's right there,” exclaims one young woman's voice.

“Can you read it - or – can you tell us what you think it is – can you all find something?” I ask. “One part of everything we have read from our notes and the notes on the board today and speak about it?’ I look round at all of them. I wait for a minute and then ask again, “Can you pinpoint those places?”

Over the next several minutes most student voices read aloud from the notes that have been constructed for chapter 21. They refer to most of the phrases that have been noted for this chapter.

“It's about Miss Emma and she needs him for herself – she wants Grant to change everything for all of them.”

“If Grant saves Jefferson, then he is saving Miss Emma too.”

“He's making things right – she wants – they all want him to change the cycle.”

“They don't want him to run away.”

“He thinks he can't have a life for himself and for them too – he gettin’ split up – he sayin’ everybody need him for everything.”

“It's sayin’ that – he got – he – they pressurin’ him to stand up – make up for all what the white man been doin’ for three hundred years.”

“Who is saying all this?

“Grant! Grant he – he – he be the one talkin’ – sayin’ this – he sayin’ it.”

“And do we know anything about what he's doing – how he is responding?”

“He bought the radio for Jefferson – he axe him what he want and Jefferson – he say he want a whole gallon a ice cream – and – and – he borrowed the money.”

“So do you think he's trying to - to be that hero – you know he was talking about heroes – where was it - in chapter - ”. I flipped through the book and found the references to Jackie Robinson and James Joyce once again. “In chapter twelve,” I said, “way back there. Does Grant – do you think he's starting to listen – you know like he said then – to really listen to what Miss Emma is saying and his aunt – is he changing?”

"Maybe - he – he – maybe."

"It's him talking here right? The whole book is about Grant – he's the one telling the story right? It's his voice we hear in every chapter, right?"

"Yeah."

"He sayin' – he tellin' Vivian that he can't have his own life – that he the only one not broken – and Vivian askin' him is it ever gonna change and he say – it's up to Jefferson."

"No – but he really sayin' they pressurin' him to make things right for Jefferson – that's why he buy him that radio – he - "

"He got to make it right for everyone – not just him and Vivian but his mother and father and everyone all the way back against the white man."

"So – so," one young woman asks – one who had been quiet for most of our time together, "Do we – are we – is that what we're doin' with the projects? Like are we – are we gonna show – like in our project do we try and show that?"

"OK," I said, "I think I have to talk for awhile about where we are going here – you know with the projects and the writing – and – and – look I think I need to help you get some kind of organization for what you will – you know for how you will decide how to choose the details from the text that match – that you want to represent in each of your projects so …".

Over the next several minutes, students watch me sketch a framework that looks like yet another of those we have worked with so many times over the past weeks. As I draw it (with my stand-in manning the camera and I holding the microphone), I talk constantly about what I am doing and how the evolving structure can be used by individuals and groups to begin organizing their projects.

"Let's try something like this as we get started today – to begin a little this week – today and tomorrow over the next several days – let's try to find – let's plan on having details from - let's say about 10 chapters - maybe more - represented in our projects and in our writing."

"What's that mean?"

"Right – let's suppose we start with something like this today – and each group of individuals will get a large sheet of chart paper for planning - to start planning this – it's the same as a lot of other structures we have been working with – the - "

"It's the bubbles again!" someone calls out laughing as he watches my circles begin to take shape on the white board in front of us – in one of the spaces available given all of the previous notes made today.

"Yes, but," I add quickly, "This time *you* are the ones deciding what goes in the middle – what the central idea is as you begin to plan your project details!" This I say while repeatedly circling the central hub of the map being created.

"And," I quickly add, "You decide which chapters you think are the most important – the chapters you will include key details from." I turn and look at them and they sit waiting, watching.

"Let's say as you look over your notes so far, and what we have done today, you want to include details from chapter 1, and 2, and 4, and 6, and 8 – you know how Grant was referring to Mr. Antoine there, and then let's say – chapter 11 where he talks about the white man winning," I am flipping through my own book and all my post-it notes all the while I am talking, "and then chapter 12 for sure, 'cause he was talking about heroes there and - " I sketched another little circle in a series of them now surrounding the large hub like a ring of petals in a flower, " - and then chapter 17, I think, and then chapter 18, cause that's when Grant asks Jefferson about obligation and commitment and then - for sure – I'd choose chapter 21 where – about what - that's the one we focused on today – I'd choose these ten chapters because there are details in each of them that would connect to what I'd see as the main idea – for me in this novel so far."

"What's your idea – ah the one in the middle," asks a young man.

"I'm not saying – I'm not saying – you know that by now," I say laughing and looking back pointedly at everyone.

"But today, I'm going to ask each of you to start talking in your groups and with another person as a pair if you're doing an independent project – decide on the chapters you'd want – the chapters with details that you think are important to be represented in your final project – see if this works for today and I'll come around and chat with each of you as this all happens – today and probably tomorrow and the next day too as we read another three chapters tonight." Groans were heard all around.

"And," I continued, interrupting the complaints – "See if some reading can be done today as well – we have to move toward the completion of the reading over the next three or four days".

For the remaining time today, I circulate among groups: listening, posing questions, responding to questions, reminding students about project structures, and in some cases making specific suggestions about particular chapters that some students may not be including as they sketch an outline modeled after the one I have presented. Within these small-group configurations, students feel comfortable revealing uncertainty about the representations they are undertaking. The exchanges are varied as some students feel very certain about the work they doing and others quite indecisive. A range of such exchanges is revealed below and reflects differing degrees of embrace of the projects while all students report unqualified engagement with the novel. In the remainder of this chapter, and across the first four chapters of the next section of this book, these conversations are presented.

I stand at the front of the room watching as groups assemble with chart paper and their copies of the novel. Directing the camera toward one group, I move toward them, hand the microphone into their center and move away as they begin conversing.

"I got a question – I wanna know why is it that ah Grant asks Jefferson right here at the last minute here in chapter 22 on page 175 – 171 excuse me – why he says – let me bring you a little – a little radio – why - why at the last minute is he gonna bring him a radio – why didn't he ask him that before?

"Things changin' – before tha - before that – they – they ah – he and Vivian they are – he told – that's when he told Vivian about all that stuff – everything about – everything that's been goin' on like – it's changin'.

I edge closer and ask, "Are you guys kind of deciding on that chapter - for your project you know, do you know what you're doin'?"

"Yeah – we're - we-re - you say - "

"Yeah, we're gonna do Grant and do like a character map – we think – we're not sure – we're kind of still decidin' – is that OK?"

"Sure."

"Yeah we still don't know like – what the key concept is – what the – like what we will do for our main concept like – but …"

"So, are you kind of you know – kind of going over the chapters and deciding on which ones you think are the ones that help you – you know the chapters where you see the most significant things going on in connection with Grant?"

"Yeah – like ah – we think it's important this thing about the radio – like why did he ask him now after everything that's been going on – why now about that radio?"

"Do you think the radio represents something important going on between them – maybe for Jefferson?"

"Yeah – we don't know why and we have to read more to find out but this radio – it got to mean something – something about Grant we think and not just Jefferson and we're not sure so - "

"So can I assume you feel OK about where you're going with this and you'll finish up your discussion about this one chapter and then kind of begin zeroing in on a range of details across many of the chapters we have read and see what specific – you know ah – which chapters and which details you'll want to represent in your character map – and we'll need to meet and talk some more about the writing?"

"Yeah – for now – for now yeah."

I stand and look toward another interaction, this time a twosome discussing elements of chapter 22, recalling Jefferson's regret about the day he was to have gone hunting and instead became caught up in the robbery that killed Mr. Grope and which also resulted in his sentencing to an execution. I pass the microphone into them, aim the camera their way, and then join yet another group, hoping to learn (later) about the videotaped discussion, while listening in on and guiding another group to the extent needed. It was much later that I heard the actual conversation being recorded:

"I can relate with Jefferson when – when he was angry – I think he was angry with himself 'cause on p. 171 – they talkin' about the day when he – when he remembered the day he was supposed to go huntin' with Gable – goin' back to my critical segment he was just focusin' in on it all."

"Yeah."

"And on page 169 it refers to my critical segment too – he – he asks what day is it."

"The title – 'A Lesson Before Dying' is for Jefferson also but I think it's also a lesson for Grant, himself."

"Yeah."

"And I think maybe I think this book is like – givin' emphasis on us - you know"

"Um Hmmm!!"

"The reader – you know - "

"Yeah – it's to teach us - "

"That's right - "

"Look at things - "

"It's to teach us - "

"To say that everybody else respectin' – you know what I mean - "

"That's right - "

"I think this book – is like – is like – a lesson – is like tellin' about a lesson for Grant - a lesson for Jefferson – a lesson for everybody in the book includin' the reader – for everyone."

"Um hmmm."

"If I had read this book on my own I would never have got this much out of it - "

"Oh hecks no."

"I mean maybe when I get other books I might do these steps."

The project ultimately completed by the two young women whose remarks are presented above focused on "A Lesson". Their unifying concept featured that phrase and encircling it were the words, Grant, Jefferson, and Readers. From those three terms, various details emanate, referencing a range of details across particular chapters of the book. Many students are engaging the novel through phrases that reveal an inchoate sense of thematic sensibility, as is the case here. In saying "This book is a lesson for Grant and for Jefferson and for everyone, including the reader", these two students, like so many others, are expressing the sense of a premise that unites the varying dimensions of the text. They are aware of how the literary elements of the novel unite within their impressions of a core underlying foundation. This same phenomenological sense of synthesis happens for all of the students – eventually. Whether, and how they are able to present their impressions of the ideational concept grounding this novel through the project structures and written presentation is another matter. The students' various meandering movements toward thematic synthesis are revealed in their (a) discussions of the remaining chapters of the novel, (b) evolving planning frameworks, (c) project constructions in class, (d) final written papers, and (e) final presentations of their projects in the last week of class. Throughout this variously processed series of engagements I am able to video-document individual and group interviews as well as whole class presentations by students and myself. The third section of this book focuses on the final stages of this collaboratively experienced literary reading venture.

As with this chapter, each of the first 4 chapters of the third section of this book refers to students' discussion of 3 chapters of *A Lesson Before Dying*. For example, chapter twenty-one of this book documents students' work with chapters 23, 24, and 25 of the novel. Similarly, chapter twenty-two references students' in-class work with chapters 26, 27, and 28 of the novel, while chapter twenty-three describes their engagement with the final chapters of the novel, 29, 30 & 31.

PART III

TRANSFORMATIONS

21

BUYING A RADIO AND FINDING GOD

Today is Tuesday. Yesterday and again today the atmosphere in the classroom is charged with restlessness, fatigue, and yet also a relative sense of surety. Students know what they want to say, have become quite comfortable about referencing the text, and are now assembling project maps, beginning drafts of their papers, and music, film, visuals, and segments of the text for drama project presentations. Underlying all of this activity is a sense of focus, of committed energy. More than that, the students have something they want to say and they are more and more sure of a direction despite some wobbly progress toward it. It may be that all of the classroom structures are facilitating their work at this point, but by now I have come to believe that a certain sense of transcendent confidence and enlivened awareness of themselves as able and involved in something meaningful is responsible for their presence of mind and being. I think they are alive in the experience of this book and they are concentrating on their project assemblies because they feel confirmed in their humanity.

The students have been asked to dedicate interpretive, organizational, and emotive energy within a relatively supportive environment that has been – for the most part – respectful and encouraging. As the steps of this journey have been undertaken I have discovered just how inexperienced most of the students are with respect to literary reading of this magnitude. They too, I think, have discovered something – a source of mindfulness, or awakened belief in the essential fact that they matter. They are being asked to say something, shown how to say it, and affirmed in the process of deciding what these statements will be and how they will express them. These many projects and mapping structures, questions, conversations, and written guides and frames are supportive to be sure but underlying all of this, I think the students have learned that they can think. They have learned that their thinking has been the subject of an intensive exploratory journey, and that their phenomenological experience is at the center of this voyage. The many teaching structures would be mere artificial props if the students' core of being in this novel were not centering this collective literary enterprise. Their final, personally rendered syntheses of this continuum of experience is what matters most and the fact that it does matter most has elicited the spirit of engagement that has resulted in the spirit of focused wholeness among us. It is a unity of mind, soul, and history through the literary map of a novel's renderings.

We begin: "We have so many things going on right now, right?"

"Yeah!"

"OK – so – ah - so I talked to some of you yesterday – and I need to come and work with others today – have you read chapters 23, 24, and 25?"

"Yeah."

"Did you make some notes like we have been doing?"

"You didn't tell us to make any notes for last night!"

"What? I assumed – ah –I didn't tell you - I forgot so you didn't write out anything as you were reading - like – ah- the - as we have been doing?"

"No!"

"So – should we – do we need to – let's – maybe we should skim through together – I'll walk you through them – I do not want you to miss something you might think is important – for your projects you know?"

"Um hmmm."

"OK – so you – we - each of us needs to decide if there is something going on in these chapters that abo – that really must – that you have to have in your projects and your writing, OK?

"We're still not so sure about this writing."

"I know – I know – and ah – I – we have to – I have to still keep meeting you - you today and see if we can get something going on with this."

We gonna run out a time – we got the projects and the readin' and the writin' and then we got to present next week, right?"

"Yeah – it's tight but remember - the writing – I – we don't have to have things perfect – but I think we can push a bit right?"

No answer - they do not want to complete the writing and think I will change my mind about assigning that.

"The most important thing – it's true," I say, "Is getting the book read and the projects in place and we have the rest of this week and then a really big day on Friday – can - do you think you can get the book finished over the next few days?"

"I already got it finished – I - "

"Me too."

"Three"

"Really, this is great so – ah - we can – we can - let's talk a bit now about these next three chapters – should we – should we meet in projects groups and pairs first or - "

"No it's better when you do it with us – you - "

"Yeah Dr. Sullivan, you do it with us."

"OK but you have to make the decisions, right?

"Yeah."

"OK. OK so let's look – get out your books and let's look to page 178 – and this chapter – what's - "

"He won't do nuthin but listen to that radio – night and day and -"

"He won't leave the cell now – he won't do nothing – they went up there to his cell and he won't talk to them or nuthin' and they callin' it a sin box – they all upset with him - "

"Tha mins'ter there - "

"Rev'rent Ambrose he ah - "

"Yeah he riled up and ah - "

They say he needs God and not that – not that – what they call it?"

"They sayin' it's a sin-box!" someone exclaims and they all burst into laughter.

"Is it a sin box?" I ask.

"No! It's all he got!"

"So what's goin' on now – all over this book and now – and now - "

"Here listen to this," someone calls out triumphantly as she reads from page 182:

> *"'Last Friday was the very first time … that – that Jefferson looked at me without hate, without accusing me of putting him in that cell. Last Friday was the first time he ever asked me a question or answered me without accusing me for his condition. I don't know if you all know what I'm talking about. It seems you don't but I found a way to reach him for the first time. Now he needs that radio and he wants it'."*

"Ahhhh …," I say and then quickly realize that my tone implies that I am reading a lot into what has just been read – I have paid acute attention to the line about Grant reaching Jefferson for the first time and my exclamation about that may be too loudly signaling my sense of that significance. I stop and wait.

They catch something in what I have just done. It sparks their attention.

Someone says, "They worried about his soul and ah - "

"Yeah but Grant gettin' stubborn now – he ah – he say he won't go back 'less they keep him with – ah - "

"That radio, like - "

"Yeah!"

"They still pushin' him and now he makin' progress!"

"Who's making the progress – what do you mean?"

"Jefferson!"

"Grant!"

"They - both a them – both a them together – they – they - "

"Yeah – it's they – ah – like – like Grant say he want to be Jefferson's friend - he said that – and and – ah - "

"He brought him presents from the children and - "

"He axe him to meet them like before in that room and ah - "

"And meet with Rev'rend Ambrose – so – ah - "

"So, what's happening? What else – ah – is this an important chapter?"

"Yeah!"

"Why?"

"Cause ah – 'cause ah – he – they talkin'."

"Who?"

"They all talkin'!"

"Yeah but anyone in particular – ah – are you seeing anything in particular – anyone in particular – ah –

"Everybody in on it now – they all talkin'."

"Yeah but - "

"It's – she – what she means - Grant and Jefferson – they talkin'"

"Are they?"

"Yeah but now he got other pressures too – they – "

"But he stand his ground and then – and then - "

"What then?"

"Now you make me forget!"

"Are there segments of this chapter – details that any of you think you need for your project?

"We got our segments!"

"But we haven't finished reading the book, right?

"Yeah."

"So there might be other details from – from - "

"We – we - "

"From this chapter – there might be - "

"Yeah there are!"

"Can you – can we see if there's anything else you need – maybe from this chapter as you begin to think more now about final project details?"

"Yeah – here he sayin' - like on the last page- page 186 – he sayin' right there near the bottom - he sayin' *I caught myself grinning like a fool. I wanted to throw my arms around him and hug him. I wanted to hug the first person I came to. I felt like someone who had just found religion. I felt like crying with joy. I really did.*"

"What's all that about?"

"Jefferson sayin' – tellin' him – he sayin' thank you for the presents that the children sent from Grant's class."

"Who asked them to send the presents?"

"Grant!"

"So – so – I'm just wonderin' – is Grant still – are they the same – are things changing?"

"Yeah – but then he mess things up later – in the next chapter - no it's the next one – he - they – like ah – he mess it all up."

I know this student is referring to a bar room brawl that happens soon but for now I want to keep their attention on the arc of the book – what this chapter signifies for the arrangement of elements they might represent to display a thematic path in their projects and now in our conversation.

"But now - what's happening now – things are happening now right?"

"Yeah!"

"What?"

"What we're sayin' – they talking and Grant – ah – he happy about it."

"Is this important – is there anything significant about this – this happiness even when he is talking about how still he is being pressured by Miss Emma and they are mad at him about not being religious with Jefferson, right?

"This whole book – you know this book – it's like – it's like what we been sayin' the whole time – this book is like non-fiction – it – "

"Yeah – it - "

"It show the struggles and the pressures – and it's what Grant sayin' and everything – it - "

"Don't say that word!"

"That word," I repeat laughing with them. "That word - everything, right? Is that the word?"

"No, she be startin' a bubble again!"

"I'm just wonderin' – you know – ah – are you maybe getting a different sense of things - I've been talking with some people and they say they aren't sure what this is all about for them yet – so – I'm – I'm – I'm just askin' if you think there's things happening there – here in this - in this chapter – that are helping you – maybe - maybe – you know – that give you some sense of what you think about – what's goin' on – what you'd show for your projects – I'm just wondering – I - "

"These projects – like ah – can we like just start drawing and like – start maybe like gluing our objects and pictures and get like lines from the book and just start putting things together even if we don't know for sure about the writing like – yet?"

"Yes! I could not have said that better myself – you don't have to know – I wish I had thought of that first – you really said something critical there! That's great! Yes – let's start – it's too tight – right – we need to start messing around and see where the shape of the final project goes, right and then you maybe – then you can start writing – we need to start - "

"We like – ah – we thought – we had to know for sure like – ah – like I'm sayin' you know – we – like our group – like I'm sayin' we just wanna mess with it like – I'm sayin' – we – it's not – like - we – we - it's not like a perfect thing but we got some ideas and – we gotta like – we gotta like start just messin' with it – you know?"

"Yeah – I think you're exactly right – does it feel like I'm - like does it seem like – it has to be - am I giving you the impression that it has to be – that you have to know it all perfectly for sure - "

"Yeah!"

"Then I'm wrong – I don't want it to seem completely random but maybe – you know I think we have to have some clear sense of the details we think we want to arrange – and that way – you know I think we have to know a general concept that we are gong to organize with our details from the chapters – that's why we - that's why you know – that's why we've been doing everything – focusing on specific details and getting a general sense of what - of what – of a thematic sense of things – is that OK – can I put it like that?

"Yeah – but - "

"Yeah but you know we gotta start getting it together and see where it goes like - "

"All this stuff we doin' – you know – like I'm sayin' it – I got – we gotta - we see what's goin' on ya know – we there with it but like – like - "

"You want to get going on putting things together and stop the reading part of it and work on the synthesizing part of it maybe – is that it?"

"Yeah – what she said," says one young man pointing to another in his group.

"Like that," he says again. We all laugh.

"OK – so let me – let me – can we just look at a few more things – just because – you know how I worry – I don't want us to forget something really critical you know – can we – can we just – ah - can we just talk about the other two chapters for today for a few minutes – I won't belabor it!"

"Yeah."

"Yeah so – take me into chapter twenty four and let's – suppose – suppose – I know – let's - maybe can we really quickly – real quick – can we form your groups – with your partners real quick – just I'm dying to know – I'm dying to know how – if you think there's anything critical you know – in the next chapter – tell me with your partners if you see anything there that gives you a sense of what these projects might look like and sound like – what details give you more of a sense of where you are going – does that make sense?'

"Yeah – well sorta you know Dr. Sullivan – we got you I guess – do we know what she talkin' about?"

"We goin' through the chapter like we bin doin' - find stuff there – where are we?"

"Chapter twenty four – like - "

"Yeah."

"That where – like – ah – that's where – what's there?"

"Is there anything there that you think is critical to your overall thoughts and feelings about what's going on in this novel?"

"That's where – where – what page - "

"Is where – there – right there –

"They all go to see Jefferson now – Rev'rent Ambrose too – they all go – and – and ah – and - "

"Yeah but before that – we didn't say – he - Grant wants Jefferson to write his thoughts in a book – like axe him questions – like sometimes – now he go and get the pencil and the book and he late goin' to the jail and they mad at him again - "

"Yeah - "

"And then – that's when that Rev'rent Ambrose start prayin' over the gumbo and - "

"Grant forgot – he be startin' to eat without prayin' - "

"Yeah," they all laugh.

"And he won't stop his prayin' he - "

"He got the - "

"The spirit *move* him!" someone shouts out evangelically as another shouts out, "Praise the lord, praise Jesus!" He stamps his foot, as the classroom bursts with cackles of hilarity.

"Ok – OK," I laugh along with them and then cannot resist pressing them forward, hoping they will all erupt with startled yelps of recognition when, together, we stumble into the elements of chapter 24 that I think might move them to expressed realizations about thematic insights.

"Then what – what's happening from here – where are we going – are you seeing anything here – anything else from this chapter that - you know – that – that – that gives you insight about – you know about things in this novel?"

"You know when she axe that question – she wants us to see somethin' – Dr. Sullivan you always do that!"

"Do what?"

"You know what you doin' – it's like- ah – it's like - "

"We got to find her book treasure!"

"That's right - "

"It's there – let's git it ya'll." They laugh uproariously and my ploy is outed.

"Don't like – we got this Dr. Sullivan – we bin plannin' our project and we don't want you to do this now – we got this for our project – don't do it now!" says one young man who is part of a project threesome.

"Oh," I say disappointed, and not able to resist the chance to afford other students realizations that this chapter might provide. I cannot resist: "Give us just a taste – I know – if you can offer us a taste of some of the project – you said you were doing partially a drama project right?"

"Yeah – but – we got other stuff too."

"Yeah – so maybe if you do some of the project – you have things from chapter twenty-four I sense, right?

"Yeah but - "

"So what if you show us – if we take a minute or two now – and we all get some time to just refer to those pages – and then you kind of – ah – you know - can you offer us a piece of that chapter – maybe do some dramatic reading from that chapter – we can talk about that – it would offer us all some thoughts about our projects - you'd be maybe giving us all something to think about ahead of the presentations next week – we'd all get some ideas from that – what do you think? Can we do that for - can we take some time for that now?"

"Yeah – yeah – ah – yeah – I guess."

"That's great – let's all go into that chapter and - "

"Dr. Sullivan you tellin' us there's somethin' there!"

"I know – I ah – I know I am – ah – but I could be wrong you know."

"She tellin' us there's something there!"

"Well see what you think – see ah – see ah – see if there's something that gives you any kind of insight – but you read last night right?"

Most affirm with a headshake. The quieter students seem very certain of themselves. I remain uncertain of what they are all thinking – of how this next chapter for our discussion today figures in the assimilation students might be making of the novel's elements. Over the next 20 minutes, I walk among groups and listen. Some are talking about projects and themes, some struggling with the idea of drafting their writing, some secretly reading chapter 24, and some are actively focusing on a discussion about this chapter. After about 20 minutes, and one discussion with a group about their direction, three young men come to the front of the room. They have been vocal and secure in all discussions throughout the course and have initiated many topics for our whole-group discussions. They take over the class.

"It's gonna - ah - gonna be different for our presentation - for like ah next week, I'm sayin' but what we got — we got — it's mostly Grant and like — we're — we're each like gonna say some a his parts — like - "

"So — so - "

"Let's just do it like - "

"And when you hear them — maybe we shouldn't read along today — yeah — yeah — that's a good idea — why not just listen to them and we can feel what's - feel the book — feel it being read to us — or - "

"OK — like we're goin' now — so like — ah like — what we got — it's like ah — it's like they're all there again with more food —

"Yeah more food — more food - "

"Yeah."

"So — ah — like — Rev'rend Ambrose he prayin' again - and ah — then Grant and Jefferson — they - ah like — they talkin' - "

"Just start readin' where — where — here our part is — there."
And they do:

> *"'I want us to be friends — a friend would do anything to please a friend — will you eat some of the gumbo? Just a little bit? One spoonful?"*

One of the young men reads and the other two shuffle back and forth behind him. Then another reads and the two others not reading continue their shuffling back and forth behind the one reading:

> *"Jefferson — do you know what a hero is Jefferson? A hero is someone who does something for other people. He does something that other men don't and can't do. He is different from other men. He is above other men. No*

*matter who those other men are, the hero, no matter who
he is, is above them.'"*

The three young men shift positions again – two of them walk back
and forth behind the new reader and the reading continues:

*"'I could never be a hero. I teach but I don't like teaching.
I teach because it is the only thing that an educated black
man can do in the South today. I don't like it; I hate it. I
don't even like living here. I want to run away. I want to
live for myself and for my woman and for nobody else'."*

Again, they shift positions and the young man who first read now
steps forth and he picks up where the other has left off – on page 191:

*"'That is not a hero. A hero does for others. He would do
anything for people he loves because he knows it would
make their lives better. I am not that kind of person, but
I want you to be. You could give something to her, to
me, to those children in the quarter. You could give them
something that I never could. They expect it from me but
not from you. The white people out there are saying that
you don't have it – that you're a hog not a man. But I know
they are wrong.'"*

They shift again and the reading carries on. A pin could drop in
this room and explode in the silences that issue between some words,
some sentences, and the pauses between readers changing places with
one another. We are all transfixed, dumbfounded by the surety of the
alternating voices. One of them reads and the other two walk back and
forth behind him, passing each other, walking past, staring at the floor
and then each turns after five paces or so and walks the other way,
passing each other again. The reading stops and they alternate positions
as one steps from the path of his pacing and assumes a position in front
of the other two where he picks up the reading. It continues:

"'Those out there are no better than we are Jefferson. They are worse. That's why they are always looking for a scapegoat, someone else to blame. I want you to show them the difference between what they think you are and what you can be. To them, you're nothing but another nigger — no dignity, no heart, no love for your people. You can prove them wrong. You can do more than I can ever do. I have always done what they wanted me to do, teach reading, writing, and arithmetic. Nothing else — nothing about dignity, about identity, nothing about loving and caring. They never thought we were capable of learning these things.'"

Another shift and this time the pacing continues for three turns back and forth before a voice reads in the silent attention of the room:

"'Do you know what a myth is Jefferson? A myth is an old lie that people believe in. White people believe that they're better than anyone else on earth — and that's a myth. The last thing they ever want is to see a black man stand, and think, and show that common humanity that is in us all. It would destroy their myth. They would no longer have justification for having made us slaves and keeping us in the condition we are in. As long as none of us stand, they're safe. They're safe with me. They're safe with Reverend Ambrose. I don't want them to feel safe with you any more.'"

Again, a shift; one of the two pacers comes to the front of the room and becomes the voice that reads — Grant's voice reading:

"'I want you to chip away at that myth by standing. I want you — yes you — to call them liars. I want you to show them that you are as much a man — more a man than they can ever be. That jury? You call them men? That judge?

Is he a man? The governor is no better. They play by the rules their forefathers created hundreds of years ago. Their forefathers said that we're only three-fifths human — and they believe it to this day. Sheriff Guidry does too. He calls me Professor, but he doesn't mean it. He calls Reverend Ambrose Reverend, but he doesn't respect him. When I showed him the notebook and pencil I brought you, he grinned. Do you know why? He believes it was a waste of time and money. What can a hog do with a pencil and paper?"'

Another shift between one reader and two young men pacing back and forth, back and forth, back and forth:

"'I need you. I need you much more than you could ever need me. I need you to know what to do with my life. I want to run away but go where and do what. I'm needed here and I know it, but I feel that all I'm doing here is choking myself. I need someone to tell me what to do. I need you to tell me, to show me. I'm no hero; I can just give something small. That's all I have to offer. It is the only way to chip away at that myth. You — you can be bigger than anyone you have ever met."'

The three of them stand and face us all together and one of them steps forward and completes a final reading to us:

"Please listen to me because I would not lie to you now. I speak from my heart. You have the chance of being bigger than anyone who has ever lived on that plantation or come from this little town. You can do it if you try.

That's all we are Jefferson, all of us on this earth, a piece of drifting wood, until we - each one of us, individually — decide to become something else. I am still that piece of drifting wood, and those out there are no better. But you can be better. Because we need you to be and want you to be. Me, your godmother, the children, and all the rest of them in the quarter. Do you understand what I'm saying to you, Jefferson? Do you?"'

As those last two words were read to us, it was as though the question were being posed to each one of us sitting in that classroom. At first no one said anything. I waited, standing at the back of the room with the camera in front of me, and the long cord of the microphone plugged into it and reaching many feet across the room to where those young men stood. They waited too.

Suddenly everyone clapped. It was as though a performance was ending. What had started simply as an oral reading is now being realized as a performance. The students clap loudly and the young men bowed dramatically – again and again. As they subside, I ask all of them a question as the young men take their seats:

"What is happening here? Does this interaction between Grant and Jefferson offer us - off – ah – offer you any insights – we've been talking and talking about everything all over – all - through – throughout the book and here together – what – what - what do you think – you know for projects – for your work with that and writing – and - "

"They're talking – they're - "

"Like ah – yeah and – like this whole thing – it's been like one long fight – fight between Grant and Tante Lou and – like ah – fight between Grant and Miss Emma – and she - be – she ah – like she – Miss Emma – she fightin' everyone too - "

"Right – that's right!"

"They're – it's one long struggle and now it's the end and ah - "

"They puttin' a lota pressure on those two men – like Grant and Jefferson – they in the eye of the storm like and ah - "

"He like – they talkin' about Christmas and Easter – it's like - like he the savior – like he say - "

"This whole thing – this whole thing – they – it's all like – a war – like a – like the eye of the storm and ah - "

"Oh," I insert quickly (worrying about that), "And then what happens – what happens after that – I want to try and link this incredible reading – this – this – what you have done in letting us see Grant's thoughts here – guys - this – this – this was – amazing, right?" I turn and ask this question of the class.

"Yeah."

"So – so, then – so then – and I'll come right back to – we don't want to forget that – and then – and then we have this next chapter right?"

"Yeah."

"And so what happens there – how do we make a connection between this chapter twenty-five and what just happened and what's been happening all throughout the book – everything we have talked about you know?"

"They still – they still ah – you know - "

"No, I don't know – what?"

"She sayin' - she tryin' to say that - "

"They still – they still - like ah - "

"The minister - Rev'rend Ambrose is jealous – he – ah -"

"Grant is still worried about – you know - "

I was forgetting what they might be talking about in such veiled ways, and asked, "What is he worried about?"

"Nuthin'"

"Nothing! – no, no, no, there is something – what is it?"

"Never mind – never mind."

"What?!"

"There – you know. You read the book - "

"Yeah … what page are you talking about – is there something I am missing?"

"Page 197 – there at the top – that - that again - "

"Ohhhhh," I say reading that *I didn't think anything in the world was worth us not being able to make it well in bed.'* Springing from the bedrock of this passage I asked, "So is Grant affected by does he care – is – is – finally he has – we have heard him talking in the previous chapter right? With everything we have heard as - with the reading just now right from Alex and Chris and James, right? And now this? And then what – I'm trying – you know – I'm really wondering how things are all coming together you know – in the book – I'm wondering."

"There's a fight – he hears – Grant – he – he hears – he hears the mulattos –that's what it says – they hate the blacks and they talkin' and - "

"It's the racism again – they got – they hate – they hate – it says they hate the blacks – that's not what it says – they use that other word – that - "

"The 'N' word," says someone interjecting quickly

"Yeah."

"Grant goes crazy – they sayin' it shoulda been over before now – the execution – they sayin' it - they shoulda done it before now and Grant he - "

"He goes crazy - they - "

"They have a big fight and Grant gets creamed," one student laughs.

"Yeah."

"Yeah – and – and ah like – Vivian she there and she take him home."

"So is it rage – first you know in chapter twenty-four, right, he's saying – he's telling Jefferson all those things – I mean he's really talking right – he is being - he's – he's – can I say that he seems committed – remember our map from before, " I gesture to one of the charts, "About commitment - and how he was – he was resistant right?"

"Yeah."

"And now - and now – he's so proud right, he doesn't want to admit it – because - but he's kinda proud that Reverend Ambrose seems jealous and Jefferson is listening to him, right? And all this time – over the whole book – he – he Jefferson won't talk and Grant won't be committed, or he – he wants to run away right and now – and now…," I stop, fearing that I am saying too much. I am articulating what I want them to articulate, to see for themselves.

I ask, "Is it about heroism like he says? Does he want – does he want to be a hero for Jefferson? Do you think maybe that Jefferson is a hero for Grant – for everyone there – if he can stand tall?" I stop. I am doing it again.

"This book – this book – it's about a struggle that's been goin' on – and it's still goin' on and we're seein' – we're seein one man – one man's struggle - we got to pick up the burden for each other – to fight – fight against injustice – it's like we were sayin' before like in our group - ah with our project."

"They got – they got – like – it's what we were sayin' before – about the racism – everyone hate the other one – the whites hate the blacks, and the – ah those bricklayers they think they superior with they lighter skin - and that's when – that's when – Grant hit one a them – they wouldn't shut up."

"Yeah."

"But things were leading up to that right? He - for the first time – he – he – really talked - and - "

"They – he – they all – it's all like – ah – they got to have – they got to have someone to be mad at – they got to blame someone - "

"It's like for us – we got – we got – it's sayin' that - right now – right now?"

"Yes?" I ask, as one young man seems to strain to express views for his group with whom he is sitting."

"This is all – this is all – ah like – Grant? He – he - they both – one is free – but they are in the same chains – him and Jefferson - and now – and now - he breakin' - and Vivian too – it seems like she the one that he can depend on – but she wants him too – like he was sayin' – like that they read before – that – that they're all broken – they all want somethin' – but – like – they need each other."

"Who?" I ask, "Who needs who and what is the significance of this fight now at the bar with the mulattos?"

"Grant – he's the one they need – they all be needin' him like he said before but - "

"That's not what he's sayin' – what he – like what he said – before – there what they read."

"It is – no – what you mean?"

"Grant – he sayin' he needs someone too – he axin' Jefferson to save *him*!"

"That's right – that's what he's sayin'."

"And then when those bricklayers – they – they disrespectin' Jefferson and he losin' it – he – they – like they had that fight and now – and now – ah - "

"It's like ah – like a explosion now."

"Why?" I interject. "Why now – after they talked – they talked, right?"

"Grant talked - it's Grant talkin' from what we heard – what they read before and - "

"Now – now like now - ah – he - "

"You all – like – all forgettin' something," says someone.

"What?"

At this point the microphone is automatically passed between one student and the other and this has been the case for some time now.

"It's those women – it's – ah – it's like it's sayin' that still – that still?

"Yes?" I ask.

"He still - "

"Who still?" I asked, feeling confused about who is being referred to.

"Grant!

"Oh, OK."

"He like – ah – he like – I'm sayin – he like still afraid to look at Miss Emma – I'm sayin' - "

"So you're sayin' we missin' something – we aint' missin' nothing – what are we missin!?"

"It's those women – the white women – who was that – yeah – ah – yeah Sheriff Guidry's wife – they meetin' in that special day room now and – and – and – ah like – Miss Emma, she the one that – it was her idea in the first place and - "

"Right, but, but she could never have made Grant – got Grant to really – to really feel committed – now it seems like he's really – he and Jefferson are really connecting right? Is that right?"

"I'm sayin' it's the women – that's all I'm sayin'."

"Dr. Sullivan I see what you're sayin' – I - "

"But – but what we - what they just did – what they read – it's like – it's comin' down to those two men – it's like – it's - this book is heavy. It's simple you know – these words – all these words – they - they – you know we readin' them – like ah – it's all - it's just like real simple – one thing and then one day and it's not hard right, but like ah – what we gotta do now, it's hard!"

"What's hard?"

"We – like we gotta - now – it's makin' my head hurt!

This last utterance spurts out with such vehemence that we all burst into laughter.

"Well, tell me – what's hard – what's hard exactly?"

"OK," the young woman says, adjusting her posture and assembling words in some definite order, "It's like – it's like – I don't know!" she exclaims

"I know - I know what she sayin'," says another, quickly reaching for the microphone, "Maybe I don't know – but like - "

"I do know!" quickly interjects another voice.

"What?" asks the previous voice, seeking someone to phrase for her what she cannot quite bring to words for herself.

"Well – I – I - like – it's like these *projects*! These projects right?!" she asks.

Many say, "Yeah!"

"Like – we gotta – now we gotta – like put things down – right? And - and – now – like – ah – we know – like it's cool – this book – we – we – like this book it's sayin stuff and we – we - I - "

"Now it's changin' things – doin' these projects – like it's – it's like – it's - it's makin' it seem - like – it's freezin' things up right?"

"Yeah – like – like that."

"It's stoppin' things."

I listen, with a great clutch of fear in my stomach. I am ruining everything. I know it. They are saying that the project work is actually interfering with their transactional reckonings of the book. Anticipation of the work of the projects is ruining the student's experiential dynamic of the novel, I fear they are saying. I swallow, ask one question and continue listening.

"What do you mean?"

"No – no – not like that," says one young man.

I'm not sure I completely follow the trail of exchanges or underlying contour of intent at this point.

"Yeah – no – it's just ah – like – it's just that – I – we don't know how to put it all down, like."

Some students clearly do know what they want to express with the projects and they are silent. Some feel constrained and are not quite articulating what I sense they are worrying about – that the formalities and structural guidelines of the projects are stymieing their expressive formulations. They are feeling constricted by the course's formalities now and are trying to say so. This was expressed in varying terms across all three classes.

"But – but," I stammered, hoping that some semblance of clarity might come forth as I address their semi-lucid worries.

"Just do it," called out one of the young men who had just presented a portion of his group's emerging final project presentation, due next week for all students.

"We didn't know what we were doin' either," laughed another member of that group."

"I think – I think – maybe – maybe we just need to do them – you know – we need to finish with the reading and you – you know – just plunge into the projects and – it's just like the reading I think – we have to see how it will emerge – how the shape of things will fall into place – I think maybe we have to trust ourselves that it will work out – that it will fall – it will have its own energy one we get started – is it – is it – let's see – can I ask – who is doing the visual collages?"

Several hands shoot into the air.

"And do you – do you have your images gathered yet and the objects that you will use?"

"Mostly – but we gotta - like we gotta get the rest of them – we gotta finish the book - "

"Yeah."

"OK what about – who is doing film, and music projects – we saw some of them kind of started a few week ago, right? When we did some of the mini-presentations?"

"Yeah we – like we know what the movies are - "

"Yeah me too – us too."

"So - "

"Yeah that's fine – that's no problem – we know - like we ah – we know what to say but - "

"What?"

"It's like – it's like ah – it's like sayin' it!"

I laugh nervously as do others.

"So, can we - can we – can I – should we spend some time each day for today and the next two days working on projects and writing and I can meet with individuals and groups and see how it's going? Can we do that? And I can help you – you know with the writing and your thoughts about how this is all coming together?"

"Yeah but – but - "

"But – it's like – it's like - "

"We just gotta do it!"

"Right but I do see – I do see - I think I can see the point you are making. It's like – maybe it's like a birth."

"Whoa Dr. Sullivan – that's nasty."

"No I mean – I mean I just had my second daughter you know six weeks before this class started right?" They are now listening with rapt attention.

"And, it's – as you're waiting and you know this will happen, you can't imagine how this - how it's possible you know? But – but once things start, once you are – once things get going, it all works. You know?"

"Can I – can we - can we continue with the sketching we were doing a day or so ago – you know, do you want to look over the book some more and trust - you know I think it's about trusting yourselves - "

"Yeah but you readin' this right? You gonna give us a grade for this and - "

"Yeah!"

"And – and ah like we don't know – what that – what that - "

"You axin' a lot Dr. Sullivan."

"So what if - what if I say that you – we - you engage in this creative process with the projects and the writing – the drafting – like we have been doing – and the projects come together and you have a reasonable draft of the writing, right – what if you receive - if you complete all of the required details for the course to the best of your abilities – you know with honest integrity – what if I guarantee that you pass the class with at the very least a solid B range and from what I can see that's really everyone – what if we can say that?"

"That's what you're sayin?"

"That's what I'm saying – if – if we can just get into the final work and meet and work on – work on the projects and the writing – just get into it."

"We cool with that!"

"Are you sure?"

"Yeah – we just – you know – we're here and we're working on things but - "

"Let's assume that - that – that we can really express something beautiful – that you have some guidelines but you know – that this project can be your synthesis of creative beauty – your expression of the – all of the passion and pain and insanity of the world that is in this novel – this is your personal moment for – for – this is your rendering - your – you know – this is a creative masterpiece – your statement – your assembly of the universe of this text – your aesthetically-driven creation of the - of your unity of this literary world – what is that vision – that – you know – what is that unity of elements for you – and I know – I know sometimes I use all these fancy words but you know - you know what I'm saying – you know, right?"

"Yeah."

"Yeah but the last thing I want now is some formal – some formal tight correct thing – you know? This is – this is still supposed to be an inspired structure of your passion about this novel – use the - use the assignment structure for guidance and – for guidance – OK?"

"It's like – it's like what happened when we saw Chris and Alex and James read - how they – why did they choose what they did - and read like that – that was amazing right? That was amazing and you all have similar passions and creative energy – and that's what we need to find and bring to shape with the work we have now to finish for our presentations next week."

"Yeah but – yeah but – we don't – like ah – like we don't know where to start."

"Do you mean with the writing? Or with the project? Or both? Or what?"

"Both!"

"I suspect - I don't know, but ah – ah I think that maybe we need to stop thinking about the writing for a few days and just start thinking more – start thinking more about the project – about the books – and about how you will choose elements – you know – how you will and – why you will choose – the particular details – the particular details you choose will tell you what your core ideas are about the novel. I think maybe we should start thinking of things that way. Let the novel tell you what you think, right? I know it sounds a little – well – how does that sound – you know letting the novel – letting it – kind of allowing your thoughts to emerge as you kind of – you know kind of listen to it, breathe as you walk through it, see it, hear its voices, feel its essential meaning and impact? How does that sound?

"Like – like – like you sayin' – what are you sayin'?"

I laugh, realizing that my guidance may have sounded more like mumbo jumbo than guided assistance for those who are stymied by the wall of uncertainty and resistance that is up against their initiatives for project work.

"I think you – if you are still feeling like these projects – and that's not everyone I know but if you are – if you are feeling as though you can't start – that you have to put something together and it feels like it's all too much – then – then – then just stop trying so hard to know what you're doing and allow your life within these pages to emerge one detail at a time – choose what's important for you – we have the - the project structure tells us something about how to – how to – what we need to collect – you know to gather in terms of chapters and ranges of details, right? So just gather, look through and walk through and walk through the path of the book – we know it almost – we are almost finished reading it right? As you work today, just let go and start identifying what you know are powerful and evocative images and words and feelings and places and events – let it wash over you – let go and find those most urgent and emotive elements – more big words from me right there, right?"

"Yeah but - "

"We have to start – I need to push you to talk and gather and allow your conversations and meanderings through the book - allow yourselves to feel your way along and see what emerges as you allow a structure to come forth. I know it sounds like - kind of like – like maybe a little - "

"Sounds - "

"Sounds kinda loose!"

"Great! That's great – keep it loose if you're having - if you're feeling like this project assembly is resisting you – or you are resisting it – let it happen. I'll come around and talk and listen and let's see what emerges – let's just do that, OK?

Students assemble, some still recalcitrant about giving into such indeterminate direction. I stand urging them on toward revisiting the text, to look over their mapping charts, to walk among others, to listen in, and look at what others are doing. Then I amble among them, capturing sample snapshots of our exchanges:

"What have you got?" I ask, rather abruptly inserting myself among a seemingly wayward threesome. Marcus shows me a segment of text he is thinking about pinpointing for this planning framework; I read it aloud in a mumbled rush which sounds something like this in the video-record of it: *"'Rev'rend Ambrose and I go to pray and visit over Jefferson's grave-site. This may - '*Ok what's the key concept of the novel do you think – in your opinion? I kind of get the idea you – you all have finished reading the whole novel right?"

"Yeah."

"Um - "

"What should the underlying idea be?"

"What do you think is going on?"

"I think resolution?" Marcus says, glancing up at his partners uncertainly. The background cacophony of student voices sounds productive, busy, involved.

"Ah," I say, smiling, suddenly more attentive, interested in this moment of realization. I wait, looking among this group of three, hoping they might spontaneously volunteer details about issues and people related to this resolution. They don't. Our quick conversation proceeds, phrase-by-phrase, my questions punctuated by their answers, the quality of the exchange suggesting that they are building a solidity of understanding bit-by-tentative-bit:

"Who's involved in this resolution?"

"Like … Grant and Jefferson and like – Miss Emma and Tante Lou and the Rev'rend and even the white people ' cause it was that deputy – what was his name – Paul – yeah Paul – he said he was the strongest one there – and so everyone."

"OK – do you know the textual elements you are – you have – have you – so you know the characters – and what is the project you are doing?

"We're doin' the concept map."

"Great – that's great – so – so we'll see – what will we see?"

"It's like a ring – like of people – from the beginning to the end."

"Yeah – we want to put in some images – and some key quotes – around the center – we want to put the word 'resolution' in the middle and have – like – have like – people, and places – like the fight and the trial and Grant and Vivian and Grant and Jefferson – and the jail and the school and white people all around – to show the power."

"This is fantastic - this is fantastic – it sounds like – with your presentation when you show this and read your textual segment – it sounds like we get to see the novel again through your eyes, right? And we will have some questions and comments from everyone, and maybe – maybe – we can hide – if that's a good idea – maybe you can hide that word – you know hide the word 'resolution' in the middle and have people guess you know? Based on how you – how they see and hear your comments and what you read and they'll see the rest of the poster board, right?"

"Yeah."

"Well that's just an idea. It will emerge just fine once you start assembling everything. Just you are planning it quite deliberately right?

How everything will appear and why it goes – why and how the details will be arranged in a particular way?"

"Yeah."

"OK. Anything else? I have a lot of confidence in where this is going – I can't wait to see it completed – it will be so interesting to see what everyone produces don't you think?"

"Yeah – just – just – what do we write?"

"Right. The writing has everyone kind of thrown doesn't it?"

"Yeah."

"So, let's see, everyone's writing will - it will be determined by the project – and you know – it seems like that will begin – to start shaping up pretty soon – maybe tomorrow or the next day, right?"

"Yeah."

"So why not – I'm never sure exactly - you know I don't want to tell you what to say right?"

"Yeah but - "

"I know – you want me to tell you what to say right?"

"No but - like ah - "

"Right. Right. Um – how about – if you can imagine right now what the poster board will begin to look like – and we're not sure right – 'cause it isn't assembled yet – but let's just say you can see it in your mind's eye right now and you - you know – you might think about explaining it to me – or even better – you know how that dramatic reading caught us - caught our attention and interest 'cause those guys knew what they wanted to read for us – they seemed to know why they chose those segments right?"

"Yeah."

"Well if you were - you know – you were playing around right now and you were starting to – just starting to tell – to pretend you were presenting the project, what would you say?"

"Ah – we'd say – ah we-d – we'd say ah – this project – is about resolution – if we were just showin' it right out, right? Ah – we'd say like - ".

The young woman talking now pauses, waiting me for me to say something and I wait, listening with my head down, expecting words to follow. They do:

"Like – we'd ah – we'd ah – we'd say that – and like it shows like each of the characters – and we'd tell about them – and then we'd ah – we'd show the connections to the parts from the text we're putting, and we'd go around the board like that – I guess." She looks to her partners. They look at me.

"I think you could start writing your draft just like that – just kind of write things out and add some details for the text segments – you know – you could write, 'We have included this detail about Grant at Sheriff Guidry's house because it shows - ". I don't know – it shows … ." Two of these students have quickly grabbed a pen and are scripting my words to them.

I continue, saying, "I don't want to write it – you know to dictate it – but I'm suggesting that once the project details are – once they emerge and you can see them, I think that will be the basis for the details and order for your thoughts – that that structure of your project will be a frame and as you write you can be sure to explain the connections between your key detail and key quotes and why – how that – how these details are related to your idea about resolution – you know?"

They look at me, and I guess they are disappointed about why I won't say more than this.

I tell them, "I will continue to check in with you every day this week as we head into the weekend, and just let it grow. Let things emerge." I move to another group, this time two young men, each writing a project based on the Situation Identification guidelines. I ask if he will read what has been written so far, and willingly Sean assents as he also comments on his work to this point of it:

"What I got so far is like how I feel like – 'cause I'm doin' situation identification."

"Um hmmm."

"You take the situation from the book and relate it to yourself, right?"

"Sure."

I listen as he reads aloud from what he has written: "Finding out who I am took me eighteen years to get a grasp on a portion of my life.

Confined to a room with four walls closin' in. You can call it solitary. I call it my personal monastery. My life gets so many memories," he reads.

"Wow," I effuse, seeing right away, (and not realizing I may be incorrect in that moment) that Sean sees his own life as a parallel to Grant's confused meanderings, offered through numerous textual disclosures featuring him as a first-person narrator. I stare up at Sean, and he seems to be shyly pleased, relieved, unlike his awkward reluctance when I first joined him and Ebbie. Now he exudes a certain diffident pleasure, I sense. He reads, now a little faster, his body posture more relaxed:

"Being poor is very depressing. The weight from being poor is very stressing."

He continues to read from his text, and stops after two pages.

"OK", I say, asking him if I can look over what he has written."

"Yeah."

"Let's look and see – you feel like this is rough draft – like – first – a first draft – like getting' it all out here kind of thing."

"Yeah."

"So, maybe – maybe – I would say maybe – once you – I'm not sure – let's see, " I muse looking back and forth among the three pages Sean has written.

"Would you say – you know - would you say there are definite you know – definite segments you know – parts of your life you are writing about here – you know?"

"Yeah – like mostly about the - like always struggling – watchin' people – like my family – never getting a head and – and – and ah – ah – like – like now I'm here and I got a chance to got to university – and all the stresses leading up to here and everything."

I smile to myself, thinking, 'There's that word again.'

"So there's more maybe, you know – there's more you'll write about maybe."

"Yeah."

"So I'm thinking – I'm thinking – I'm wondering how – you know – how we can talk about how your life circumstances get connected to the book you know… ."

"Yeah."

"To how you see the core ideas – the central focal point of the book in your own opinion, you know?"

"Yeah."

"So could you say - are you identifying with one of the characters in the book in particular?"

"Yeah – like Grant and Jefferson – they both trapped – he is sayin' that you now – Grant – he – like ah – he is sayin' that he's the one talkin' like we've been sayin' – and he's sayin' that."

"He's saying that," I repeat hoping that Sean will elaborate. I wait.

"He's saying that …" I begin, prompting what might become a conclusive statement from Sean about what Grant is saying - hoping he will be more explicit about Grant's exact statements so that I can verbalize a parallel between those details and the thread of Sean's own first-person narrative identification.

"Yeah – like – he's - he's all the time – he's sayin' he wants to get out, to – to – leave with Vivian – to get away and leave – and now – like what we've been readin' – like today – now he's facing things – like – like – he's fightin' back against those bricklayers and he's – he's committed like – he wants to stay and work with Jefferson now – like keep talking it seems like."

"So have either of you finished this book?"

"Amost says Ebbie."

Sean says, "Naw, I just – I just readin' what you say each night – I'm keepin' up."

"OK. OK," I say, "OK so here is what I am thinking – I think this is what I am thinking you know? I think so - what if we can find say – I don't know – a series of definite points from the text about Grant – what he is going through like we have been saying – and then – like you have just said Sean, and - then perhaps you might feel like – you might begin to see if there are specific parts of your own stories that you have here in the draft – in both of your drafts – and you can – you can put things in order – like alternate between the details of your own story – and make a connection to the details in the novel - and write specifically what you are seeing in your own life – then what you are seeing in the text that links with your own life – you know kind of fit those explanations in just very simply here and there."

I look through Sean's text again and pinpoint possible places that might become definite junctures – places he might choose to align with particular aspects of the novel. I suggest phrases he might use to link his text with particular aspects of struggle as he sees this presented in the novel:

"You could say, 'My life is similar to aspects of Grant's life and – or Grant's feelings here in chapter ____ when he …' - I don't know – maybe when he talks about – like we have said – when he talks about how his options as a teacher are so limited by his lack of materials – or when he talks about how – when he talks about Mr. Antoine – maybe there are people in your life that you will bring into your own story – do you see what I am saying? I'm trying to find a way for you to go back and forth between your own text and selected key aspects of core issues in *A Lesson Before Dying*, you know?"

"Yeah."

"Those are some ideas and maybe we can talk some more tomorrow you know as things emerge further in your writing and our final reading, right?"

"Yeah."

"So here is my question as I leave – you know – I'm wondering – there may not be an answer right now – but when you write about – in your own story there – and the relationship to Grant – the connection between your story and Grant's – what is the key connection - what is the common theme – you know – the big idea – what's the big idea you are sharing – the thematic thread you have in common – you might not know right now but that's what we're doing right? I wonder - "

"Overcoming obstacles – like racism – like he said and poverty – and everyone else's expectations – and like – like makin' something of yourself."

"OK, fair enough – that's enough right? You have plenty of ideas that form the basis for your text then and - and - that are shared with - that you know – that are also presented in the novel – the thing to do is expand your own text and keep in mind that you are going to be showing you - you – how you share your own critical life story – life segments – your core aspects of being and identity with what happens with Grant in the novel – and you have that – you have just expressed the core idea – what you see for the book and for your own life so – so when we talk more tomorrow and the next day, we can see how this is fleshed out perhaps a little more deliberately – is that enough for you?"

"Yeah," Sean says with relief.

We talk about Ebbie's ideas which are not in draft form yet and I move to another, and another and another group, in each case attempting to elicit students' statements about the conceptual foundations for their projects, their project details and structure, and how their written text might elucidate these ideas.

As we stop for this day, I urge students to work on drafts tonight and complete chapters 26, 27 and 28 if they have not already done so. They are reminded to bring poster boards, visual images and objects, their planning frameworks, and their notes. Tomorrow is a day, I tell them, when their thoughts and ideas will take shape ever more fully. I think they believe me.

* * * *

There is a proliferation of reading skills courses for "underprepared students" (Cox, Friesner & Khayum, 2003). They write that "students who enter college underprepared to read at the college level and who take and pass a reading skills course experience significantly greater success in college over the long term compared to similarly underprepared students who either do not take, or do not pass, such a course" (p. 189). We must bear in mind that the "reading skills" the students have been engaged with are literary reading skills and we must also pay close attention to the nature of those reading skills. Marshall (2000), writes that the reading of literature can be regarded, respectively, as having a salutary moral effect, a formative effect or spiritual balm. I proceeded with the work with these thoughts in mind but was primarily focused on the range of processes that would be engaged by the students given what I presumed would be a deep aesthetic reading. I was also cognizant of the place that such reading had having "arrived" out of the context of formalist new-critical reading earlier in the 20th century.

Our work went forward respectful of three groups of theorists – those that find the source of literary meaning in the psychological identity and autobiographical history of readers, those that posit literary reading as a set of conventions, and those that locate the "source of readers' responses in the sociocultural context in which they are reading" (Marshall, 2000, p. 387). But more importantly, the work was conducted in light of an empirical tradition "whose interests are more closely associated with teachers, students and schools ..." (Marshall, 2000, p. 389). In that sense readers' responses were seen to be characterized by Rosenblatt's (1978) descriptons of aesthetic reading, aesthetic synthesis, and individual and social consciousness. Given that this work happened in a day-by-day processing of a novel, it happened that a great range of responses were forthcoming. It must also be said that the art and media-based response vehicles and the classroom context was channeling students' responses toward an aesthetic synthesis. These three broad categories from Rosenblatt's work deserve more discussion.

Aesthetic reading was seen as related to four categories of response: (1) active experiential participation, (2) personal experiential significance, (3) a range of feelings and ideas, and a (4) beginning response structure. Rosenblatt uses specific words and phrases for each of these four categories of response related to aesthetic reading. About ***active experiential participation***, she writes that the reader is "highly active" (p. 22) and that "the reader's attention is focused primarily on what will remain as the residue *after* the reading – the information to be acquired, the logical solution to a problem, the actions to be carried out" (p. 23). Also she writes that the reader "fixes his attention on the actual experience he is living through" (p. 27), that the reader focuses on the "actual moment-to-moment participation" (p. 28) and "emotional responses" (p. 136) of the literary work being read.

She writes as well about ***personal experiential significance*** saying that the reader "actively draws upon past experiences and calls forth the meaning from the coded symbols" (p. 22) and that "recognition of the individual consciousness mediating between symbol and referent is essential to an understanding of any reading and especially of aesthetic reading" (p. 43). Further, we read that "the individual subject is seen as the center of activity, the mediator among the various structures that present themselves to consciousness" (p. 42). Most importantly Rosenblatt speaks repeatedly of the literary reading act as an "experiential process being lived through" (p. 43), and "permitting rather the view of meaning as experienced" (p. 44) and that in fusing the cognitive with the emotive the reader "lives through the experienced meaning that is for him the poem" (p. 44).

That aesthetic reading encompasses a ***range of feelings and ideas***; Rosenblatt writes that the reader "pays attention to the associations, feelings, attitudes and ideas that these words and their referents arouse within him" (p. 25). We read further that "the reader who adopts the aesthetic attitude feels no compulsion other than to apprehend what goes on during this process, to concentrate on the complex structure of experience that he is shaping" (p. 26) as an inner-oriented focus of attention brings about "absorption in the quality and structure of the experience" (p. 27). Rosenblatt speaks of a "moment-to-moment participation" (p. 28) and a "complete absorption in the process of evoking a work from the text, and in sensing, clarifying, structuring, and savoring of that experience as it unfolds" (p. 29). We see an insistence on a quality of attention that is "consciously focused on what the words are stirring up" (p. 31).

These varying attributes of aesthetic reading lead us toward a fourth one – that of a ***beginning response structure.*** I proceed to discussing this ***beginning response structure*** in light of a very important point about aesthetic reading which is best espoused yet again in Rosenblatt's very words. She writes that "[e]mphasis on the reader's role does not in any way minimize the importance of the text" (p. 34). We apprehend that the reader makes an active contribution to what is read: "Recognition of the individual consciousness mediating between symbol and referent is essential to an understanding of any reading and especially of aesthetic reading" (p. 43). Yet further we discover the insistence on this process of "awesome complexity" (p. 49). Finally, we are led to a series of statements that focus on the very rudiments of a response structure, "an organic and vital kind of synthesis" (p. 50). This last phrase leads us toward the second of the three elements of literary reading discussed by Rosenblatt, that of aesthetic synthesis.

About aesthetic synthesis Rosenblatt writes about (1) possible beginning frameworks, (2) refining coherent frameworks and a (3) personally significant synthesis. About ***possible beginning frameworks*** she writes in reference to Coleridge that the author attempts to satisfy "some such organizing or synthesizing urge" (p. 51). Claims Rosenblatt, "[a]ll the more strange, therefore, is the general failure to do justice to the parallel synthesizing, organizing activity of the reader" (p. 51). We appreciate her insistance on the "element of creativity in even the simplest reading act" (p. 51) and further discover her insistence that the aesthetic stance "provides the differentiating factor as the reader builds up and contemplates a unique synthesizing of his responses". She says that "[t]his active synthesizing aspect of the reading process has been largely neglected" (p. 52) and that "the shaping spirit, the synthetic and magical power of the imagination which Coleridge attributed to the poet, can also be claimed for the reader" (p. 52). Assuming the aesthetic stance, the reader "selects out and synthesizes [while carrying on] a continuing, constructive, "shaping" activity" (p. 53).

In ***refining coherent frameworks*** the reader works to refine a framework while also simultaneously carrying on with the aesthetic experience of the literary reading. We read that "the more closely knit the text, the greater the reader's need for refinement of synthesizing responses" (p. 54) and that "one begins to develop a tentative sense of a framework within which to place what will follow" (p. 54). The text, writes Rosenblatt, "bears the potentiality for a reasonably unified or integrated, or at the very least coherent, experience" (p. 54). As she discusses aesthetic synthesis she writes about adoption of tentative frameworks, selection and synthesis of further responses, sometimes a revision of the framework, rereading and then if all goes well a final synthesis or organization. She writes, "underlying all this organizing activity … is the assumption that the text offers the basis for a coherent experience. It may seem to "organize itself" if the reader proceeds smoothly with the process I have sketched above" (p. 55). She continues:

"Sometimes the reader may need quickly to grasp the framework ... before rereading it more slowly to attend to all the details and finer shadings. ... If such a putting-together, such a com-postion does not eventually happen, the cause may be felt to be either a weakness in the text or a failure on the reader's part" (p. 55).

A ***personally significant synthesis*** arises with a "click of insight" such as we saw earlier expressed as a student felt that *A Lesson Before Dying* was about resolution. This moment may be the result of adopting a framework within which all the experiential and textual elements are organized. Rosenblatt writes that "[t]he very general term "framework" has served to cover the great variety and complexity of kinds of organizing principles that the reader may require" (p. 56). Past literary experiences and memory "function in an important way in this selecting, synthesizing, organizing process" (p. 57). For the experienced reader, says Rosenblatt, this degree of organizing has become automatic. But as we can see for many readers in this book, that is not the case. Many of the readers with whom I am working are reading a book for the first time and so their moments of synthesis are not necessarily automatic. I have led them a day at a time through reading and rereading. Rosenblatt writes repeatedly that the aesthetic reading process entails a selective synthesizing urge, and that "[t]his kind of tentative synthesis and revision goes on in less drastic ways in all reading, and especially in aesthetic reading with its attention to fine shades of thought, sensation and feeling" (p. 62).

Individual and social consciousness is characterized by Rosenblatt in two dimenions: (1) awareness of self-in-the-world, and (2) compassion and empathy. As to ***awarenesss of self-in-the-world*** Rosenblatt writes that the reader "can be made aware of the needs, the assumptions and sensitivities, and blind spots that he had brought to the transaction" (p. 145) and that reflection on our "meshing with the text can foster the process of self-definition in a variety of ways" (p. 145). She further writes that the reader "may be stimulated to clarify his own values, his own prior sense of the world and its possibilities" (p. 145). As the reader reflects on the world of a literary text and on his or her responses to that text s/he can "achieve a certain self-awareness, a certain perspective on his own preoccupations, his own system of values" (p. 146). We are reminded that the literary transaction "has social origins and social effects" (p. 157). The individul consciousness is seen as "a continuing self-ordering, self-creating process, shaped by and shaping a network of interrelationships with its environing social and natural matrix" (p. 172). Through reflective self awareness the reader achieves a certain objectivity as s/he "seeks to understand how his own sense of life, his own values, coincide with, or differ from the world that he has participated in through the transaction with the text" (p. 174). These characterizations offer a theoretical glimpse of awareness of self in the world.

What Rosenblatt has characterized theoretically we see transpiring moment-by-moment spurred on by the teacher's guidance in all of the classroom engagments. The vital and organic syntheis is a messy process that for these students happens through the constant intercession of a supportive teacher. None if it was scripted. The teaching arose through the dynamism of the students' rapture with the text. The text itself was being made manifest through language and project structures that in various ways erupted, evolved, and were shaped gradually. What is important here is that we are hearing the voices of students who have never read a text before – we see their struggles and progress. We are able to witness the small moments of progress possible or students who have almost no background in reading texts. The teacher's role is critical here in such cases. They were urged to shape the fabric of their engagement with the text in much the same uncertain way as Jefferson's and Grant's relationship transpired. Neither teacher nor individual student knew exactly what final shape might evolve yet all parties were forged through commitment. For Grant and Jefferson, the commitment came through forces that came from outside them and ultimately settled within. For me, the journey began with commitment yet travelled the same uncertain path toward completion.

22

LEARNING TO WRITE AND FINDING GOD

We have been engaged over all of this time in a kind of collaborative thinking apprenticeship that has been nourished by constant conversation and support for students' efforts. The classroom environment has fostered reading and writing as active and mindful literary engagement. It is clear that students are still in various throes of readiness to complete this thematically oriented process. All the while, a multitude of sociolinguistic processes are being aroused – in many cases for the first time. Constantly it is emphasized that students' personal interpretations are at the center of this experience, yet for most of the students the depths of reading, writing, listening, speaking and artifact construction is vast and demanding relative to their backgrounds. This means that, though students have become relatively sensitized to the depth of literary reading and response that is being prompted, many are still tender about how they will complete the varying dimensions of final project details. It is as though the first several days and weeks of this thinking emporium is honing a readiness for the final moments when they will present their projects and related written expressions. Like Jefferson's responses to Grant Wiggins, the students' consummate embrace of this work is, finally, sincere yet arrives uncertainly and with feeble footing in its development. We must recall, now, that many have still not quite finished reading the novel. Given all these considerations, they are present in the work at this point as we turn to conversation about chapters 26, 27, and 28, and final flushes of reading and classroom work emerge.

From a phenomenological research perspective, it must be acknowledged here that many students, at this time, lunge into deeply emotional revelations about the interpretive process *and* thematic realizations about this novel that seem to transcend the contextual boundaries of the classroom. Now, thematic realizations seem to erupt out of individual consciousnesses that have been nascent, perhaps for many years. It is hard to say why this is so and a matter of conjecture to be sure. It should also be stated that, once settled into the reading habits of this literary enterprise, very few students (perhaps two altogether) displayed reading difficulties per se. There were some challenges here and there with reading fluency and occasionally very minor difficulties with word identification issues. The point being made is that 'these students' became relatively able readers in accordance with the demands of this set of circumstances. It is not as though they *could not* read but that they *had not* read. Students' limitations in coming to terms with the literary reading demands of this course had to do with reading history and experience rather than reading ability. Given these considerations, perhaps it is not surprising that as this day, and the next few, and the final week proceeds, depths of insight and coherent realizations emerge with sudden, expressive leaps. Certainly these observations are borne out in today's events.

We assemble and I ask if anyone has insights about chapters 26, 27 & 28. In particular, I ask, "Maybe something has happened here for those people who have not finished reading the book – maybe some of you read last night and see things that give you insight into this novel – this – and your own thoughts about it – you know – your ideas for your work and - "

"She pissed at him now I know that much."

"He coulda got hisself killed!"

"Now he got her in trouble too – now – that's what she mad about!"

"So we're talking about chapter 26, right?"

"Yeah."

"Yeah and now after all this - Vivian is – I'm sayin' – she's – she's like upset!"

"Why?"

"'Cause – cause – you know – you know – he – Grant he got hisself knocked out in that fight and now – and now he at her place – and she might lose her kids – and   if they find out he there – and she sayin' she's – what she say – she say – she say - "

"She's disgusted, that's what she say."

"Yeah and he sayin' he'll leave but then – but then – like then he say – he's happy – he say things went good at the jail – he happy about that!"

"Yeah but – it's like – it's like – now he actin' - "

"Who?" I ask, "Who are we talking about?"

"Grant – who – that's who – Grant who!" Laughter bubbles up.

"OK," I prod again, "Why are they - are they fighting? Is that what's going on?"

"Yeah!" says a voice. The tone implies, 'Dah! – Yes they're fighting – what do you think is going on?'

"Now her husband won't give her a divorce unless he can see the kids every weekend, and now – any now - "

"She – she thinks Grant is turnin' into big trouble – just like all the others – like it said before."

"She want to know if he really love her – not just like you know - "

"Yeah."

"That – you know."

"And then he does leave – and and - "

"Yeah but he comes back and – and - "

"It's all like a big explosion now – all the pressure – it's like explodin'!"

"Oh," I say and stop and they all look at me.

"Oh … ." I wait, wondering if I should really be stopping the proceedings in such a provocative tone. Everyone looks at me.

"What's exploding?" I ask.

"Whaddaya mean?"

"Someone said, everything's exploding and I'm just wondering – can we – can we look back and just do a quick synopsis – you know – just quickly note the past new chapters – I promise it'll be quick. I know you want to work on your projects and I want to talk to you all again - you know with groups and partners – but - but – ah – can we just keep track for a minute about what's been going on you know?" I turned and notate chapters 21 through 26, one after the other in a list and someone says something:

"Dr. Sullivan, we read those chapters already."

"I know - I know but can we just really quickly – can we see what has been going on – like you know just make a little path – like keep track of how we got to this point with Vivian and Grant here in chapter 26, you know?"

No one days anything. They are tired and I think they resent having to look back and go over previously discussed elements.

"Just – you know – can you – can you just page through quickly with me – or do you want me to – I don't want to put words in your mouth."

"That's all right Dr. Sullivan. You know, just tell us what you want to say. Just tell us."

"OK, look," I say resolutely. "You know it just seems like we have been leading up to this point – you know there – look on pages 166 and 167 – you know after they hear about the execution date, Vivian comes and Grant talks to her, right? We read that right? He tells her that Miss Emma wants a memory – he starting to explain things – 'cause he's starting to see things – maybe see it – have some perspective right?"

Everyone looks up at me and listens and I can't help myself – I keep on talking.

"So then – so then we move into the next chapter, right? And he's at the jail and they're talking – him and Jefferson, and he gets this idea about bringing Jefferson a radio and people - we talked about that right? So, he gets the radio – Grant gets it - and then we move into the next chapter, and Rev'rend Ambrose calls it sin company right – there on page 181," I say, paging through and following my own post-it notes and margin notes.

"And Rev'rend Ambrose asks him, what about his soul, and Grant says that radio was the first time - the first time," I read searching for a comment, and then find it on page 182, 'was the first time that Jefferson looked at me without hate' is what he's saying."

"And then we keep reading, right, and then in that same chapter Grant says he will bring him a notebook and he asks him to write out his thoughts, right, and – and he told Jefferson he wants to be his friend. They are talking a bit and Grant is really – finally – he's becoming involved – maybe committed right – that was one of our words from early on in our discussion – and – you know – then Jefferson says thank you for the gifts, and we go onto the next chapter – chapter 24 right?"

"And that's when – that's when – the guys – no that was another class – so in that chapter – Grant really talks to Jefferson and he says he could never be a hero and – but Jefferson could – he tells him – what does he say?" I ask myself looking into my book, as the students stare at me.

"He – he says Jefferson can chip away at the myth of white superiority - and tells him he has the chance of being bigger than anyone – it's like he is saying only Jefferson can - can – and then the fight on chapter 25 and he gets konked on the head right, and now they're fighting – and someone said – someone said everything's exploding and I want to know what's exploding - and why now? You know? Now you have me curious."

Again, there is silence and this time I wait. I wait.

A nervous voice begins: "The only way for something new to come is if they – if you can break out of what was before – so – so – that's what I think is happening – they're – it's all like – they had to rip away something – he had to ah break – like something had to get broken for something to be fixed so – so – they were all tearing at him except – except Jefferson and when he heard them calling him you know – the N-word – then he lost it – ah like he lost it – and now – and now like - "

"Y'all it's like I said, this is non-fiction."

"Right – I hear you – I hear you – but – I know I'm being a little pushy – but why – why – why now are they having a fight just after everything you know – seemed to becoming clear and fall into place – and – and I wish we could talk more about – like someone said – about exploding now - "

"Yeah – maybe – maybe – it's like she said – like Grant – who he was before – it was getting pressure and now he tore – now – everything – the way he was before – now he cares!"

"Like she said – like - "

"Right – it's everything he said, right? Now – like – like – ah – he said – that school play – I was gonna say – that play – maybe like – it's like – with the fight and now – and now – like that school play – maybe it's crazy you know but like Jefferson is like – is like – is like like ah – Jesus."

"I see what you're sayin' – you sayin' that – that Jefferson – he the one – like Grant said – he the one that gotta save them all and break the cycle – all that cycle over - what Grant said – over three hundred years - "

"I don't know - "

"It's all comin' apart – everything – everything – like – ah – like – now it's all comin' apart – things are - they're all - they are all on him – and now – and now – it's been eatin' away at him – eatin' away at him from the inside out and now – he – he got to come to terms – it's all comin' down to one thing!"

"What's the one thing?" I ask.

"Love!" calls out a female voice.

"That's right!" says another, a member of the same group as the young woman who has just spoken.

"She want – Miss Emma want – he right – what Grant says - that's right – they got to stand for each other – ain't no one done it before now and now – and now - "

"It's the women – it's always the women – they – it's like – they the ones – they the ones that make all this happen – Vivian she support Grant – and Miss Emma – she make him go there – and when you say – when you – ah – like when you said about those chapters – you know – it's like peace can only come after – after the storm – after everything falls apart – then – none of it is fair – it's all racism and poverty – and they got to find – to find their dignity – like - "

"So – so we are – you are saying a lot! A lot of things".

Students express many more burgeoning realizations of the thematic whole of this novel. They refer, for example, to it being about communication, struggle, transformation, strength, overcoming resistance, and fighting racism. At this point, their premises and conjectures are blurted in fragmented statements such as those just presented. It is as though several united factors are underpinning conclusive moments of synthesis: projects and written statements are being shaped and constantly discussed just as the novel's final resolution of elements is coming forth. Thus, the classroom context now is an environment altogether poised for summation. Perhaps the combined intensities of this literary landscape, students' personal histories, and the classroom's dynamism are arousing a need for final realizations. Certainly, as I speak with students today and in ensuing days, they speak in passionate terms about the novel's final impact on them. Many such expressions are presented in this chapter, word-for-word from videotaped interviews with individuals and small groups of students who have finished reading the book. The impetus to begin work on projects today stems from what seems a natural urge toward completion. Despite their protestations to move into project-based work, focus on writing, and meetings about same with me, I urge them toward the next chapter, holding their surging focus on project work as though restraining horses.

I ask, "All these things you're saying – these statements you know about transformation and everything - you know everything we just read about Grant from those chapters, right - and now – now – then we have the next chapter right – and I wonder if it affects – if it – what happens there with Grant and Rev'rend Ambrose – can we talk about that and - "

"It don't change nuthin!"

"He still sayin' the same thing – that –

"Grant's making Jefferson go to hell – is what he's sayin – it's the same as what we said – like ah - like when he was jealous cause Jefferson was talkin' to him instead of - "

"Who was talking to who – when?" I asked, confused as I often am about uncertain pronominal references.

"Yeah – you know – when Jefferson – at the jail – when Grant and Jefferson was talkin' and the Rev'rend was there and he was jealous 'cause Jefferson wasn't talkin' to him – we talked about that - "

"Yeah, I see what you're sayin' " I respond.

"Yeah – and like – and like – ah – now it's the same – so ..."

"So you don't think this chapter says anything that affects your sense of the coherence of things – you know the overall synthesis you are building with these projects - your work you know?"

"Not really."

"Nothing at all – can we look at one thing here?"

"Yeah."

"For example on page 215 – do you think Rev'rend Ambrose is saying anything that might make Grant reflect on his own his story – I mean you know he talked about the past three hundred years at one point right?"

"Yeah."

"And all about heroes and the past and what he learned – finally – learned - that was several chapters back about – you know – do you remember – about really listening to people and so - "

"Yeah."

"So I was wondering if there is anything here in this chapter that might – I don't know – might you know – ah – expand your sense of the importance of his people - thinking about his people – does that affect Grant – and perhaps alter your own sense of the structure of your ideas – any details from here that play into your own thinking?"

"Like where?"

"Well - can you have a look – or maybe in your own reading you noticed something here?"

"He's sayin' he ain't really – he's not really educated – but Grant said that before - "

"He's talkin' about street smart and book smart kinda thing."

"He sayin' that Grant is book smart but he is not thinking about his own people."

"But that's not true."

"No Reverend Ambrose is talkin' about religion – he's talkin' about Jefferon's soul!"

"Can we read just a little in particular from that chapter – can we have a - maybe someone can read some of the significant bits from that page I have referenced?"

"Where?"

"Well have a look and see if you can find - "

"Here! I know what you're talkin' about here," says an emphatic voice.

"Read it for us."

"He sayin' *'No you're not educated boy. You far from being educated. You learned your reading, writing, and 'rithmetic but you don't know nothing. You don't even know yourself'.*"

"Grant – he said – he said the same thing to Jefferson from what we read before."

"Maybe this is all about self discovery!"

"But it's not Grant talkin' now – it's that Rev'rend, what's his name?'

"Rev'rend Ambrose."

"Yeah but - "

"He sayin' there's only one way – everybody got they own way – Grant is not religious and that - the Rev'rend Ambrose he think that's the only way for Jefferson to – to – to – for him to be a man before he dies!"

"But it's the same – they still - it's still pressurin' him – that's what I'm sayin'"

"Yeah but then he say – look there on the next page – he sayin' that all want to give up at some point - "

"But Grant is not givin' up – this part does not make sense!" says a young woman with frustration.

"Does it mean – is what he sayin' that the only way is for Grant to get religion too. Can you just tell us Dr. Sullivan?"

"Let me push things a bit here," I say. "Look with me to page 218 and tell me what this – what Rev'rend Ambrose is saying here – he is talking about lying right? What is he saying? What is he saying here? And I have to be honest with you I am a little confused about this chapter – a little but anyway … I have some questions really more than answers for this part. But – but – can we just look for a minute – look there?"

"Where?"

"Page – the past page of this chapter – chapter 27 on page 218, I think – is that right?" I ask aloud turning to the page to be sure.

"Yes, just have a look here with me for a minute. What is Rev'rend Ambrose saying here – can - can - would anyone find something significant here and read it for us?"

"Yeah."

"OK."

"Look here – here." The students read: "*Reading, writing, and 'rithmetic is not enough. You think that's all they sent you to school for? They sent you to school to relieve pain, to relieve hurt – and if you have to lie to do it, then you lie. You lie and you lie and you lie. When you tell yourself you feeling good when you sick, you lying. When you tell other people you feeling well when you feeling sick, you lying. You tell them that 'cause they have pain too, and you don't want to add yours – and you lie. She been lying every day of her life, your aunt in there. That's how you got through that university – cheating herself here, cheating herself there, but always telling you she's all right'.*"

"Is that what you mean?" asked the student, looking up.

"Can you read just a little more?" I asked him.

"Yeah, *'I've seen her hands bleed from picking cotton. I've seen the blisters from the hoe and the cane knife. At that church crying on her knees. You ever looked at the scabs on her knees boy. Course you never. 'Cause she never wanted you to see it. And that's the difference between me and you boy; that make me the educated one and you the gump. I know my people. I know what they gone through. I know they done cheated themselves, lied to themselves – hoping that one they all love and trust can come back and heal the pain'.*"

"So – but – Grant said all that before."

"Yeah but maybe- maybe Rev'rend Ambrose he got the wrong impression – "

"You know - "

"So my question you know about this chapter – and I honestly don't know - why – my question is this – why is Ernest Gaines putting this in here – he's the one that's controlling everything right – he's the one telling – the – he's the writer, right? Why is he telling us - why is this happening here? I mean do you think he's saying - I just don't know - he's saying that Grant still does not care enough – that he isn't thinking deeply enough about Jefferson's soul – but it seems he does care right? He has said – we have heard him – it's his voice – I mean Gaines is controlling it all – Gaines is the writer – but he has revealed Grant's voice in deep reflection with Vivian right? And with Grant – a lot of time so I just don't know why – why Rev'rend Ambsoe – why this is here about Rev'rend Ambrose right here. I really don't."

"Maybe – maybe - he sayin' he's sayin' that – maybe it's the same as what Grant said before but now it's different 'cause someone is sayin' it to him – it's not just him thinkin' it - he got to hear it from someone and have hum – humilate – what's that word?"

"Humility – you mean – it's different when he hears it from someone else?"

"Yeah – he really got to hear about his own people – I mean his *own* people – about how they sacrificed for him – like really – he maybe – maybe he really did not know that before."

"OK. OK. I see what you're sayin'."

"So – so – so like ah - "

"So he got to feel the pain – really – he got to feel it – maybe - "

"But he knows they want someone – they need someone to – to – to make everything right! He been sayin' that hisself!"

"So it's like – it's like healing – this whole thing maybe – this whole thing is about healing and – listening."

"But like Dr. Sullivan, if you are askin' if this changes anything - no really – not really like for what we are gonna say but - "

"But no – maybe – maybe a little like - "

"But no – it's all – it's all like – like – ah – like carrying the burden for your people – it's the same as what Grant said before – now this Rev'rend Ambrose is sayin' it – that's all."

"Does that make any difference - I mean he is telling Grant he is not really educated – because – because he does not know the pain of not just his people – his own black race, but you know his own - his aunt. And what about lying – what is he saying about the lying – you know – he says he is lying when - Rev'rend Ambrose I mean - that he is lying when he says - when he is at weddings and funerals that - "

"He is sayin' that – that you know – that Grant has to have compassion – it's about compassion and havin' someone you know – ah like -

"It's hope – it's hope – to have something to believe in – you have to have some hope – that's what he is saying I think – that's what – he has to give hope – I - "

"That's right!"

"So do you have – do we have other insights from this chapter that add to our – to our sense of things as we are concluding our reading and begin final assemblies – anything from this that - "

"It helps us see things from before I guess – you know it - "

"It's - it – it's still – still pressure – just maybe a bit more pressure this time about the same thing."

"Well is this all about two men – you know Grant and Jefferson – or is it about something bigger than that – is there an essential idea underlying everything or is – is it – is it – what is it – why am I seeing that there is more to all of this here now – I don't know – I don't know."

"It's just all gonna – soon we're gonna see how – what - how they're both gonna deal with all this pressure - both of them – both of them – but it's – it's what – it's what - it's like all of their history – the whole thing with these two people."

"Maybe – maybe – like Rev'rend Ambrose he is sayin' that – he is sayin' that – like – like ah – like Grant is still like – not deep enough like - you know - you know before – we said - they said like – he ask him, 'what you think deep in you, right?' He ask him that and - "

"That's right! That's right! That's a great point – I never thought of that, "I burst in, perhaps inadvisedly at this point, since the young lady speaking sits looking at me, waiting for me to say something when clearly she has something to say which I have interrupted. She waits. Realizing my error (yet again), I say, "No – no you go – I am interrupting – you go ahead Stacey."

"Yeah – you know," she looks at me somewhat reticent now and continues in a slightly more diffident tone, "It's like – you know – you know – he is there, like we b'in sayin' but he still is not right there – he still does not really know the whole story – it's the same what Vivian told him too in that last chapter – she tellin' him – where is it – here – she sayin' that he does not give her enough – what – where is it – yeah here - she sayin," Stacey says looking up now from the pages of the book, continuing: "she sayin' he does not give her consideration, and it's the same that this Rev'rend Ambrose is sayin' before and now – about – about – like deep in you – about giving them hope – that's what I think anyway – like."

Students' viewpoints are offered now with far more automatic textual reference and developed perspective. They respond to each other, attend to substantive comments, and exchange viewpoints and argumentation readily. We are now engaged in degrees of exploratory depth that comes forth with attention to the broader conceptual territory of the novel. It is difficult to know if such relative sophistication is a function of constant attention to their thematically oriented projects, or the novel itself invites probitive wanderings, or if perhaps the contextual emphasis on constant discussion influences the far more extensive commentary than was the case when we began this course. Is it significant that the students' viewpoints, cultural and experiential backgrounds are dignified? Is that a key factor influencing willingness to probe this novel and express points of view that are more and more forthcoming as points of synthesis - ones that fairly respect a breadth of literary elements? It is not the case that all students are presenting such statements, but all are involved and attentive to the classroom exchanges I am now referencing.

I ask, "So we are saying that – it sounds like we are saying that there are varying interpretive possibilities still emerging – still – we are - we have been reading this book for - we are into our fourth week – and still – still we are finding things - new questions – I see new questions to ask and it seems as though we are all – you are all probing and thinking – we are still thinking about what it all means and you – I hear you saying that it may be – a - it may you know a matter of compassion, hope, humility, personal realization – you know for Grant anyway – all of their history I heard someone say and – and – carrying a burden – and maybe about healing – but I think each idea – you know – each idea is richer because it is influenced by what everyone else is saying you know? I mean if we consider that the essential idea about this book for us is a matter of healing, we can also consider that the idea of hope and compassion and carrying burdens might all be a part of that healing right? Hope and healing and compassion and carrying a burden – and we talked about transformation before, and struggle right – but each one of those ideas can be connected to any other of the ideas you are all talking about I think, right?

"Can we use all of the ideas? Like other peoples?"

"Yes, if – and this is important – if you are sure how you can fit the other big ideas to your key conceptual platform – sorry – I know – more of my fancy phrases – but you know what I am saying – you know right? You have to be able to really fit the ideas you want to include in your projects by drawing specifically on textual elements and your own explanations – in your own words - in your own words very simply – you have to make connections to the text as much as possible as you explain things – as you draw in the other ideas we are all talking about. Does that make sense?"

"Yeah."

"Really? I am not so sure I made - that I really explained it all that clearly but the point I am trying to get at is that we are here discussing all these ideas so that we all do have access to everyone else's thinking. We can adopt ideas we hear others express as long as we can link them to our ideas and really – you know really explain why and how those other ideas are related to the text and our – your own individual thinking."

"I got a – I got a question – like – like I'm sayin' these projects, right? These projects – like it's personal right – we each got our own personal way of thinkin' and we can say it that way, right – like - "

"You mean in the first person? With your writing?"

"Yeah that – but like – like ah – it's like my project right? It's - "

"Yeah?"

"It's like – it's personal – I'm bringin; in all of my personal stuff – like it's about – this book is about my life – I'm sayin' can we do it that way?"

"I think so - I'm not completely sure what you are saying – let me think – are you – are you asking – for example I know some of you are doing projects – just the project on SITUATION IDENTIFICATION – so the whole idea there is that you are writing about how the core conceptual essence of this novel – in your opinion – relates to your life in some critical way, right? So in those cases you are going to be aligning the novel with your life, your feelings, your experience, your universe *but* – and this is the important word, *but* – there will be constant alternation between your core details and those that align with the novel in terms of how the key idea of this book connects to core elements of your own life – and I know I have been talking and talking about that – and I have been saying the same thing – but now we are asking about it - and so when I say this again now – does it make sense - this is not exclusively a project about you – it is a project about the connections – the core similarities between the novel and a conceptual essence of your own life."

"Yeah but – but – but – we can make it like – we can make it – ah – like from our point of view – it can be – the project can be about us personally right?"

"If I am uderstanding you, yes, - yes as long as you are linking your own personal approach to a core essential idea of the novel - the way we have been talking about it – I will come around again today after we talk about this next chapter and see if – see if I am following you and where this is going – am I more or less making sense with my answer?"

"Yeah."

"So, what about – what about the next chapter - I know we need to work on projects, and writing and I have to meet with you – as many as possible for today and tomorrow as well – when we talk about the last three chapters – but what about – what about this next chapter – what's going on here that we can relate to the ideas that are emerging more and more – you know your ideas about the core theme or maybe themes of the novel - we are talking about many of them today – we seem to have these ideas very much in mind today – is there anything going on in this next chapter – chapter 28 that helps you refine or expand or sharpen your thinking about project ideas?"

"This chapter - this chapter – is sad - is sad - "

"Yeah."

"This is where I think all the religion comes in, right?"

"What do you mean?"

"Like he talkin' – Jefferson – he talkin' about when he die – he writin' about it – on Good Friday – he axin' is that when he gonna die – like he say that's when he die – he talkin' about Jesus – when he die – and – and like – it seems like – it seems more now like it's about a sacrifice – like Jefferson – he the sacrifice - "

"No he sayin' he is the savior – he got to save everyone – and that's what Grant told him before – he got to be the strong one."

"But here – he writin' – he sayin' about his dreams – that he a hog - that like he is dreamin' – he is writin' about his dreams in that notebook that Grant gave him and then he axe about when he gonna die and then – and then and that's when they talkin' about religion again – like - "

"Grant tell him to talk to Rev'rend Ambrose and pray and Jefferson's askin' him does he believe in God and Grant says yes – and – and he should pray with Rev'rend Ambrose for his aunt – he tell him that again and about God and stuff."

"No but he still sayin' he don't believe in nuthin' - "

"Grant tellin' - he - he don't know what to do – same as before."

"OK – but - OK can we – can we - you know we have been talking about a range of ideas and I don't want to lose sight of all of those discussions – you know we mentioned struggle and sacrifice and here – well – is there – is there a particular point or segment of special importance here in this chapter - you know maybe after these things you are mentioning – can we do what we did before – can someone – can someone maybe read for us – can we – everyone take 2 minutes – look through – I think there's something we should hear – I think we need to hear Jefferson's voice – I think we need to hear his voice - what he says here. Can you have a look?"

"I got – I got somethin' right here."

"Yeah – let's give everyone a chance to find - you know to really look over what's going on here and see if new thoughts arise about this interpretive path we are on about the thematic essence of this novel – personally – analytically – you know?"

I wait a minute as students read – skim through this chapter. The camera scans their faces. They are absorbed.

"What are you seeing?" I ask quietly, murmuring, bringing them together, away now from separate musings within the pages of this chapter.

"I got somthin'," says the same voice.

"What is it?"

"It's long – it's about a whole page - should I read it all?"

"Where are you – where are you starting from? What page?"

"It's page 224, near the top – sort of near the top."

"OK, why not start where you think it makes sense to start - it's Jefferon's voice we will hear now right?"

"Yeah."

"OK."

"Yeah here; he reads: *Me Mr. Wiggins. Me. Me to take the cross. Your cross. Nanna's cross, my own cross. Me Mr. Wiggins. This old stumblin' nigger. Y'all axe a lot Mr. Wiggins.'* And then there's more but when he talk again – this is what I'm readin' now, OK: *'Who ever car'd my cross Mr. Wiggins? My mama? My daddy? They dropped me when I wasn't nothing. Still don't know where they are at this minute. I went in the field when I was six, driving that old water cart. I done pulled that cotton sack, I done cut cane, load cane, swung that ax, chop ditch banks, since I was six.'* Then there's more and he says, right here, *'Now all y'all want me to be better then ever'body else. How, Mr. Wiggins? You tell me.'* So it's sayin' – he's – it's sayin' they – maybe he's – he's sayin' - "

"But then – Grant says – Grant says he more than - he more a man than him – they all - "

"Yeah – they all need him – that's what he's sayin' right?

"Yeah."

"So, when you were asking about making this personal – you know before – I am wondering is it because – are you identifying with Grant in particular – or Jefferson or – I don't know, you know – I guess I am – we finally hear Jefferson speak – and we have been talking about you know core ideas grounding this text from varying perspectives, points of view you know how we have been discussing this – kind of for weeks now – and so – so "

"It's not like one or the other – it's the whole situation – it's the whole thing."

"The whole thing?" I am now straining to ask, 'What is this whole thing?' but resist, realizing that I pushing for a conceptual tag right now would undermine the inchoate sense of holistic phenomenal realization I am sensing among us today. I wait.

"It's comin' down – comin' down to it now – now Jefferson is talking too – they all talkin' now – it's all comin' out now "

"It was out for the women from the get go!"

"Naw it's "

"Yes it was – they are – she was – his aunt saw it all – it's like it said here about her being on her knees with scars and cuts she picked it up when his parents left – she been doin' it all these years just like her people before her and she don't say nothin' about it – and now the men – the – Grant and Rev'rend Ambrose – I don't know about him – really – but now Jefferson he talkin' but these women they say it all from the beginning and they b'in doin' it all from the – from ah like – since forever and "

"No but "

"It's true but "

"But right here – right here it's sayin' – I'm sayin' – like – like – ah – it's gettin' – now it's gettin' we seein' it all now – about the way she – she axe him "

"But it's all like we – like you b'in sayin' to us, " says a young lady looking at me as the microphone is virtually thrown back and forth among them, "You b'in sayin' – it's Grant like – he's the one that's got to listen to everyone and he don't want to and it's what – what – now like – they gittin' – now it's gittin' – like ah – like – right? Like – now it's down to when – now like when he and Jefferson is talkin' and he sayin - he still sayin' that Jefferon gonna be the one to stand tall and save all a them – and – nobody is gettin' everything – now nobody – they all torn up – they all sufferin' – the only one that maybe ain't sufferin' is Vivian but now she might lose her children 'cause Grant had to stay there after that fight and - "

"They are all in this situation – this – this – like – this thing from the start – like in their community – he accused of murder, right? And he never had a chance and then Grant – they got him involved and that set him – he b'in – he b'in – like he's in the middle like bein' pulled like – I'm sayin' and Jefferson – he – like – he the one that's pullin' everyone together really and - "

"But he got to die – he gonna die – he got like life – but - "

"There's one thing - like one thing that -"

"No like – I - "

"I think maybe we need to let each person finish their thought before we – you know – before we kind of – I think we might be interrupting each other a bit - "

"Yeah but - "

"It's true – like but – ah - "

"No but – I mean – I'm sayin' – y'all – I'm sayin – like I'm sayin' – I'm sayin' that this is all – this is all like – we know what it is right? We know 'cause like – it's what we see every day – it's the same - "

"It's worse – there's more freedom now – they got no freedom at all – they got – all they got is poverty and this one – this one – this one guy - "

"But it's not one guy - it's the three of them men – and all the children that bring Jefferson the presents – they all – it's their whole world and - "

"I just wonder – I have to say I wonder if it's a story about that time and that place and those people or if it is allegorical – like I was saying awhile back and I know I have mentioned it here and there – if this story is a comment on race and America – the history of black people in this country or if it is simply a story about these individual people – I wonder – I - "

"It's not just - well it is – but - "

"This story is non-fiction – it's real – it's what happens all the time – all the time - "

"So why is Ernest Gaines telling us this story – why?"

"'Cause he – 'cause he – he is sayin' – he is showin' maybe he is showin' - "

"He wants to show strength!"

"Whose strength?"

"Not just that – it's showin' – it's tellin' – it's – it's – it's easier to say it with – when we did like before – when we – when we – made the – showed the movies and stuff."

"OK, OK. Well do you think - "

"Yeah, and when you come now and talk to us about what we're makin' and what we're thinking and sayin' like".

"OK – things are coming together – can we – do you want to stop for now and go to project work – group work and I'd like to try and talk to as many of you as possible over the time we have left today – about projects, writing, the reading – everything – shall we do that?"

"Yeah."

"I think we have about an hour – so – I'll come – or can I talk – can I talk to one person at a time today and then tomorrow, I will come to groups agin? Will that work?

"Yeah but Rachelle and I have to come to you - have to ah – like – we have to come with you both a us."

"OK."

"OK – but can I come first," asks Keenan.

"Yeah – I can keep – can I record us – you know set up the camera there first," I ask pointing to the middle of the room, with plans for various individuals to sit with me at my desk at the front of the room.

"Yeah – like – yeah."

"That's OK?" I ask, pushing the camera, holding the microphone under one arm, and talking to him, while another few groups seemed pressing with questions, answered briefly before Keenan and I can sit together at my desk.

I ask him, as I ask all others with whom I speak in individual interviews during these last few days of our shared work: "Can I get your impressions of this book and about this reading experience – can you tell me – talk to me about your thoughts, feelings, ideas, and you know raise any questions you might have about this whole experience?"

"Oh," Keenan responded immediately, in a steadfast and low voice, "Oh – this book you don't know – you don't know … it like changed my life – I never read a book before – never – ever - every time I started a book in high school I would just stop reading it – but this – this book – I read it – I never told you but like I read it the first week – a lot of us did – the guys I am working with – we sat down every night - like the three of us and we read it out loud to each other – we could not like put it down. It was like – like – I don't know – I never knew about a book like this – like this book – it made me see everything in my life – in my own life – for real – and no matter what happens – I know - I know I'm gonna finish – get my degree – after I read this – it gave me strength and made me believe in myself for who I am – what I want and I did not know that for sure – this book – this book – it got – it got – it – me – it really made me think about what I want and what I can do."

I did not ask Keenan a direct question about the thematic platform for this project, nor did I do so with any of the other students who I interviewed in this manner from this point forward; it seemed now crude to reduce the reading expeience to a banner phrase. The impact that was expressed in this first of such meetings comes as a shocking surprise. Keenan's comments to me reveal a level of intimacy that arises in a completely spontaneous manner indicating perhaps that our classroom exchanges, as wide-ranging and honest as they are and have been, may still have forestalled – or not entirely fostered – the level of emotive candor that individual conferences are allowing. Or, it is possible that we have reached a maturity of exploration in our work that now unites analytic and personal approaches to processing. It is difficult to know with certainty why such statements of profound impact came at this time but they emerge with similar intensity for many students.

I met with Marielle whose comments also signify deep insights about her reading experience:

"I really liked the book – I don't know – it affected me in a big way – I don't know how yet. Like I'm sure maybe some day when I'm old or something, I'll be able to tell my grandchildren but ... the book just makes me think like – how much," her voice lowers, "how much we had to go through. Everything had to like be silenced and you couldn't say much you had to beg for just a little bit. It just makes me feel that I'm very, very lucky to live in this – in this era and not back then. I couldn't put this book down – sometimes I *had* to put it down but you know – it's like – like what they went through – all of them – what it took – what it took for you know – for this – this like – this struggle and basic communication – it was like a miracle to keep your dignity – well you didn't and now we can 'cause a them – I have opportunity – I have so much – so much – 'cause a them."

Marielle stops; she can't say anything else. She swallows and shakes her head. She looks down at the book in front of her.

"They – they had more strength than I ever could – we owe them so much – so much – like everything – we owe them everything."

I wait. Again, asking specific questions now seems wrong. The thoughts she is expressing seem to touch a subjective chord of being that resonates somewhere within an historical vestige of consciousness. As Marielle concludes her reflections about the mid-twentieth century events of *A Lesson before Dying,* she stares blankly ahead. She shakes her head again.

She says, "I guess you had to be there to really know what they went through – it's amazing reading this now in our day – it's amazing."

I speak with Christine who is much more matter of fact in her reckonings about the work:

"I feel that it has like something to do with change – like evolution of emotion – like everyone in the book went through something – like just everybody," she draws a large circle with her hands as she glances down at the book. She says, "Like they're all connected in some sort of like a domino effect."

I ask her, "Who specifically is connected?"

She says, "Well like the women for sure – they are at the core – at the center of everything – without them – it would just be like a story – like another story of – about like – well like racism and wrong – like 12 white men accusing – convicting a black man – and it is that – that is the story- but it's not at the same time – that's like the backdrop – it's more like it's a story about like I said – how the emotions evolve – that's what starts everything off - like at the beginning when Grant like was there – like we keep saying and he was not here – but then – he grew and changed and everyone grew and changed like Stacy said and Jefferson too – so it's really about like that – all the way through – it keeps expanding – from one scene to the other until like at the end when Grant is crying – 'cause I read the whole thing already."

"Yeah, it sounds like at least some of you have finished it, right?'

"Yeah."

"I think that next week – you know next week when we do our presentations, people are still going to keep getting's ideas from each day as they go by – don't you?"

"Definitely – we keep talking and talking and talking about this book – there's more and more and more - it's got so much in it."

Rayne's testimony about the book is as follows:

"Like the reason I picked the Pink Floyd music – 'cause that's what my final project is about is because - like when they ask, hello is there anybody in there – it's like that hollow sound that echoes - like when Grant is trying to reach Jefferson – and he's – he's like empty – after being convicted – sentenced to die – like – and so - it fits with Grant too because he is - everyone is tryin' to reach him too – so it's – it connects with both of those two men – and it's kinda weird sounding too – because it gives you the feeling like in the jail – it's dark and gloomy and kind of scary too – like – ah – and - and like – like maybe it's what – how Vivian feels too – I don't 'know like when she – when she wonders if Grant gives her any consideration – like kinda – but anyway I like – just someone trying to run away and get away from all their problems – that's how it seemed a lot of the time – they were all wrapped up in it – I - I liked the book a lot – it helped me a lot - like in the last – the last couple of weeks because one of my friends committed suicide – he was only 16 years old and he hung himself from a water tower - it kind of helped me like – like the feelings that everybody in the book went through kinda helped me like come along with – to overcome like me not seein' him ever again and stuff like that ... so that's – that's how I felt about the book."

Complete silence reigns for a moment. I nod and Rayne looks down at the tabletop in front of us. He is deeply overcome, seemingly exhausted and dejected.

"So the reading – the way you are responding to this book through music you know – through the Pink Floyd music, is that – is that maybe that music is expressing things for you that come through you know - with that mood – you know – the depths that that music reaches in you."

Yeah." He nods.

"Are you OK?"

"Yeah – not really – but yeah – it's like I said this book really helped me a lot – like if they can go through all of that – then I – it helped me a lot – to read it like now you know?"

"Yeah."

I want to ask him about particular characters but it would not be appropriate to pose such a query. It would rupture a sense of privacy, an intimacy, a trust. I am learning that for many students, their deeply rooted responses to this book are sometimes virtually ineffable. I find myself wondering if its import will be rendered most vividly through the medium they choose to present next week when final statements are presented, and final moments of discussion arrive.

I speak with several other students before our time ends. Their comments range from objective accounts of how they will assemble their character and concept maps and the details they feel are important for their thematic unity, to those that are much more emotively centered as many above are.

Tomorrow is another day. We conclude today's work with reminders to read the final three chapters, if they have not yet been read. Some students ask for others to bring in as many magazines as possible as I have promised to do. We leave the room.

23

MIND, MEMORY, HEART AND LIFE

On this day, there is the sense of an ending. It is not a listless feeling – no, it is one of quiet completion. Though much work remains for students on their projects, today is the last day we will talk about the book upon completion of a reading segment and it seems we know this and celebrate this sense of closure with a certain degree of serenity. We begin as we always do: I set up the camera and the microphone, students idle into the room, and bantering pleasantries are exchanged. It will be busier in another hour after we have talked about these last three chapters, 29, 30, and 31. I learned yesterday (and perhaps should have known much sooner) that the true depth of engagement students have about this book will not necessarily be revealed through direct, objective probing. The many venues of experiential response have, in fact, yielded vast depths of personal insight alongside responsible textual references. I realize now that final personal commentary and projects will probably be an amalgam of mind, memory, heart and life experience. Knowing also that chapter 29 is unique within the book, I begin rather tentatively.

"I wonder – we're done right – I mean I think we have all – some of us before today – some of us last night – but we're finished the reading right – and now I – now I just wonder what you saw - you know – what did you see – what did you hear – 'cause now we have Jefferson's journal right – the one that he writes in – when Grant brought him that journal – we saw before he wrote a little bit but now this whole chapter – chapter 29 – this whole chapter – it's Jefferson. Do you – can we – I mean - I wonder if we can just hear his voice you know – just read a bit from him – and listen – and see what we might want to say about that … "

"You mean like read the whole chapter out loud?"

"No well – no maybe not the whole chapter but - "

"Like maybe pick some parts like we always do – like that?"

"Yeah – I mean what speaks to you – you know – what are you hearing him say here – it's his – I mean – he is writing here – the whole chapter is what Jefferson writes in his notebook so - "

"It's hard to read – the way it's spelt – like – it's hard!"

"So why - "

"Yeah – it is! I almost – like I could not read that!"

"Why?"

"'Cause a the way he - the way that it's spelt!"

"Yeah, Gaines is revealing Jefferson's level of – his – you know – just perhaps that Jefferson's experience with literacy maybe – well you know – it seems like this is the first time he ever wrote anything, right?"

"Yeah."

"Yeah, he says – he tells us what he did mostly all his life – right?

"Yeah – like bein' on the water cart - bein' the bucket boy for the – for the people in the field all the time."

"Yeah and there – right there – right at the beginning of this letter – that's the whole of chapter 29 right – it says, *I don't kno what to put on paper cause I aint never rote nothin but homework I aint never rote a leter in all my life'* – that's the first thing we hear Jefferson say – that's the first thing he writes, right?"

"Yeah."

"So we kind of - that's the first impression the chapter makes on us right?"

"Yeah."

"So – what are you thinking when you see that – what do you think?"

"He don't know what to say – or think – he never done this before – he done never wrote nuthin' not ever – not really – like not really."

"OK, and … anything else?"

"It makes – it seems like he getting' started – and he write a little bit each day – like in each one a these – these – like these …"

"You mean the various paragraphs?"

"Yeah, like – like – they got the paragraphs and they got the stars underneath right there on that first page, page 226 – like - "

"So maybe it – seems – it seems like – that's the first day – maybe each day he writes a bit more and with each new day, they show a break with those stars – maybe that's where he stops for each day."

"Yeah."

"Can we try to hear him – do you want to look and find some things he is saying – even if it is a little hard to read because of the spelling and – you know the way he is saying things – his grammar maybe?"

"It's hard but – but – it's like you got to get past – past the way it looks and you kind of – you do kind of hear him – it's his voice - "

"But they don't have – it don't have – like it's hard 'cause all the – like all his – what he sayin' – all his sentences – they all – like – they all like together like."

"Right – there are no capitols or periods, or really any punctuation – right? It's like – you know – it seems like it's all free-flowing thought from him, right - from one thought to the next, there's no breaks – we kind of get used to the formalities of written English and we don't even realize it and now reading this – it's – it makes you slow down to read it I guess. I don't know."

"Yeah."

"Well, can we – I mean – do you want to take a few minutes with a partner and maybe find some significant elements - maybe can we – you know – I just think it might be interesting to hear his voice – and maybe have you comment about what you're seeing and hearing from him now – you know - as we are pulling everything about this book together you know?"

Students agree to spend some time with a partner to decode the phonetically written presentation of chapter 29's letter to Grant from Jefferson.

"What do you think?" I ask as various group mumurings subside ever so slightly after about fifteen minutes.

"It's sad," says one young woman in a weak voice.

"Can we hear something – when you say sad – is it – can you read something in particular?"

"It's just like – everything – not one thing – it's just – like sad," she repeats.

"Yeah, why is it sad? What is particuarly sad? I'm just wondering about that."

"Like – everything," someone else starts. "He never did have a chance – like not really – not really."

"Nobody had a chance – it's like the whole book says, 12 white men say he got to die and someone else – like white person - picks the date – that's it – they don't have no freedom – no chance – nuthin'," concludes another voice.

"And why he getting' a grade for this writin' - that don't make no sense."

"What?!"

"Yeah – he say he getting 'a grade like – there."

"Where!?"

"Right – where – where was that – I know it said that somewhere ..."

"You mean there on page 228?"

"I – I – yeah – maybe – I – where?"

"There it is – like – at the bottom there – he sayin – there – look there," the student points to his place on the page to another.

"Can you read - "

"Read it yeah – that's what I'm doin' - right there," he repeats again as he starts: *'mr wigin you say you like what I got here but you say you stil cant give me a a just a b cause you say I aint gone deep in me yet an you kno I can if I try hard an when I ax what you mean deep in me you say jus say whats on my mind so one day you can be save an you can save the chirren and I say I don't kno what you mean an you say I do know what you mean and you look so tied sometime mr wigen I just feel like tellin you I like you but I don't know how to say this cause I aint never say it to nobody before an nobody aint never say it to me'* – and that's the end of one day – what he wrote one day."

"So like – like – he's sayin – what he says next too – that's what – that's the same thing really – he sayin' he never done this before – all this thinkin' and writin' – like."

"Then – what's that?" someone asks.

"That – there – that where they say – Jefferson – what he writes there – about a bet – when did they make a bet?"

"What bet?"

"There he say – there - "

"Where?"

"There at the bottom a the next page – page ah – like 229 – he say," she reads: *'an I yer mr mogan say it aint fridy yet an mr picho say you want double that bet you want add that troter an mr mogan say it still aint Friday yet'* – they're talkin' about a bet – what was that bet?"

"Yeah," responds a male voice – they did – they said that – a long time ago – they bettin' that Grant won't do no good – they make that bet – they sayin' he'll crawl – he can't walk to that chair – that's what that is."

"Right in front of him – like he ain't even there!"

'That's what he's writin' –

"Then he say everybody comes up from the quarter – all the children – is that what that's sayin' on the next page – it's hard to read."

"Yes, I think so – he's referring to the childen coming and all the people from the quarter there – right on page 230 – I think that's what he is saying there – yes I think so."

"Then – like then - "

"It's talkin' about – I think – it – I think – it's sayin' – sayin' that - "

"It say's he was cryin' after those kids left – and somethin' about – somethin' about a marble – what does it mean when he says – says he was cryin' 'cause of the marble someone give him – is that right?"

"Yeah – he – they all gave him – brought him something and – and – then it says he don't want to sleep ' cause – 'cause of the dreamin' – he dreamin' about that day."

"So – so so I just – I – can we maybe stop for a just a second 'cause I'm – now I'm wondering if you see any connection between this bet that we kind of skipped over – just now – just a moment ago – you know - what Lauren referred to at the bottom of p. 229, right? Did you notice that – really when you read last night and if you didn't are you noticing that now – and I mean – I'm wondering do you see any connection between that – you know- and various comments Grant has made – we have kind of emphasized several times various significant passages of – various comments that Grant has made and now we are hearing about this bet so - "

"What do you mean?"

"Well, I'm saying you know – I mean what has Grant said to him before about – about … ." I stop and page back through my own text as someone sits in yet again adjusting the camera lens to where I stand now as the microphone is passed along, "You know there – in – in where is that – chapter 24 on page 192 – I don't need you all to look back now because I don't want to disrupt this focus now on this chapter but I'm thinking that Grant has told him – told Jefferson he can chip away at the myth of white superiority and be bigger – be stronger than anyone ever was before – all his comments you know about the past and heroes and listening and so here we read now in this chapter about this bet – and I wonder what kind of connections are you seeing?"

"He just – he just – he don't remember that now – he ain't sayin' nuthin about that here – he just - "

"Yeah – he's just learnin' to think – to you know like - put down things on paper and he can't even spell the words – and like - "

"But he's sayin – like he writin' about – he talkin' about those men – the ones that are talkin' – like there in front of him about that bet – yeah -"

"Yeah they're sayin' - he's sayin – he's – "

"I'm not finished - "

"Oh sorry - "

"Yeah like – like – they axin' him does he want his pencil sharpened and he say yes - and they axe him does he want a – an – erase – like an eraser and he says no he don't 'cause he kinda – like – he's just writin'

things down like Mr. Wiggins – like Grant told him to to get his "A" –
you know - like really puttin' down what he's thinkin' 'n stuff – so –
now – now like on the next page – it says - like he's sayin' that – who is
that – Old Clark – he's – who that – I don't remember him – but he's
sayin' that this guy Clark is comin' around tryim' to act youman – does
he mean human?"

"Yeah."

"OK – like tryin' to act human but Jefferson – he sayin' – he says - "

"Can you read it – where are you?"

"Yeah – he's sayin' like at the top of the next page – there on page
230 that *'ole clark been comin roun too tryin to act like a youman but I
can see in his face he ain't no good an I don't even look at him when he axe
me if im doin all rite and can he git me something no I jus go on ritin in
my tablet an I don't care if he do see it after im dead and gone'* – like he
knows - and so - "

"It's like what you're sayin' Dr. Sullivan – now he's – now he's
like – maybe he's – maybe it's sayin' that now – now – he the one – he
knows – it's sayin' he sees everything – he sees them all and he's the one
that – that – that like - "

"It's like maybe it's like – like ah - like now they're all comin'
around – and like maybe they're seein' that he's calm now – yeah he's - "

"Yeah he is."

"Yeah like he's – like he's – he's how you say - "

"He's quiet and still."

"Maybe he's the wise one now – I never thought of that before – like
the wise men in the school play – I never thought of that you know."

"OK yeah maybe that's it – like that – but -"

"That's right!"

"But he's cryin'!"

"Yeah but that don't mean he ain't strong too – it's both things
true!"

"What else?"

"It's sayin' it's sayin – like he's strong – I mean he's sayin' that!"

"Can you read it?"

"Yeah – there – it's all right there on the next page – at the bottom a the next page – it's sayin - he's sayin' -"

"Where?"

"At the bottom of page 231 – there – right there – he's sayin like - "

"Are you gonna read it?"

"Yeah like at the bottom there it's sayin' – like what he's writing', *'when they brot me in the room an I seen how ole she look'* – he's talkin' about his nannan right – right there – that's Miss Emma he talkin' about – *'an how tied she look an I tol her I love her an I tol her I was strong an she jus look ole and tied an pull me to her an kiss me an it was the first time she never done that and it felt good an I let her hole me long is she want cause you say it was good for her an I tole her I was strong and she didn need to come back no mo cause I was strong an she jus set ther wit her eyes mos shet like she want to go to sleep lookin at me all the time til reven and mis lou have to hep her up an take her back home'* – so sos like – that's what he's sayin right there – what he's writin'."

"And that sheriff it – says – like when you go further there in that chapter – it says he axin' Jefferson do he treat him right and was he good and like all that – and Jefferson just say yes – they – they all – they tryin' ta make it seem like they bin good and fair – they want him to – he says to Jefferson to write that in the book – in his journal book - "

"They all lookin' ta get credit now for bein' decent and – and – it's like – they all want to get let off a tha hook – they want to feel like they the good guy – but he seein' everything now so – so - "

"So I'm dying to ask – you know I have to ask you know – what is Ernest Gaines doing here – it's the end of the book almost right – and we hear Jefferson – we see his voice kind of really – how he writes and what he sees and so I'm wondering how this affects your thinking and your feelings about everything as we – you know as well build our final structures and impressions – you know why are we hearing from Jefferson now – why is Gaines showing us this now – he's writing to Grant right? Jefferson is writing to Grant - the whole joural is written to Grant - "

"Cause now he trusts Grant – now they have like a – like a bond – like they trust each other!"

"Right but – yes – and – so – what – how does this chapter kind of you know – kind of – do you think it – maybe it – finally we see whether or not everything Grant has said is revealed through Jefferson kind of?"

"Like – like – what you mean?!"

"Well I'm wondering how you're seeing this chapter in relation to everything that's developed up to this point and I think we've talked about it all quite well – you know? We've talked about everything that's happened – what Grant has said – his resistance – how he was there and not there - and finally – I mean all of his struggles with what he was being asked to do – and now – before how he really seems to finally get some things – the way he talks to Vivian about it in earlier chapters – and now - I mean he is the one who has set up this writing - the radio and the writing – the things that seems to give Jefferson some voice and some sense of humanity – and how finally we see what Jefferson says - his feelings – and I hate to put words in your mouth – you know how I never want to say – so I'm asking - why – how is this coming together for you now as we read Jefferon's thoughts in this way – how is it all coming together for you for this book and our work?"

"It's like – like – he got – they got – she got what she wanted – like!"

"Did she – who?"

Miss Emma and his aunt – they forced him and everything and – and he like – he kind of – Grant – he went there - 'cause of Vivian – that's what it said – and now – he is strong – that's what he's sayin' – now – that's what – that's what - "

"That's what it's sayin' right to the end of the chapter – right at the end it's sayin' – I'm strong and I'm a man – and that's what – that's what - "

"That's what they wanted – that's what they all wanted."

"And he did it – they did it – he did it his own way."

"So Ernest Gaines is telling us all things really – right? Why – he is showing us now – here at the end in Jefferon's words - with Jefferson's voice – I'm wondering what you think of that – about that – how all of that is coming together for you."

"It's – from the start – he got accused and on trial and sentenced and noone said anything – he never – nuthin' mattered what he said – and now it's the whole story."

"Ahhh … it's the whole story," I repeat, hoping that more will be said about this. It is quiet.

"Why – how is it the whole story?" I insist on asking.

" 'Cause – like he's writin' to Grant – it's him and Grant really – all the way through in the middle of everything they all goin' through - "

"It's the women – he sayin' that stuff – he sayin' it to his aunt at the end!"

"No he ain't! He *writin'* it to Grant – that's tha difference – that's why it's about –like about them two, really."

"They down to it now – it's all what Jefferson can do – like how he feel – when – after – like they all want him to ah think they doin' right by him now – and – and ah - like - like he the one that got the power kinda - "

"But he gonna die!"

"Yeah but – what it's sayin - is like – it's showin' that he's scared – and he's cryin' – yeah and he don't want to sleep no more 'cause a those dreams about that day but – but like – like I'm sayin' - he's sayin – he's talkin' – like writin' out his words to Grant and he's sayin' - "

"Can you read it – the part you're thinking about?"

"Yeah – yeah – there like at the end – it's sayin, *good by mr wigin tell them I'm strong tell them im a man good by mr wigin im gone ax paul if he can bring you this'* – he got the final word – like."

"And Grant – you think he gonna take that journal to Miss Emma so she can see what it say?"

"No it said before – well – he - I - "

"Jefferson told her before – we read that part!"

"She knows – that's true."

"So we have all of this book in the voice of Grant and now we are reading that – you know all of Grant's struggles and frustrations and realizations and now this powerful chapter – I think it's such a touching and powerful chapter if – if I can say – I just want to say that I guess – and so – so I keep wondering I know – but ah – all of the book we hear from Grant – it is him writing and we are hearing his voice and how deeply conflicted he is feeling about being with Jefferson – with everybody – he has had all this friction and internal confusion about it

and it brings him to memories of all of the people in his life and now –
and now – and we have heard him speak to Jefferson and to Vivian with
truths – about his realizations and I know I have tried – we have tried
to talk about that a great deal right – and so – so can I ask – can you
say something about why - how we hear from Jefferson – what we read
and maybe other things you want to read from this chapter you know?"

"They in it together – like he sayin' – like he said before."

"What do you mean?"

"Like it's sayin' – I'm sayin' like – ah like – he got to die and he the
one that can give Miss Emma what she wants – what they all want –
they got they hero – and – and – that's it."

"Why are we seeing this – you know – why do you think we are
seeing this through the voice of Jefferson and in his words – and I – I
have to say as I ask this I am kind of – can I say this – yes I am going
to say this – Grant told him right? Grant told him that he - where was
that?" I page again through the previous chapters and to strategically
placed post-it notes. "Grant told him – here – here it is – page - now
pages - these two pages, pages 224 and 225 – look there – can you find
it with me? Jefferson is saying *'Yes I'm youman Mr Wiggins. But nobody
didn't know that 'fore now. Cuss for nothing. Beat for nothing. Work for
nothing. Grinned to get by,'* right? And then Grant tells him – I don't
know if we read that out loud before but Grant tells him on the next
page *'You're more a man than I am Jefferson. … My eyes were closed before
this moment Jefferson. My eyes have been closed all my life. Yes, we all need
you. Every last one of us.'* Right? So one dies to save the other – is that
what this is all about – it's amazing right?"

"It's like – its like – yeah …"

"It's – he still - "

"Who?"

"They makin' it seem like – he gonna die and everything be
different – ain't nuthin' gonna change! It's still – they still be throwin'
black men in jail all the time!"

"But this story – like this story – "

"Like they leadin up to this – all a this – that dark cell all the time and now – he ain't eatin' food offa the floor and calling hisself a hog – it's sayin' that - "

"Yeah! They all stand up for him now – with the children and all - "

"That marble!"

"They all around him – his community - she makin' food for him all the time – all through it all – and – and ah – like he tole her he strong and she can rest now – and - "

"Vivian – she – she – he – they – like her and Grant – now like – they got their own – like what it said about when in that chapter with Jefferson like – he sayin' in that journal he writin' that they all axin' him now – do he think they treat him right – they all need him now to make things right for them – for him – for all a them!"

"Right - OK so I'm saying – I'm asking – when you stand back from it all and you look now and see all this and I hear many voices speaking about this – how do you – when you read this now and look back over everything we have done and talked about and all the wall charts, right - and the maps and the journals and all of our conversations – everything – and you see his words now here – like this – what – how – I mean - "

"It's like the end – they shoulda made this the end a the book – I mean Ernest Gaines – like he shouda stopped there – like that!"

"Ahhh – he should have stopped there – but he couldn't stop there – right? He couldn't because it's Grant's story – oh – I shouldn't have said that should I. Anyway – sorry ah – I - "

"What you mean? Why you can't say that?!"

"Well I always feel like I am putting words in your mouth and I talk to you and I realize that maybe I think it is Grant' story but when I – you know when I talk to you – sometimes when I listen to your – when we meet you know I realize this book is – maybe it's – it's I don't' know – it's more – not a book – well it's a book I know that – but it's more than a book – it's – someone said it before better than me – it's life I guess – and well I'm always wondering what you think and – it's not one story I guess – you are all going to say – you are saying how this story – all of the elements are spinning into a particular form and substance for you so - ”

"So – so – like you think he can't stop – like – it - the book – it has to keep going sorta like - ”

"It has to keep going – that's really interesting,” I pause, repeating that phrase slowly, and seeing reverberated layers of metaphoric depth therein. In saying the story 'has to keep going' will one or many (any?) students feel enfolded within a collective forward movement of that phrase? Will any pause and reflect that Grant's pilgrimage through the soil of personal and historical landscape might be picked up by them? Some have spoken about how his or her place at the university doors represents a triumph for family and community. Will they perceive that the voices of Grant and Jefferson speak allegorically, perhaps realizing that at these closing moments of the book?

It's as though there are two levels of phenomenological engagement taking place altogether. One transpires in the day-to-day conversation and the other at the moments of project construction. I wonder which of these two levels of experience are truest – the verbal classroom discourse, or the yet-to-be-seen synthesis projects? I wonder about redemption, about the transformation that seems to be presented in both Grant and Jefferson and I also worry that I have not fully arbitrated students' conversational exchanges toward the full impact of the book. Then I also realize that their realizations are their own and that the impact of the book on them is taking place in ways that may not necessarily come across through the formal structures of the project or even in formal words, despite the ease and fluidity with which conversation is flowing.

We turn to chapter thirty and students – almost all of them across all three classes – don't want to say much about this chapter. I have read and reread that *'My aunt did not sleep at the house the night before. Like many of the other older people in the quarter, she spent the night with Miss Emma'* (p. 236). This chapter tells us that *'the minister did not sleep at all that night'*, that he had *'chosen the Twenty-third Psalm to read at the jail; he had made that choice soon after the sheriff had given him permission to be one of the witnesses'* (p. 237). We see that *'at six-thirty, the sheriff sat down at the table in his dining room to eat his breakfast* and that he tells his wife that *'he wished this day had never gotten here, but now that it had, he had to do what he had to do'* (p. 238).

I read Gaines' details about all of the townspeople who see the truck carrying the chair in which Jefferson will die. Jaunita tells Melvina, for example, that *'she wished something like this could be done somewhere else. What about those poor children up at the school? She just hoped they would not hear that thing. Melvina knew she was speaking of the white children at the white school'* (p. 240). The white people call the chair Gruesome Gerty and that it would be heard today between twelve and three - the same time as when the Lord died. *'Yes,'* says another, *'Yes and so did two thieves, one on either side of Him'* (p. 241). The white people are affronted: *'The whole town can hear that thing. ... It was just horrible. Just too horrible'.* People are worried about the effect the chair will have on their white children and on the serenity of their white streets.

I read that Jefferson's head must be shaved, that birds are chirping outside, and that Jefferson asks about one of the deputies' wives. He asks that his journal be taken to Mr. Wiggins and offers Paul *'that marble that Bok had given him'* and *'He told Paul to be sure that Mr. Henri got the pocketknife and the little gold chain'.*

For the most part, students' responses are that "'it's the same thing – the same old thing – the racism – and what he said – what we said – before – like with the other chapter – it's what he told his nanan – he's strong – the day is breakin' and the sun is comin up'".

It is quieter in the room now – in all three of the classrooms at this point in the literary experience. It is quiet as well as we move into the last chapter. I defer to what seems an unspoken need to say very little about chapter thirty. I have many questions.

"Can we read a little bit from the last chapter – it's been – we've been reading for all of these weeks and now we're done with reading and will complete - we'll complete projects I know. But for now, before we start to work and I come around and talk to each of you – in groups and with individual people, can we look into this last chapter and maybe I can ask – we can talk about how everything – that word 'everything – how it all – how you see everything we have talked about coming together – is that all right?

"Yeah."

"OK well, where are we now?"

"It's in this classroom – in Grant's classroom – with the kids – he got them on they knees from twelve until he hears from the courthouse."

"Yeah, he told them to be quiet and he went outside – he couldn't teach – that's what it says."

"Yeah."

"Maybe – can we – can you find a segment - for – for our final reading together of the book – one sentence or more that sums up – that – I don't know – that expresses something about how you see this final chapter – kind of the final words of the text, right?"

"Yeah."

"So Jefferson says he is strong and we see him give his things away – the journal – those thoughts in particular go to Grant, right?

"Yeah."

"Right, and Jefferson has asked about people and has given his few valuable possessions away – does it – I want to ask – does it seem that he is kind of the savior – I have to ask – I am wondering."

"Maybe – yeah."

"He has forgiven – it seems – like he has reached his peace and he has – he is I guess - it seems he is at peace, that he is strong – and no one is saying too much about chapter thirty – other than that – I am not sure why ..."

He said it – it said it in the other chapter - the one with the journal – the rest is is - that last chapter – that's just all the white folks – it's the same about the racism – it's the same – like it's been sayin' that – Jefferson's – it's like – he's bigger now – he's like – he's now it's like – he's the center of everything – and everyone else is on the outside - that's what it seems like – like the rest is like – it's all the same – he's the one that's changed – him and Grant like – so – so so – yeah so that's why – that last chapter – it's – it's like – it's – it's just like a that's the way it's always been and the thing that's changed is Jefferson and now we seein' Grant in this chapter.

"OK – OK – well ... maybe that's it then – let's – shall we try and find some aspects of this chapter and see maybe if anyone wants to make a statement – yeah – maybe we can all – you can all make a statement about the impression this reading is having now that it's ending – how is the final experience of this book together now – reading some segments - how is that affecting – you know influencing the structures and thoughts related to your projects? I am kind of wondering about that, you know?"

"It was a nice day, that's what it says."

"Can you read a bit?"

"It's just – that's what it says – I *am* readin' it!"

"Where are you?'

"Page 247 – it says, *'It was a nice day. Blue sky. Not a cloud. Across the road in the Freeman's yard, I could see a patch of white lilies on either side of the walk that led up to the porch. An old automobile surrounded each flower. Behind the house was the sugarcane field.* Then it goes on a bit and then they say, *'Even those who worked up at the big house for Henri Pichot or for other white people along the river had taken the day off. This had been discussed and agreed at church last Sunday. Those who were not at church were told what the others had decided, that he, Jefferson, should have all their respect this one day.'*

"So now it's Grant telling the story again, right?"

"Yeah."

"How does this chapter feel for you?"

"What do you mean – like feel?"

"Well, you know – it seems – well it seems kind of I don't know how it seems – how does it seem to you?"

"You mean now in the classroom where they are right now?"

"Yeah, I guess so – I mean over the whole chapter – I am wondering about – I don't know – I just wonder how this chapter after everything we have talked about – how it - you know how it kind of feels to you."

"It's quiet."

"Yeah – it's quiet."

"How does Grant seem – I mean this chapter is about Grant right? It seems that way to me. Does it seem that way to you?

"I guess."

"So he's – he's talking about what he did that day it seems, doesn't it?"

"Yeah."

"So – so he seems nostalgic - sad to me – how does he seem to you – I mean - "

"He lookin' back at things – like - "

"Can we read some of that – just this one last time we will be reading some parts of this book together – this is the last day we will do that, really."

"Like – it's the whole chapter – like - "

"Maybe – can we – can we look at some thing – maybe a few things on each page – I don't know – it won't take that long really – we have some time – no one wanted to say much about that last chapter, really."

"Like he's sayin' he's talkin' about the school he went out back near the church and he's talkin' about the cement blocks holdin' up the church – it was a long time ago."

"He sounds wistful."

"What?"

"Wistful – you know – looking back with memories that take him somewhere deep inside himself it seems – I don't know."

"He's remembering playing in the school yard near the church."

"Yes, and he's asking about people from back then, right?"

"Yeah."

"Can someone read something about that?"

"There – yeah – right there."

"Where?"

"There on page 248 it's sayin' *'Where were all the others now. Most had gone. To southern cities, to northern cities, others to the grave. Had - "* Should I keep reading?"

"Yes, can you read that part a little bit more?

"Yeah – like – like *'Had Jefferson ever hit a home run? He was as big as anyone else, stronger than most, but to hit a home run off a rag ball was a feat. Brute stregth was not enough. Timing and luck were needed. You had to hit it just right, and that took timing and luck. Lily Green hit as many as anyone else, I supposed. But her luck ran out before she was twenty. Killed accidentally in a barroom in Baton Rouge. What a waste. Such a beautiful girl. All the boys loved Lily Green.* So like – he's thinking about back when."

"It sounds like – it reminds me of that chapter about Matthew Antoine – do you remember that – that teacher that told him to – no back in – where was it, " I asked them, paging quickly back to the many notes that were sticking out from one point or another of my book.

"There it is – back in - way back in chapter 8 – do you remember – when he was talking about all those who had died – yes – there it is – back on page sixty-two – yeah – there it is – you know when he is remembering again – hmmm – you know I never realized before how much of this book is about memory – he says that to Vivian once too – remember that? That Miss Emma needs a memory?"

"Yeah."

"So – anyway, I just thought of that – but here – here he is remembering all those who had gone and how he hears about them – someone being killed, sent to prison, stabbed, and some who stayed but just died slower – so – so – we have talked about all this before – I know but – so on this day he is also remembering that – you know about Lily Green and what a waste it was for her too – so I'm wondering if it seems like he – it – if he is - you know – bringing things together – if everything is coming together for him now - "

"He says nothing will ever be the same after today."

"He says he wants to lose all memory – he does not want to remember at all – he still sayin' he wants to go – he still wants to run away!"

"Then he starts talkin' to Jefferson – he axin' him – he sayin' to - that now Rev'rend Ambrose is there and that Jefferson can believe in their God – that that's all there is right now."

"He's askin' a lot of questions – like - "

"Yeah but he's sayin' - that - he won't believe - he's sayin' *I will not believe*'"

"Yeah but then at the end he's cryin' so – so - "

"He doesn't know – even though like you say he writin' all this – he rememberin' like looking back at it all – mostly he – he like – he wishes he was there but he says – he - "

"Can you read it for us – what you are thinking about? Is it something specific from this chapter?"

"Yeah – like – yeah – there – here – *Don't tell me to believe. Don't tell me to believe in the same God or laws that men believe in who commit these murders'* but then at the end of that he kinda sayin' that they have to believe – it's the only way to be free and he's a slave – that's what he's sayin' – I think that's what he's sayin'."

"Can you read that whole segment for us – I think that's important, right? We - I think we do realize that this is Grant's story in many ways – that he is the allegorical voice – sorry – it is through his words and his experience that we are seeing the story of – well maybe a big part of - a key part of the story of African American people – it seems like that anyway – so we are hearing from him here in these pages for the last time and he's struggling right – we know Jefferson is dying any minute here and we see Grant – we hear him now in his final reflections about it – so what is it there – that part we were just hearing, can you read that part – more of that part?"

"Yeah – it's – he's sayin' he won't believe in the same God of the men that commit murders against black people – I think that's what he's sayin' and then – and then – it's - here on that same part - "

"Page 251," I say.

"Yeah, - it's *Don't tell me to believe that God can bless this country and that men are judged by their peers. Who among his peers judged him? Was I there? Was the minister there? Was Harry Williams there? Was Farrell Jarreau? Was my aunt? Was Vivian? No his peers did not judge him – and I will not believe'* but then something else - "

"Yes! Something else, right? What is it?"

"Yeah, he says – it says *'Yet they must believe. They must believe, if only to free the mind if not the body. Only when the mind is free has the body a chance to be free. Yes, they must believe, they must believe. Because I know what it means to be a slave. I am a slave.'* It's like – it's like – like – that's what it means the whole time – all the way through this book about that thing we've been sayin' – all those things about running and leaving – and like bein' trapped - like - "

"Runnin' in place - "

"And like tired a commitment and about bein' alive - "

"It's like – like that minister - "

"Rev'rend Ambrose - "

"Yeah - "

"He's the one that's there now with Jefferson – he's the one - "

"That's what Grant is sayin' - "

"It's like Jefferson is – he's the sacrifice – he's like all the others that died too but this time maybe it made a difference."

"What was the difference?"

"It said – like it said – he did walk like a man – it says that later when the white deputy comes and talks to Grant and brings Jefferson's – brings his journal to Grant – that's when they said he was the stongest one there and he walked like a man so he had his dignity and maybe he saved Grant – maybe - "

"That's right!"

"It doesn't say that."

"No but – like you can see in the end that Grant was crying and it was peaceful really – like we were saying – and it's like now Grant maybe is freed – when that butterfly came up it was like Jefferon's spirit was released and he as free and maybe Grant got a bit healed too – now he does not have to feel like he has to run any more."

"But he's still angry - "

"No, but when he said – what – like what we read before – he – maybe he knows that.

24

I SAW THE TRANSFORMATION

This chapter summarizes the latter four days of our time together. It recounts briefly some of the many moments of project presentation that took place and offers final thoughts about the work we completed together. Students are offered guidance about the format of their final-project presentations: (1) they will present their various projects, (2) read a core segment from the novel that aligns with the theme of their project, (3) explain what the novel meant to them and (4) respond to final questions and comments. We have seen and heard them make similar presentations earlier in the course as they were learning to take hold of the projects in the first place; then they presented a range of their work and completed similar presentations. Now we see completed projects and hear students' comments about the many thematic impressions they have made about the novel.

We see film segments presented, music segments heard, visual collages discussed and varying mapping projects articulated. All of them discuss a thematic vantage point, many of which have been presented in earlier chapters of the novel. Each student reads pertinent sections of the novel as part of the final project presentations and as we have done many times throughout these weeks, we respond to what is presented. The rabble of conversation is intense; one student comments, "I almost feel as if I was in a book!"

One-by-one, and group-by-group students stand and make their presentations over the last four days of the course. Various projects are presented and conversation ensues after each one. As these days pass students comment that they see more of the book through the presentations; they'd have added more detail if they had known about others' ideas many comment.

It is more clear then ever that the experiential dynamic of the past four weeks is enlarged even further through the presentations. Students talk about salvation, resolution, struggle and transformation. They present analyses about Grant and Jefferson – one student has merged the two of them in her visual collage. She represents one whole face that is comprised of two men and a hog and as she presents her commentary she says, "All the individual faces make up the - make up one whole face 'cause they have come together and make a whole new person. That's what my project is about – it's about – about – how everyone but mostly Grant and Jefferson are transformed – they save each other and when you see the butterfly at the end you know that Grant's soul is free and Jefferon's soul is free too. He saved tham all and brought them altogether."

Students have all assembled one of the project choices, all make a presentation and complete the written portion of the assignment. Day after day we entertain project presentations and see more in the book as a result of each one. We talk about all of our renewed interpretations as I continue to raise questions. The camera records everything.

All of the interpretive processes we have employed, all of the talk and listening, and all of the reading has changed them somehow. They have a voice. They have defininte opinions. They have learned to speak to one another about a book. How lamentable it is that this marks the first time such a phenomenon has occurred.

In a project such as this, there remain as many questions as there are answers: did the work refine the students' academic abilities? Did affirming them as literary readers and writers forward their abilities to negotiate other texts? Would they achieve success as they continued on their academic journeys? I broke the rules in setting up this course as I did as has been mentioned. Their phenomenological experience was designed to immerse them in a novel – to have them aesthetically explore the complexities of that text as a way of teaching them to read deeply, read to make connections, and read to make a personal expression of synthesis as they lived through the aesthetic transaction of the reading. We heard them do this on many levels as the course ensured. We have also learned that the processes they engaged are very new for them. For many, in all of their years of school, they have never read a book -- ever -- and thus have been hamstrung by school, in fact.

We place readers in classes throughout their schooling that are designed to help them and often enough those very classes enervate the vibrancy of their beings. Students become listless and apathetic and in many cases we turn them away from school. We have all been fortunate to participate in this reading voyage. We have heard a rare story – one that has allowed us to be there in a classroom where a whole book has been read and responded to through dynamic projects. It should not be an extraordinary event! One has to wonder if *these students* had been involved in such reading experiences throughout their school years would they have remained as remedial readers. I don't think so. All so very often we divide reading up into so many finite pieces through skills approaches that we lose the very essence of what it means to unite reader and book. *These students* have shown us that they can read in all of its complexities. Having peeked into their experience of a book, I hope that we, too, are transformed in our realizations of what it means to teach. Surely, we teach to redeem in our own students a sense of their humanity just as we saw it raged about in *A Lesson Before Dying*.

25

A LESSON BEFORE TEACHING, OR FINAL THOUGHTS

What I see of *these* students' phenomenological literary experiences is characterized, as has been earlier mentioned, by the following themes:

- A profound attraction to the literary text;
- Life relevance with the literary text;
- Naiveté, or inexperience with literary reading and writing;
- A sense of play;
- An invested collaborative dynamic among class members;
- A sense of voice and ownership as discussion ensues;
- Ongoing and caring teacher interaction.

A cavalcade of elements has come together to produce this aesthetically-driven, lived experience with *A Lesson Before Dying* (a la Rosenblatt, 1978). To now deliberately look back on *and* in future successfully and consciously choreograph such a phenomenological literary experience bears one more brief reflection. Thoughts to this end are invaluably offered to us by Muhammad (2020); they leave us with a touchstone of current grounding in what matters for disenfranchised adolescents as they experience literature.

In her path toward constructing a liberating education – especially for marginalized black and brown students - Gholdy Muhammad looks to black literary societies of the 1800's, seeing them as transformative spaces for the improvement of self and society. She grounds her blueprint for Historically Responsive Literacy on these intellectually invigorating models from the past, as she emphasizes culturally relevant and responsive theories of education that nourish identity development, skill development, intellectual development, and criticality. Muhammad writes:

> Each time early Black readers came together to read, write, think and learn, they were making sense of who they were (identity), developing their proficiencies in the content they were learning within (skills), becoming smarter about something or gaining new knowledge or concepts in the world (intellect), and finally, developing the ability to read texts (including print texts and social con-*texts*) to understand power, authority and anti-oppression (criticality) (2020, p. 12).

To be critically literate, writes Muhammad, is to be able to read, write and shape an understanding of power, privilege and oppression and deliberately work toward social transformation. Her universal teaching and learning model helps teacher cultivate the genius within students and within themselves as they "… create spaces for mutual empowerment, confidence, and self-reliance" (2020, p. 15) toward that end.

Based on her study of black literary societies, Muhammad speaks of literary presence, literary pursuits, and literary character as these thematic qualities emanated from such groups. Black citizens made themselves visible and "present" within the intellectual community through their writings. They engaged in such literary pursuits as "reading, discussing issues, giving lectures, offering peer critique and publishing original writings (2020, p. 28). And, they refined the ultimate goal of developing literary character, accumulating literary and literacy skills such as self-discipline, intellectual curiosity, civic responsibility "…and the ability to use reason, self-expression, eloquence, and agency" (2020, p. 31). Reflecting on literary presence, literary pursuits, and the literary character of Black literary societies, Muhammad concludes with ten literacy lessons that she imagines might be tenets for educators to rethink learning in classrooms. They are worth mentioning and aligning with the seven phenomenologically oriented themes outlined at the beginning of this chapter.

First of all, Muhammad refers to how literacy learning in Black literary societies encompassed cognition as well as social and cultural practices. She writes that "[w]hen I investigated the theories that framed literacy learning in literary societies I found that multiple perspectives shaped their engagement in literacy development, including critical theories, social learning theories, and cognition" (p. 32). Such emphases contrast with current school classrooms' focus on solely cognitive perspectives such as decoding, fluency, and rote vocabulary. Indeed, we saw adolescents reading the words of the text to see the world(s) around them in their work with *A Lesson Before Dying* as per Friere and Macedo (1987). Readers will remember that I eschewed a contractual obligation to teach *these* students through an emphasis on strict literal comprehension, decoding, and other skills emphases. I hoped that my students would read to shape their identities and to find personal relevance in this novel as they built resonance through their synthesis projects and many weekly journal writings, discussions, and mini presentations. Their own personally and thematically rendered day-to-day and week-to-week engagements were oriented to their own interpretive stances and multiple perspectives as these were negotiated in accordance with the novel's elements.

Secondly, Muhammad writes that in black literary societies literacy was the foundation and central to all disciplinary learning. She says that "[l]iterary societies focused on literacy development but were grounded in the learning of the disciplines" (p. 32). In fact, my hope in facilitating students' engagement with this novel was that it might refine their level of confidence and authority in approaching all other texts they might encounter in their future years as baccalaureate students. In expressing their thoughts through written language in journals, in collaborating with one another, in shaping mini-projects, in aligning text-to-text segments across the novel, and in exploring a range of graphic concept maps, I was hoping to teach a process of synthetic thinking that would ground students in their confidence with written language in general. In my thinking, it was as though their fledgling literacy engagements would establish a valuable foundation of security in textual territories. As I look back at the seven phenomenological themes foregrounded at the beginning of this chapter, I am given to think that their life relevance with the literary text along with their invested collaborative dynamic among class members made for an intensively successful basis for all literary and literacy learning.

Thirdly, Muhammad refers to the fact that in black literary societies literacy learning involved print and oral literacy simultaneously. Muhammad tells us that "[a] tradition among Black people involved the cultivation of reading, writing, and oral literacies together, layered upon their contextual readings of the world" (p. 33). We have seen students' reading and their writing and oral literacies tumble over one another seamlessly as they were guided to repeatedly express themselves in accordance with many types of mini presentations, small group, and whole group exchanges. Reading and writing were two sides of the same coin with oral language being the emollient for the two. There were multiple levels of writing ongoing as there was a constant thematic exploration at the reading of the chapter, multiple-chapter, and whole text level. It was never the case that reading was focused on to the exclusion of writing and oral language. Voice and ownership of the novel developed at many simultaneous levels with students seeking and constructing thematic signifance through multi-faceted engagements.

Fourthly, Muhammad writes that in Black literary societies literacy instruction was responsive to the social events of the time. Again, Muhammad tells us that "[o]ftentimes, when Black readers of the 19th century engaged in literacy learning, it called for them to not just read printed text but to also read their social world" (p. 33). Did we not hear students say that this book was not just back then, it was now?! It told about something that was happening for them in their own worlds with their family and friends. The novel brought them inside a world that resonated for them in the present tense. They were reading their own social lives as they read the text. And so, their profound attraction to the literary text came about as through the gaze of a culturally meaningful object. *A Lesson Before Dying* really was a social environment that the students read, wrote, and talked within as the literacy instruction favored and supported their life relevance in that book.

Fifthly, literacy was tied to joy, love, and aesthetic fulfillment in Black literary societies of the 19th century. And so it was with our adolescent readers. Rosenblatt's (1978) work was foregrounded as the very firmament of aesthetic reading – of reading as a live experiential circuit between each reader and the novel. These students of color were not encouraged to focus on rote, linear, and prescriptive teaching practices even through such work formed the basis for the contract I signed in preparation for my work with them. No, they were working with joy and love and aesthetic fulfillment, just so. Through their reading, writing talking, and project constructions they were refining both their hearts as well as their aesthetic sensibility toward education. A sense of play emerged between the teacher and students, and among students themselves and could be characterized much like the state of flow described by Csikszentmihalyi (2008). He writes that what makes an experience genuinely satisfying is a state of consciousness called *flow*. During flow, people typically experience deep enjoyment, creativity, and a total involvement with life. With some rare exceptions, what I saw with these students was what Rosenblatt (1978) and Csikszentmihalyi (2008) were emphasizing in their respective works.

Sixthly, Muhammad focuses on how learners of different literacies and experiences came together to learn from one another in Black literary societies. The invested collaborative dynamic among class members that was evident in our two summers of work together very much aligns with this principle, or lesson. Collaboration was a keystone of our work together. We talked and talked and talked. Some of it was unscripted and much was very much designed to deliberately draw on the collective mind that came together in each of these three, 25-person classes. Using others' experiences and abilities as resources to nudge and guide one another was very much present throughout and jibes with Muhammad's characterization: "it was a practice for brothers and sisters who were enslaved to learn how to read and subsequently teach one another. Also, other family members, young and old would teach one another" (p. 34). One begins to wonder if this one unique experience with literacy that the students had with *A Lesson Before Dying* would have been so solitary and isolated an experience if students had been educated to work deliberately and collaboratively together throughout their educational pathways.

Seventh, as just previously mentioned, Muhammad tells us that literacy learning was highly collaborative and created within a shared learning space; this tenet of Black literary societies was evident in our work together. The collaborative aesthetic that was evident was playful and student-with-student based. Students did have a social responsibility to one another - an increasing one - as they came together each day to share their journal writing, along with insights and feelings that the novel aroused. We could see this unfolding each day! Collaborative, oral language and students' shared written language, as we saw, was elicited through relatively unstructured general frames as well as more focal prompts. The collaborative language shared ran a continuum from being loosely prompted, as by the critical elements of the novel each day, and via the more narrowly focused (teacherly) insistence on textual reference(s), for example. Readers will recall many such pages of collaborative dynamically focused language exchanges. What was not so well documented in this book was the reading and rereading and revision acts that were implemented as the final project writings were conducted. Another tale. The shared learning space(s) of Black literary societies and this collaborative contextual background of multi-voiced adolescent have much to share.

Eighth in the corpus of Muhammad's lessons is how literacy learning in Black literary societies involved reading diverse text genres and authorship. This tenet could be seen in our work together as we read *A Lesson Before Dying* when students drew on comedy riffs, music, film, and any other of the few texts they had read and embraced. But, in terms of our 5-week teaching and learning segments, our focus was on one book and not multiple ones outside the intertextual referents just mentioned. We have explored how these other "texts" served as pivots as per Vygotsky (1978). One might consider: if curricular pathways were established among school courses so that multiple texts could be explored around thematic foci, it would pave the way toward adolescents increasing their range of diverse subjects and authorship. That in turn, would build both efferent and aesthetic embrace, confidence, and literacy depth.

Muhammad continues in her lessons learned from Black literary societies with her ninth precept as she discusses how literacy learning was also focused on "how to reclaim the power of authority in language through critical literacy" (p. 35). She speaks of how Black forebears read with a critical lens, with their writings becoming transcriptions of resistance, and of how "[l]anguage was the means to assert one's own existence as well as one's voice and stance on political issues" (p. 35). While it cannot be said that our adolescents read with an aim of transforming society, I had hoped they would establish an authentic critical voice and find societal connections with which they identified - that the strength of their involvement with the novel would engender a staunch and confident identity. Change not for the sake of humanity at large but change of one's school and literate identity was part of the key to our work together. In having one isolated yet fulsome experience with literature as we did, would our adolescents go forth and flourish across dimensions of schooling and society? Would they - did they — proceed into their first year of university with a confidence of voice and political righteousness as a result of those finite five weeks? I am left to wonder ... . We can say, though, that the experiences related to their engagement with *A Lesson Before Dying* appeared to be relatively liberating. We heard them say so when they claimed, among other things, that "this one book — it's lesson for not only Jefferson but for the reader, for everyone." Looking back now all these years later, I am left to ask many more questions about the work, about whether or not they claimed the power of authority in language as Muhammad puts it.

Finally, Muhammad outlines that identity and intellectual development were cultivated alongside literacy learning in Black literary societies of the 1900's. "Identity and intellect were two important facets to literacy learning," (p. 35) writes Muhammad. Making sense of the students' phenomenologically-oriented individual and collective identities was part of the grounding premise of the work as the classroom dynamics clearly paved the way toward them unravelling how Grant and Jefferson, how Tante Lou, and how the school children and those community confreres related to their own identities. "This is a story about us – about now" they said. I think that the students' individual identities and their intellectual development were curated simultaneously as they first began to write in their journals with their own voices, opinions, thoughts, and feelings. This phenomenon continued with classroom oral discourse and was leavened yet further by playful and yet full investment in the events of the novel as we will recall.

While Muhammad offers us invaluable lessons about literacy learning for black and brown children and perhaps *all* those disenfranchised students in our society, we must depart from the lessons momentarily as we consider the one phenomenological theme from this book that has not yet been aligned with her work. And that is the element of naiveté, or inexperience with literary reading and writing. Many, many teachers work with adolescents whose backgrounds include no invested embrace of a literary (or any other genre of) text. Many liberate while others crush the spirits and identities of those who come to them innocent of invested, confident, and uplifting literacy experiences. This book tells a story about seventy-seven adolescents with a paucity of rewarding literacy experiences; in the telling I've come to realize that this mini-slice of school society represents a crisis-level bulk of our North American population. Can it sway teachers to reframe literacy lessons? Does the story teach us that the educationally dispossessed can be redeemed through their aesthetically-driven embrace of culturally relevant literature? Do we not yet realize that the naiveté of which we have spoken cannot be met with one-size-fits-all frameworks that stultify and Stepfordize the adolescent soul/identity? It does seem that one of the lessons the books offers is that our malnourished adolescent readers need and can achieve, as Jefferson did, dignity!

REFERENCES

Allington, R. (2000). *What really matters for struggling readers: Designing research-based programs.* New York: Allyn & Bacon.

Alvermann, D. E. (2001). *Effective literacy instruction for adolescents.* Executive Summary and Paper Commissioned by the National Reading Conference. Chicago, IL: National Reading Conference.

Alvermann, D. (2002). Effective literacy instruction for adolescents. *Journal of Literacy Research, 34,* pp. 189-209. DOI: 10.1207/s15548430jlr3402_4

Alvermann, D. E. (2006). Struggling adolescent readers: A cultural construction. In A. McKeough, L. M. Phillips, V. Timmons, & J. L. Lupart (Eds.), *Understanding literacy development: A global view* (pp. 95-111). Mahwah, NJ: Erlbaum.

Alvermann, D. (2009). Sociocultural constructions of adolescence and young people's literacies. In L. Christenbury, R. Bomer, and P. Smagorinsky (Eds.). *Handbook of adolescent literacy research.* New York: Guildford Press.

Alverman, D. and Hinchman, K. (2011). Reconceptualizing the literacies in adolescents' lives (3rd ed.). Taylor & Francis.

Alvermann, D., Hinchman, K., Moore, D., Phelps, S. and Waff, D. (2006). *Reconceptuializing the literacies in adolescents' lives.* Hillsdale, NJ: Laurence Erlbaum

Apple, M. (1999). *Power, meaning, and identity.* New York: Peter Lang.

Apple, M. (2004). *Ideology and curriculum* (3rd ed.). New York: RoutledgeFalmer.

Arnheim, R. (1969). *Visual Thinking.* Berkeley, CA: University of California Press.

Aronowitz, S. (2000). *The knowledge factory.* Boston, MA: Beacon Press.

Au, K. (1980). Participant structures in a reading lesson with Hawaiian children: Analysis of culturally appropriate instructional events. *Anthropology and Education Quarterly, 11,* 91-115.

Ayers, W. (2004). *Teaching the personal and the political.* New York: Teachers College Press.

Bahktin, M. M., (1981). *The dialogic imagination.* University of Texas Press.

Ball, A. (2000). Empowering pedagogies that enhance the learning of multicultural students. *Teachers College Press, 102,* 2, 1006-1034.

Ball, A. and Ellis, P. (2008). Identity and the writing of culturally and linguistically diverse students. In C. Bazerman (Ed.). *Handbook of research on writing: History, society, school, individual, text* (pp. 614-632). England: Taylor & Francis.

Banks, J. (1994). *An introduction to multicultural education.* Massachusetts: Allyn and Bacon.

Banks, J. & Banks, C. (Eds.). (1995). *Handbook of Research on Multicultural Education.* New York: MacMillan.

Barr, R., Kamil, M., and Mosenthall, P. (Eds.) (1984). *Handbook of reading research, Vol. I,* New York: Longman.

Barr, R., Kamil, M., Mosenthall, P. and D. Pearson, (Eds.) (1991). *Handbook of reading research, Vol. II. New York: Longman.*

Bartolomé, L, (2009). Beyond the methods fetish: Toward a humanizing pedagogy. In A. Darder, M. Baltodano, and R. Torres (Eds.). *The critical pedagogy reader*, (pp. 338-355). New York: Routledge.

Bateson, G. (1972). *An ecology of mind*. New York: Ballentine.

Beach, R. (2000). Reading and responding at the level of activity. *Journal of Literacy Research, 32*, 237-251.

Berliner, D. (2006). Our impoverished view of educational reform. *Teachers College Record, 108*(6), 949-995.

Biancarosa, G. & Snow, C. (2004). *Reading next – a vision for action and research in middle and high school literacy: A report to Carnegie Corporation of New York*. Washington, D.C.: Alliance for Excellent Education.

Bleich, D. (1978). *Subjective Criticism*. Johns Hopkins University Press.

Bronfenbrenner, U. (1978). Who needs parent education? *Teachers College Record, 79, 773-774*.

Bruner, J. (1990). *Acts of meaning*. Cambridge, MA: Harvard University Press.

Buber, M. (1965). Education. In M Buber (Eds.). *Between man and man* (pp. 83-103). New York: MacMillan.

Callow, J. (1999). *Image matters – visual texts in the classroom*. Marrickville, N. S. W.: Primary English Language Association.

Callow, J. (2003). Talking about visual texts with students. *Reading Online, 6* (8).

Casey, H. (2009). Engaging the disengaged: Using learning clubs to motivate struggling adolescent readers and writers. *Journal of Adolescent and Adult Literacy, 52*(4), 284-294.

Cazden, C. B. (1988). *Classroom discourse: The language of teaching and learning.* Portsmouth: Heinemann.

Christenbury, L., Bomer, R., and Smagorinsky, P. (Eds.). (2009). *Handbook of adolescent literacy research.* New York: Guildford Press.

Claggett, F. and Brown, J. (1992). *Drawing your own conclusions: Graphic strategies for reading, writing and thinking.* Portsmouth, NH: Heinemann

Clark, K. (1965). *Dark ghetto: Dilemmas of social power.* Hanover, NH: Wesleyan University Press.

Clifford, J. (Ed.). (1991). *The experience of reading: Louise Rosenblatt and reader- response theory.* Portsmouth, NH: Boynton Cook.

Cochran-Smith, M. (2004). Multicultural teacher education: Research, practice and policy. In J. A. Banks & C. M. Banks (Eds.). *Handbook of research in multicultural education* (2nd ed., pp. 931-975). San Francisco: Jossey-Bass.

Cochran-Smith, M. (2013). *Transformative leadership in education: Equitable change in an uncertain and complex world.* New York, Routledge.

Collins, J. (1997). *Strategies for struggling writers.* New York: Guildford.

Cowan, K. & Albers, P. (2006). Semiotic representations: Building complex literacy practices through the arts. *The Reading Teacher, 60*(2), 124-137.

Cox, S., Friesner, D. & Khayum, M. (2003). Do reading skills courses help underprepared readers achieve academic success in college? *Journal of College Reading and Learning, 33*(2), 170-96.

Cresswall, J. (2007). *Qualitative inquiry and research design: Choosing among five approaches (2nd ed.).* Thousand Oaks: Sage.

Csikszentmihalyi, M. (2008). *Flow: the psychology of optimal experience.* 1st Harper Perennial Modern Classics ed. New York, Harper Perennial.

Cummins, J. (1986). Empowering minority students: A framework for intervention. *Harvard Education Review, 56* (1), 18-36.

Darling-Hammond, L. (1994). Performance-based assessment and educational equity. *Harvard Educational Review, 66*(1), 3-30.

De La Luz Reyes, M. (1992). Challenging venerable assumptions: Literacy instruction for culturally and linguistically diverse students. *Harvard Education Review, 62* (4), 427-447.

Delpit, L. (1995). *Other people's children: Cultural conflict in the classroom.* New York: Free Press

Dewey, J. (1910). *How we think.* Chicago: University of Chicago Press.

Dickens, L. & Watkins, K. (1999). Action research: Rethinking Lewin. *Management Learning, 30*, 127-140.

Driver, R., Asoko, H., Leach, J., Mortimer, E. and Scott, P. (1994). Constructing scientific knowledge in the classroom. *Educational Researcher, 23* (5), 5-12.

Eagleton, T. (1983). *Literary Theory: An Introduction.* University of Minnesota Press Minneapolis.

Eisner, E. W. (2002). *The arts and the creation of mind.* Yale University Press.

Ellison, R. (1980). *Invisible Man.* New York: Random House.

Fish, S. (1980). *Is there a text in this class: The authority of interpretive communities.* Cambridge Massachusetts: Harvard University Press.

Flood, J., Heath, S. B., & Lapp, D. (1997). (Eds.), *Handbook of research on teaching literacy through the communicative and visual arts*. New York: Macmillan.

Franzak, J. (2006). *Zoom*: A review of the literature on marginalized adolescent readers, literacy theory, and policy implications. *Review of Educational Research, 76* (2), 209-248.

Friere, P. (1970). *Pedagogy of the oppressed*. New York: Continuum.

Friere, P. and Macedo, D. (1987). *Literacy: Reading the word and the world*. Westport, CT: Bergin & Harvey.

Friere, P. (1998). *Pedagogy of Freedom: Ethics democracy and civic courage*. New York: Roman & Littlefield Publishers.

Friere, P. (2005). *Teachers as Cultural workers: Letters to those who dare teach*. CO: Westview Press.

Gaines, E. J. (1997). *A Lesson Before Dying*. New York: Vintage.

Galda, L. and Beach, R. (2001). Response to literature as a cultural activity. *Reading Research Quarterly, 36*(1), 64-73.

Gay, G. (2000). *Culturally responsive teaching: Theory, research and practice*. New York: Teachers College Press.

Gay, G. (2002). Preparing for culturally responsive teaching. *Journal of Teacher Education, 53*, (2) 106-116.

Gee, J. (1991). Socio-cultural approaches to literacy (literacies). *Annual Review of Applied Linguistics, 12*, 31-48.

Gee, J. and Crawford, V. (1998). Two kinds of teenagers: Language, identity, and social class. In D. Alvermann, K. Hinchman, D. Moore, S. Phelps, & D. Waff (Eds.). *Reconceptualizing the identities in adolescents' lives (pp. 225-246), Mahwah, NJ: Erlbaum*.

Gee, J.P. (2000a). Teenagers in new times: A new literacy studies perspective. *Journal of Adolescent & Adult Literacy, 43*(5), 412-420.

Gee, J. (2000b). Discourse and sociocultural studies in reading. In M. L. Kamil, P. B. Mosenthal, P. D. Pearson & R. Barr (Eds.), *Handbook of Reading Research* V.III. Mahwah, NJ: Erlbaum.

Gee, J. (2001). Reading as Situated Language: A Sociocognitive Perspective. *Journal of Adolescent & Adult Literacy, 44*(8), 714–725.

Gee, J. P. (2002). Millenials and Bobos, Blue's Clues and Sesame Street: A story for our times. In D. E. Alvermann (Ed.), *Adolescents and literacies in a digital world* (51-67).

Gee, J. P. (2008). *Social linguistics and literacies: Ideology in discourses* (3rd ed.). New York: Routledge.

Gilligan, C. (1982). *In a different voice.* Cambridge, MA: Harvard University Press.

Goodlad, J. (1984). *A place called school.* New York: McGraw Hill.

Goodman, K. (1976). Reading: A psycholinguistic guessing game. In H. Singer & R. Ruddell (Eds.). *Theoretical models and processes of reading, 2nd ed.*, 497-508 International Reading Association

Gibson, E. and Levin, H. (1975). *The psychology of reading.* Boston: MIT Press.

Graham, S., Harris, K. and Mason, L. (2005). Improving the writing performance, knowledge, and self-efficacy of struggling young writers: The effects of self-regulated strategy development. *Contemporary Educational Psychology, 30*(2), 207-241.

Groenewald, D. (2003). The best of both worlds: A critical pedagogy of place. *Educational Researcher, 32* (4), 3-12.

Groenewald, T. (2004). A phenomenological research design illustrated. *International Journal of Qualitative Methods, 3*(1),

Harklau, L., Losey, K. and Siegal, M. (1999). *Generation 1.5 meets college composition: Issues in the teaching of writing to U.S. educated learners of ESL*. Mawah, NJ: Lawrence Erlbaum.

Heath. S. B. (1983). *Ways with words: Language, life and work in communities and classrooms*. New York: Cambridge University Press.

Heron, J. (1996). *Cooperative inquiry: Research into the human condition*. Thousand Oaks, CA: Sage.

Holland, N. (1975). *5 readers reading*. Yale University Press. hooks, b. (1994). *Teaching to transgress: Education as the practice of freedom*. New York: Routledge.

Howard, T. (2003). Culturally relevant pedagogy: Ingreidnets for critical teacher reflection. *Theory into Practice, 42*(3), 195-202.

Husserl, E. (1931). *Ideas: General introduction to pure phenomenology*. New York: Macmillan Company.

Hynds, S. (1997). *On the brink: Negotiating literature and life with adolescents*. New York: Teachers College Press.

Ingarden, R. (1973). *The cognition of the literary work of art*. Northwestern University Press.

Intrator, S. and Kunzman, R. (2009). Who are adolescents today?: Youth voices and what they tells us. In L. Christenbury, R. Bomer, and P. Smagorinsky (Eds.). *Handbook of adolescent literacy research*. New York: Guildford Press.

Iser, W. (1980). *The act of reading: A theory of aesthetic response*. Baltimore: Johns Hopkins University Press.

Jacobson, W. (1998). Defining the quality of practitioner research. *Adult Education Quarterly, 48*, 125-138.

Johannessen, L. and McCann, T. (2009). Adolescents who struggle with literacy. In L. Christenbury, R. Bomer, and P. Smagorinsky (Eds.). *Handbook of adolescent literacy research*. New York: Guildford Press.

John-Steiner, V. and Mahn, H. (1996). Sociocultural approaches to learning and development: A Vygotskyian framework. *Educational Psychologist, 31*(3/4), 191-206.

Kamil, M., Mosenthal, P., Pearson, P.D. and Barr, R. (Eds.). *Handbook of reading research, Vol. III*, Mahwah, NJ: Lawrence Erlbaum Associates.

Kohlberg, L. (1981). *The philosophy of moral development: Moral stages and the idea of justice.* San Francisco: Harper and Row.

Kozol, J. (2012). *Fire in the ashes: Twenty-five years among the poorest children in America*. New York: Crown Publishers.

Kress, G. (2000). Design and transformation: New theories of meaning. In B. Cope & M. Kalantzis for the New London Group (Eds.), *Multi-literacies: Literacy learning and the design of social futures* (pp. 153-161). South Yarra, Vic: MacMillan.

Ladson-Billings, G. (1994). *The dreamkeeprs: Successful teachers of African American children.* San Francisco: Jossey-Bass.

Ladson-Billings, G. (1995). Toward a theory of culturally relevant pedagogy. *American Education Research Journal, 32*(3), 465-491.

Ladson-Billings, G. (2000). Fighting for our lives: Preparing teachers to teach African-American students. *Journal of Teacher Education, 51*, 206-214.

Ladson-Billings, G. (2006). From the achievement gap to the education debt: Understanding Achievement in U.S. schools. *Educational Researcher, 35*(7), 3-12.

Ladson-Billings, G. and Tate, W. (2009). Toward a critical race theory of education. In A. Darder, M. Baltodano, & R. Torres (Eds.) *The critical pedagogy reader,* 167-182.

Ladson-Billings, G. (2009). Fighting for our lives: Preparing teachers to teach African American students. In A. Darder, M. Baltodano, & R. Torres (Eds.) *The critical pedagogy reader,* 460-468.

Latour, B. (1986). Visualization and cognition: Thinking with eyes and hands. *Knowledge and society: Studies in the sociology of culture past and present, 6,* 1-40.

Lee, C. (1995). A culturally-based cognitive apprenticeship: Teaching African American high school students skills in literary interpretation. *Reading Research Quarterly, 30*(4), 608-630.

Lee, C. (2007). *Culture, literacy, and learning: Taking bloom in the midst of the whirlwind.* New York: Teacher College Press.

Long, L., MacBlain, S., & MacBlain, M. (2007). Supporting students with dyslexia at the secondary level: An emotional model of literacy. *Journal of Adolescent and Adult Literacy, 51*(2), 124-134.

Marshall, J. (2000). Research on response to literature. In M. Kamil, P.

Mosenthal, D. Pearson, and R. Barr (Eds.) *Handbook of Reading Research, III.* Mahwah, NJ: Lawrence Erlbaum.

McLaren, P. (2014). *Life in Schools: An Introduction to Critical Pedagogy in the Foundations of Education* (6th Ed.). New York: Routledge

McLaren, P. and Leonard, P. (1993). *Paulo Friere: A critical encounter.* New York: Routledge.

Mezirow, J. (1991). *Transformative dimensions of adult learning.* San Francisco: Jossey Bass.

Moje, E., Young, J., Readance, J., and Moore, D. (2000). Reinventing adolescent literacy for new times: Perrenial and millennial issues. *Journal of Adolescent & Adult Literacy, 43,* 400-410.

Moje, E. (2002). Reframing adolescent literacy research for new times: Studying youth as a resource. *Reading Research and Instruction. 1* (3), 211-228.

Moll, L. and Whitmore, K. (1993). Vygotsky in classroom practice: Moving from individual transmission to social transaction. In E. Forman, N. Minick, & C. Stone (Eds.). *Contexts for learning: Sociocultural dynamics in children's development* (19-42). New York: Oxford University Press.

Moustakas, C. (1994). *Phenomenological Research Methods.* London: Sage.

Muhammad, G. (2020). *Cultivating Genius: An equity framework for culturally and historically responsive literacy.* New York: Scholastic.

Nagda, B. and Gurin, P. (2007). Intergroup dialogue: A critical dialogic approach to learning about difference, inequality, and social justice. *New Directions for Teaching and Learning,* no. 111. DOI: 10.1002/tl.284

New London Group. (1996). A pedagogy of multiliteracies: Designing social futures. *Harvard Educational Review, 66* (1), 60-92.

Nieto, S. (2000). *Affirming Diversity: The sociopolitical context of multicultural education (3rd ed.). New York: Longman.*

Noddings, N. (1983). *Caring: A feminine approach to ethic and moral education.* Berkeley: University of California Press.

Nowotny, H., Scott, P. & Gibbons, M. (2001). *Rethinking science: Knowledge and the public in an age of uncertainty.* Malden, MA: Blackwell.

Oakes, J. and Lipton, M. (2007). *Teaching to change the world* (3rd ed.). Boston: McGraw Hill.

Olshansky, B. (1998). *Crafting collage stories: Image making within the writing process.* Durham, NH: Center for the Advancement of Arts-Based Literacy.

Ong, W. (1982). *Orality and literacy.* New York: Metheun.

Olson, D. (1994). *The world on paper.* Cambridge, England: Cambridge University Press.

Owens, L. and Ennis, C. (2005). The ethic of care in teaching: An overview of supportive literature. *Quest, 57* (4), 392-425.

Pearson, P. D. et al (Eds.). (1984). *Handbook on Reading Research, VI,* New York, Routledge.

Persky, H., Daane, M. and Jin, Y. (2003). *The nation's report card: Writing.* U.S. Department of Education, Washington, DC.

Raynor, K. and Pollatsek, A. (1989). *The psychology of reading. Hillsdale, NJ: Lawrence Erlbaum Associates.*

Richards, J. (2002). Integrating visual arts literacy: What do you need to know? How can you begin? *Journal of Reading Education, 28*(1), 42-43.

Rosenblatt, L. (1978) *The reader, the text, the poem: The transactional theory of the literary work.* Carbondale: Southern Illinois University Press.

Rosenblatt, L. (2005). *Making meaning with texts.* Portsmouth, NH: Heinemann.

Rudell, R. & Unrau, N. (Eds.). (2004). *Theoretical Models and Processes of Reading, 5th ed.* Newark, DE: International Reading Association.

Scammacca, N. et al (2007). *Interventions for adolescent struggling readers*. Center on Instruction at RMC Research Corporation.

Schmandt, D. and Erard, M. (2008). Origins and forms of writing. In C. Bazerman (Ed.). *Handbook of research on writing: History, society, school, individual, text* (pp. 7-26). England: Taylor & Francis.

Scribner, S. and Cole, M. (1981). *The psychology of literacy*. Cambridge, MA: Harvard University Press.

Sedlacek, W. (2006). Teaching minority students. *New Directions for Teaching and Learning, 16*, 39-50. DOE: 10.1002/tl.37219831606

Shields, M. (2013). *Transformative leadership in educaton: Equitable change in an uncertain and complex world*. New York: Routledge.

Sleeter, C. (2005). *Un-standardizing curriculum: Multicultural teaching in the standards-based classroom*. New York: Teachers College Press.

Smagorinsky, P., Zoss, M. & O'Donnell-Allen, C. (2005). Mask-making: An idenity project in a high school English class: A case study. *English in Education, 31*, 60-75.

Smith, F. (2004). *Understanding reading, 6th ed*. Mahwah, NJ: Lawrence Erlbaum Associates.

Smith, M., & Wilhelm, J. (2003). *Reading don't fix no chevies*. Portsmouth, NH: Heinemann.

Suhor, C. (1984). Toward a semiotics-based curriculum. *Journal of Curriculum Studies 16*, 247-257.

Sullivan, M. A. (1995). Reader response, contemporary aesthetics, and the adolescent reader. *Journal of Aesthetic Education, 29*, 79-95.

Sullivan-Palinscar, A. (1998). Social constructivist perspectives on teaching and learning. *Annual Review of Psychology, 491*, 345-375.

Taylor, S. and Bogdan, R. (1998). *Introduction to qualitative research methods (3ʳᵈ ed.).* Hoboken, NJ: John Wiley and Sons

Tarlow, B. (1996). Caring: A negotiated process that varies. In S. Gordon, P. Benner & N. Noddings (Eds.), *Caregivers: Reading in knowledge, practice, ethics, and politics* (pp. 56-82). Philadelphia: University of Pennsylvania.

Tatum, A. (2000). Breaking down barriers that disenfranchise African American adolescent readers in low-level tracks. *Journal of Adolescent and Adult Literacy, 44* (1), pp. 52-64.

Tatum, A. and Gue, V. (2012). The sociocultural benefits of writing for African American males. *Reading and Writing Quarterly, 28,* (2), 123-142.

Valeboncoeur, J. (2006). Engaging young people: Learning in informal contexts. *Review of Research in Education,* 30, 239-278.

Van Manen, M. (2007). *Phenomenlology and Practice, 1* (1), 11-30.

Vygotsky, L. (1978). *Mind in Society: The development of higher psychological processes.* Cambridge, MA: Cambridge University Press.

Vygotsky, L. (1981). The instrumental method in psychology. In J. Wertsch (Ed.). *The concept of activity in Societ psychology,* pp. 134-144. Armonk, New York: Sharpe.

Walsh-Piper, K. (2002). *Image to word, art & creative writing.* Lantham, MD: Scarecrow Press.

Wells, G. (1995). Language and the inner-oriented curriculum. *Curriculum Inquiry, 25*(3), 233-269.

Wertsch, J. (1991). *Voices of the mind: A sociocultural approach to mediated action.* Cambridge, MA: Harvard University Press.

Wilhelm, J. (1995). Reading is seeing: Using visual response to improve the literary reading of reluctant readers. *Journal of Reading, 27* (4), 467-502.

Wilhelm, J. (2008). *You gotta BE the book: Teaching engaged and reflective reading with adolescents.* New York: Teachers College Press.

Wise, B. (2009). Adolescent literacy: The cornerstone of student success. *Journal of Adolescent and adult literacy, 52*(5), 369-375.

Wolk, S. (2009). Reading for a better world: Teaching for social responsibility with young adult literature. *Journal of Adolescent and Adult Literacy, 52*(8), 664-673.

Yorks, L. (2005). Adult learning and the generation of new knowledge and meaning Creating liberating spaces for fostering adult learning through practitioner- based collaborative action inquiry. *Teachers College Press.*

Zoss. (2009). Visual arts and literacy. In L. Christenbury, R. Bomer, and P. Smagorinsky (Eds.). *Handbook of adolescent literacy research.* New York: Guildford Press.

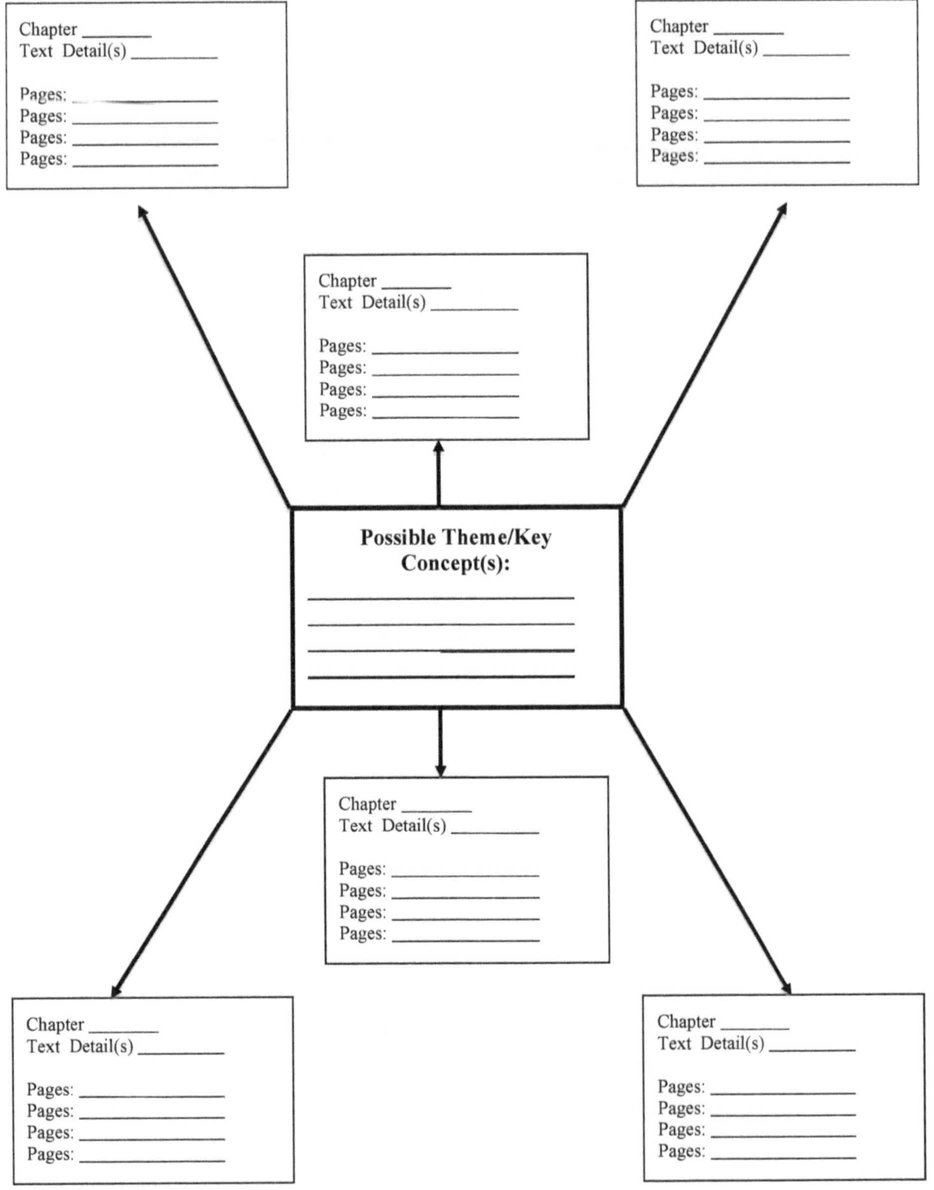

Chapter ________
Text Detail(s) ________
Pages: ________
Pages: ________
Pages: ________
Pages: ________
Chapter ________
Text Detail(s) ________
Pages: ________
Pages: ________
Pages: ________
Pages: ________
Chapter ________
Text Detail(s) ________
Pages: ________
Pages: ________
Pages: ________
Pages: ________
Possible Theme/Key Concept(s):
____
____
____
____
Chapter ________
Text Detail(s) ________
Pages: ________
Pages: ________
Pages: ________
Pages: ________
Chapter ________
Text Detail(s) ________
Pages: ________
Pages: ________
Pages: ________
Pages: ________
Chapter ________
Text Detail(s) ________
Pages: ________
Pages: ________
Pages: ________
Pages: ________